The Struggle for Recognition

The Struggle for Recognition

The Moral Grammar of Social Conflicts

Axel Honneth
Translated by Joel Anderson

The MIT Press
Cambridge, Massachusetts

This book was printed and bound in Great Britain.

Library of Congress Cataloging-in-Publication Data

Honneth, Axel, 1949–
    [Kampf um Anerkennung. English]
    The struggle for recognition: the moral grammar of social conflicts/
    Axel Honneth; translated by Joel Anderson.
        p.   cm.—(Studies in contemporary German social thought)
    Includes bibliographical references and index.
    ISBN-13 978-0-262-58147-9 (pbk. : alk. paper)

    1. Social conflict.   2. Social sciences—Philosophy.
3. Recognition (Psychology).   I. Title.   II. Series.
HM136.H59813   1996
303.6—dc20   96–21276
                                                                     CIP

10 9 8 7 6

Contents

Acknowledgements

The author, translator, and publishers wish to thank the following for permission to use material:

The University of Chicago Press for excerpts from George Herbert Mead, *Mind, Self and Society*, ed. Charles W. Morris, 1934;

Wayne State University Press for excerpts from Leo Rauch, *Hegel and the Human Spirit: A Translation of the Jena Lectures on the Philosophy of Spirit (1805–6) With Commentary*, 1983.

Every effort has been made to trace all the copyright holders, but if any have been inadvertently overlooked the publishers will be pleased to make the necessary arrangements at the first opportunity.

Translator's Note

Although most of the cases in which the original German terms defy easy translation are indicated within square brackets in the text, four cases deserve special attention here. In English, the word 'recognition' is ambiguous, referring either to 're-identification' or 'the granting of a certain status'. The former, epistemic sense translates the German '*Wiedererkennung*', which is distinguished from the practical sense with which Honneth is concerned here, expressed in the word '*Anerkennung*'. Throughout the present translation 'recognition' and 'to recognize' are used in this latter sense, familiar from such expressions as 'The PLO has agreed to recognize the state of Israel.' It is perhaps useful for understanding Honneth's claim that love, respect, and esteem are three types of recognition to note that, in German, to 'recognize' individuals or groups is to ascribe to them some *positive* status.

Honneth's general term for the failure to give someone due recognition is '*Mißachtung*', which is translated here as 'disrespect'. It should be noted that this concept refers not merely to a failure to show proper deference but rather to a broad class of cases, including humiliation, degradation, insult, disenfranchisement, and even physical abuse.

Whereas the terms 'ethical' and 'moral' are often used interchangeably in English, there are important differences between the German terms '*moralisch*', '*ethisch*', and '*sittlich*'. The first of these is bound up with Kantian, universalistic approaches to the question of what is right and is rendered here as 'moral'. The other two terms both refer to conceptions of what is right or good that are based on the substantive customs, mores, or *ethos* of a particular tradition or community, or to practices that are motivated by such. They are both translated as 'ethical', although the phrase 'customarily ethical' is sometimes used to indicate the more traditional connotation of 'sittlich'. A related term, 'ethical life' [*Sittlichkeit*], denotes a concrete, integrated social arrangement in which norms and values are embodied in the basic attitudes and ways of life of members of the community.

Finally, in translating the discussion of Hegel, the pronoun 'it' has been used as the referent for 'the subject', not so much because '*das Subjekt*' is neuter in German, but rather to reflect the formal character of the concept for Hegel.

Translator's Introduction
Joel Anderson

As social struggles of the last few decades have made clear, justice demands more than the fair distribution of material goods. For even if conflicts over interests were justly adjudicated, a society would remain normatively deficient to the extent that its members are systematically denied the recognition they deserve. As Charles Taylor has recently emphasized, 'Due recognition is not just a courtesy we owe people. It is a vital human need.'[1] As one scarcely needs to add, it is also a need that has all too often gone unmet. Regularly, members of marginalized and subaltern groups have been systematically denied recognition for the worth of their culture or way of life, the dignity of their status as persons, and the inviolability of their physical integrity. Most strikingly in the politics of identity, their struggles for recognition have come to dominate the political landscape. Consequently, if social theory is to provide an adequate account of actual fields of social conflict, it will have both to situate the motivation for these emancipatory struggles within the social world and to provide an account of what justifies them.

In this work, Axel Honneth sketches an approach to this dual task of explanation and justification that is both highly original and firmly rooted in the history of modern social theory. Rather than following the atomistic tradition of social philosophy going back to Hobbes and Machiavelli, however, Honneth situates his project within the tradition that emphasizes not the struggle for self-preservation but rather the struggle for the establishment of relations of mutual recognition, as a precondition for self-realization.[2] Like Hegel, George Herbert Mead, and, more recently, communitarians and many feminists, Honneth stresses the importance of social relationships to the development and maintenance of a person's identity. On the basis of this nexus between social patterns of recognition and individual prerequisites for self-realization – and with constant reference to empirical findings of the social sciences – he develops both a developmental framework for interpreting social struggles and a normative account of the claims being raised in these struggles.

With regard to the former, explanatory task, his approach can be understood as a continuation of the Frankfurt School's attempt to locate the motivating insight for emancipatory critique and struggle within the domain of ordinary human experience, rather than in the revolutionary theory of intellectuals.[3] As Honneth argued in *Critique of Power*, however, the Frankfurt School suffered from an exclusive focus on the domain of material production as the locus of transformative critique. In the present volume, he now proposes an alternative account, situating the critical perception of injustice more generally within individuals' negative experiences of having their broadly 'moral' expectations violated.

With regard to the normative task, the roots of his approach are to be found in the model of the struggle for recognition developed by Hegel during his early years in Jena (before the completion of the *Phenomenology of Spirit* in 1807). Honneth takes from Hegel the idea that full human flourishing is dependent on the existence of well-established, 'ethical' relations – in particular, relations of love, law, and 'ethical life' [*Sittlichkeit*] – which can only be established through a conflict-ridden developmental process, specifically, through a struggle for recognition. In order to avoid the speculative, metaphysical character of Hegel's project, however, Honneth turns to Mead's naturalistic pragmatism and to empirical work in psychology, sociology, and history in order to identify the intersubjective conditions for individual self-realization. In the course of analysing these conditions, Honneth develops his 'formal conception of ethical life', understood as a critical normative standard that is intended to avoid both the overly 'thick' character of neo-Aristotelian ethics and the overly 'thin' character of neo-Kantian moral theory.

Honneth's approach can be summarized, in a preliminary way, as follows. The possibility for sensing, interpreting, and realizing one's needs and desires as a fully autonomous and individuated person – in short, the very possibility of identity-formation – depends crucially on the development of self-confidence, self-respect, and self-esteem. These three modes of relating practically to oneself can only be acquired and maintained intersubjectively, through being granted recognition by others whom one also recognizes. As a result, the conditions for self-realization turn out to be dependent on the establishment of relationships of mutual recognition. These relationships go beyond (a) close relations of love and friendship to include (b) legally institutionalized relations of universal respect for the autonomy and dignity of persons, and (c) networks of solidarity and shared values within which the particular worth of individual members of a community can be acknowledged. These relationships are not ahistorically given but must be established and expanded through social struggles, which cannot be understood exclusively as conflicts over interests. The 'grammar' of such struggles is 'moral' in the sense that the feelings of outrage and indignation driving them are generated by the rejection of claims to recognition and thus imply normative judgements about the legitimacy of social arrangements. Thus the normative ideal of a just society is empirically confirmed by historical struggles for recognition.

Central to Honneth's 'social theory with normative content' is his account of self-confidence, self-respect, and self-esteem, along with the modes of recognition by which they are sustained, and this will be the focus here. With regard to each of these 'practical relations-to-self', three central issues emerge: the precise importance of each for the development of one's identity, the pattern of recognition on which it depends, and its historical development. Beyond this, the present introduction will provide a brief discussion of both Honneth's interpretation of social struggles as motivated by the experience of being denied these conditions for identity-formation – which he refers to as 'disrespect' ['*Mißachtung*'] – and some of the distinctive features of Honneth's readings of Hegel and Mead, found in chapters 2–4.

It is perhaps useful, at the outset, to understand what self-confidence, self-respect, and self-esteem have in common. For Honneth, they represent three distinct species of 'practical relation-to-self'. These are neither purely beliefs about oneself nor emotional states, but involve a dynamic process in which individuals come to experience themselves as having a certain status, be it as a focus of concern, a responsible agent, or a valued contributor to shared projects. Following Hegel and Mead, Honneth emphasizes that coming to relate to oneself in these ways necessarily involves experiencing recognition from others. One's relationship to oneself, then, is not a matter of a solitary ego appraising itself, but an *intersubjective* process, in which one's attitude towards oneself emerges in one's encounter with an other's attitude toward oneself.[4]

Love and basic self-confidence

With regard to the concept of love, Honneth is primarily concerned with the way in which parent–child relationships – as well as adult relationships of love and friendship – facilitate the development and maintenance of the basic relation-to-self that Honneth terms 'basic self-confidence' [*Selbstvertrauen*: 'trust in oneself']. If all goes well in their first relationships to others, infants gradually acquire a fundamental faith in their environment and, concomitantly, a sense of trust in their own bodies as reliable sources of signals as to their own needs. On Honneth's account, basic self-confidence has less to do with a high estimation of one's abilities than with the underlying capacity to express needs and desires without fear of being abandoned as a result. Because of this fundamental character, it is usually only when extreme experiences of physical violation, such as rape or torture, shatter one's ability to access one's needs as one's own and to express them without anxiety that it becomes clear how much depends on this relation-to-self.[5]

To explain the link between self-confidence and intersubjective relations of love and concern, Honneth draws on the object-relations theory of early childhood experience, particularly as developed in the work of Donald Winnicott. Against the Freudian emphasis on instinctual drives, object-relations theorists have argued that the development of children cannot be abstracted from the interactive relationships in which the process of maturation takes place. Initially, the child is dependent upon the responsiveness of primary care-givers (following Winnicott, Jessica Benjamin, and others, Honneth uses the term 'mother' to designate a role that can be fulfilled by persons other than the biological mother) and their ability to empathically intuit the needs of the inarticulate infant. Due to the newborn's utter helplessness, an insufficient level of adaptation of the 'mother' to the infant's needs early in life would represent a serious problem for the infant, since the child can neither cope with nor make sense of failures of this 'environment' to intuit and satisfy his or her needs. Of course, the failure or 'de-adaptation' of care-givers is an unavoidable element of the individuation process by which infants learn to cope with gradual increases in the environment's insensitivity, that is, to recognize and assert their needs as their own instead of experiencing the absence of immediate gratification as threatening.

Following Winnicott, Honneth argues that this formative process must again be understood as intersubjective. Because 'good-enough' infant care demands a high degree of emotional and intuitive involvement, the individuation process has to be understood as a complex, agonistic process in which *both* parent *and* child extricate themselves from a state of 'symbiosis'. Despite the fact that the 'mother' is a fully individuated adult, it is only together that children and care-givers can negotiate the delicate and shifting balance between ego-dissolution

and ego-demarcation. And it is this balance that provides the enduring, intersubjectively reproduced basis for relationships of love and
friendship with peers as well as for a positive, embodied sense of
what Erik Erikson calls 'basic trust'.[6]

Although Honneth is generally at pains to emphasize the historically contingent nature of human subjectivity,[7] he argues that this
notion of bodily integrity, together with the need for love and concern
it entails, captures something important that cuts across differences of
cultural and historical contexts. This is not to say that practices of
child-rearing or love have gone unchanged but only that the capacity
to trust one's own sense of what one needs or wants is a precondition
for self-realization in any human community.

This is part of what separates love from the two other patterns of
recognition Honneth considers essential to self-realization, for unlike
the form of recognition that supports self-confidence, the ways in which
both respect and esteem are accorded have undergone a significant
historical transformation. Indeed, the very distinction between the two
is a historical product, something that may help to explain why 'respect' and 'esteem' are still used interchangeably in some contexts (as
in: 'I respect her enormously'). In pre-modern contexts – roughly, until
the bourgeois revolutions of the eighteenth century – one's standing
in society and one's status as a moral and political agent were fused,
typically, in the concept of 'honour'. Rights and duties were rights and
duties *of one's status group or 'estate'*, never of one's status as a free
legislator in either the local kingdom or the 'kingdom of ends' (Kant).
In the modern period, however, the fundamental principles underlying the realm of law and rights came into conflict with the idea of
according legal status on the basis of class privilege. In this way, the
notion of one's 'status as a person' was historically differentiated from
the notion of 'social standing', giving rise to psychologically and
analytically distinct modes of recognition, as well as to the corresponding notions of 'self-respect' [*Selbstachtung*] and 'self-esteem'
[*Selbstschätzung*].[8]

Rights and self-respect

As Honneth understands it, self-respect has less to do with whether or
not one has a good opinion of oneself than with one's sense of possessing of the universal dignity of persons. There is a strong Kantian
element here: what we owe to every person is the recognition of and
respect for his or her status as an agent capable of acting on the basis

of reasons, as the autonomous author of the political and moral laws to which he or she is subject.[9] To have self-respect, then, is to have a sense of oneself as a person, that is, as a 'morally responsible' agent or, more precisely, as someone capable of participating in the sort of public deliberation that Habermas terms 'discursive will-formation'.

This relation-to-self is also mediated by patterns of interaction, those organized in terms of legal rights. To show why being accorded rights is crucial to self-respect, Honneth makes use of Joel Feinberg's argument to the effect that 'what is called "human dignity" may simply be the recognizable capacity to assert claims'.[10] The object of respect (including self-respect) is an agent's capacity to raise and defend claims discursively or, more generally, an agent's status as responsible [an agent's *Zurechnungsfähigkeit*].[11] But this capacity can only become a basis for 'self-respect' if it can be exercised. Indeed, in this context it is unclear what it could mean to have a capacity one cannot exercise. Hence, the importance of rights in connection with self-respect lies in the fact that rights ensure the real opportunity to exercise the universal capacities constitutive of personhood. This is not to say that a person without rights cannot have self-respect, only that the *fullest* form of self-respecting autonomous agency could only be realized when one is recognized as possessing the capacities of 'legal persons', that is, of morally responsible agents.

The specific content of these universal capacities, however, is something that shifts over time, along with shifts in the conception of the procedure by which political and moral issues are to be resolved: 'The more demanding this procedure is seen to be, the more extensive the features will have to be that, taken together, constitute a subject's moral responsibility'.[12] To understand this claim, it is important to keep in mind the distinction Honneth makes between two historical processes: (a) an increase in the *percentage* of people who are treated as full-fledged citizens and (b) an increase in the actual *content* of what it means to be a full-fledged citizen (in particular, the emergence of both political and welfare rights, as supplements to basic liberties). In the first case, the historical development involves realizing the universality clearly implied in the notion of modern law, with its basis in post-conventional morality. In the second case, the historical development involves a shift in the conception of law itself, by taking into account what skills and opportunities persons must be equipped with if processes of political decision-making are to count as legitimate. One of the interesting implications of this is that, since participation in public deliberation presupposes certain capacities, neo-Kantian moral and political theory cannot be as purely proceduralist as is often

Translator's Introduction

suggested, for it must rely tacitly on a minimally substantive conception of justice in order to be able to determine the conditions under which participants in practical discourse can be said to have acquired the practical relations-to-self necessary for engaging fully in collective or personal self-determination.[13]

With regard to these historical processes, Honneth emphasizes that the social struggles for either type of expansion are oriented to ideas of universality and self-legislation that make it normatively illegitimate (though perhaps factually accurate) to view rights as the embodiment of class interests. It is precisely this universalistic core of modern law that has been overlooked by attempts since Hegel to appropriate the model of the struggle for recognition. As Honneth argues in chapter 7, despite their insights into the non-Hobbesian character of many social struggles, Marx, Sorel, and Sartre all failed to appreciate that the appeal to rights has, built into it, the idea that every subject of the law must also be its author.

Solidarity and self-esteem

Whereas self-respect is a matter of viewing oneself as entitled to the same status and treatment as every other person, self-esteem involves a sense of what it is that makes one special, unique, and (in Hegel's terms) 'particular'. This enabling sense of oneself as a unique and irreplaceable individual cannot, however, be based merely on a set of trivial or negative characteristics. What distinguishes one from others must be something *valuable*.[14] Accordingly, to have the sense that one has nothing of value to offer is to lack any basis for developing a sense of one's own identity. In this way, individuality and self-esteem are linked.

With regard to these issues of individuality and particularity Honneth argues that Hegel's work, though ground-breaking, is marred by an unfortunate tendency to understand the relevant mode of recognition in terms of an overextended conception of romantic love. Because of this, Honneth focuses instead on Mead's discussion of personal identity. Mead claims that distinguishing oneself from others as an individual is a matter of what 'we do better than others'.[15] The immediate difficulty with this, of course, is that not everyone can stand out above others. Mead tries to democratize this 'sense of superiority' by focusing on the division of labour in modern industrial societies, that is, by allowing individuals to find their functional roles in which to excel, not at the expense of others but precisely to the benefit of the whole.

In Honneth's view, however, Mead overlooks the fact that not every job automatically serves as a basis for one's 'sense of superiority' or self-esteem. Like the evaluation of the way in which the work is done, the esteem accorded to certain tasks hinges on a range of particular cultural factors. If, for example, homemaking is considered an insignificant contribution to the common good, then homemakers will lack the evaluative resources in terms of which they can acquire a sense of personal accomplishment. In this sense, the social conditions for esteem are determined by the prevailing sense of what is to count as a worthwhile contribution to society. By situating esteem not in the division of labour but in the horizon of values of a particular culture,[16] Honneth opens up the possibility of conceiving of the conditions for self-esteem as a field of contestation and cultural struggle for the recognition of previously denigrated contributors to the common good.

'Solidarity' is the term Honneth uses for the cultural climate in which the acquisition of self-esteem has become broadly possible. Although 'being in solidarity with someone' is sometimes equated with feelings of sympathy, Honneth's view is that one can properly speak of 'solidarity' only in cases where some shared concern, interest, or value is in play. What he is concerned with here is not so much the collective defence of interests or the political integration of individuals, but rather the presence of an open, pluralistic, evaluative framework within which social esteem is ascribed. He claims that a good society, a society in which individuals have a real opportunity for full self-realization, would be a society in which the common values would match the concerns of individuals in such a way that no member of the society would be denied the opportunity to earn esteem for his or her contribution to the common good: 'To the extent to which every member of a society is in a position to esteem himself or herself, one can speak of a state of societal solidarity.'[17] Unlike the sphere of rights, solidarity carries with it a 'communitarian' moment of particularity: *which* particular values are endorsed by a community is a contingent matter, the result of social and cultural struggles that lack the universality that is distinctive of legal relations.

Honneth's position here may be usefully compared to the culturally oriented views of subaltern groups that have influenced recent debates over multiculturalism, feminism, and gay and lesbian identity. Like defenders of the politics of difference, he regards struggles for recognition in which the dimension of esteem is central as attempts to end social patterns of denigration in order to make possible new forms of distinctive identity. But for Honneth, esteem is accorded on the basis of an individual's contribution to a shared project; thus, the elimination of demeaning cultural images of, say, racial minorities does not provide esteem directly but rather establishes the conditions under which members of those groups can then build self-esteem by contributing to the community. To esteem a person simply for being a member of a group would be to slip back into pre-modern notions of estate-based honour discussed earlier, rather than acknowledging the 'individualized' character of modern esteem. Honneth insists that the point of reference for esteeming each individual is the evaluative framework accepted by the entire community and not just one subculture. It remains somewhat unclear exactly what determines the boundaries of the community in Honneth's account – what if one is esteemed only by other Jews or other lesbians? – but the central point is that, in pluralistic and mobile societies, it is difficult to maintain self-esteem in the face of systematic denigration from outside one's subculture.

Disrespect and the moral grammar of historical struggles

These intersubjective conditions for identity-formation provide the basis for Honneth's 'formal conception of ethical life', understood as a normative ideal of a society in which patterns of recognition would allow individuals to acquire the self-confidence, self-respect, and self-esteem necessary for the full development of their identities. This ideal is not merely a theoretical construct; it is implicit in the structure of recognition itself. As Hegel showed, recognition is worthless if it does not come from someone whom one views as deserving recognition. From this perspective, since the requirement of reciprocity is always already built into the demand for recognition, social struggles for the expansion of patterns of recognition are best understood as attempts to realize the normative potential implicit in social interaction.

Although the teleological language of 'potential' and a hypothetically anticipated 'final state' of this development may raise eyebrows, Honneth is careful to avoid suggesting a philosophy of history in the traditional sense of a necessary progression along a knowable, preordained path. He insists that history is made less at the level of structural evolution than at the level of individual experiences of suffering and disrespect. His point is that one misses the 'moral grammar' of these conflicts if one fails to see that the claims to recognition raised in them can only be met through greater inclusion, the logical extension of which is something like the state of society envisioned by the formal theory of ethical life. In this way, Honneth argues, normative theory and the internal logic of social struggles mutually illuminate each other.

The idea of social conflict having a 'moral' dimension is not, of course, entirely new. It is a central focus of much recent work in social history inspired by the ground-breaking studies of E. P. Thompson, and Honneth looks to that tradition – particularly to the work of Barrington Moore – for empirical support for his position.[18] Where he departs from this tradition, however, is in arguing that 'moral' motives for revolt and resistance – that is, those based on a tacit understanding of what one *deserves* – do not emerge only in the defence of traditional ways of life (as Thompson and Moore suggest) but also in situations where those ways of life have become intolerable.

Because key forms of exclusion, insult, and degradation can be seen as violating self-confidence, self-respect, or self-esteem, the negative emotional reactions generated by these experiences of disrespect provide a pretheoretical basis for social critique. Once it becomes clear that these experiences reflect not just the idiosyncratic misfortune of individuals but experiences shared by many others, the potential emerges for collective action aimed at actually expanding social patterns of recognition. Here, the symbolic resources of social movements play a crucial role in showing this disrespect to be typical of an entire group of people, thereby helping to establish the cultural conditions for resistance and revolt.

Hegel and Mead

As Honneth demonstrates, many of the ideas outlined above – in particular, the tripartite distinction among three relations of recognition as social prerequisites for identity-formation – are already found in the work of Hegel and Mead, and Honneth's interest in these thinkers lies largely in reconstructing a systematic social theory from their often fragmentary proposals. Beyond this, however, Honneth's discussions also represent significant contributions to the secondary literature on these authors.

The discussion of Hegel focuses on the elusive and little-discussed early texts from the years in Jena. His reading of these texts not only uncovers the resources for reconstructing a 'recognition-theoretic' social theory but also identifies important tensions between the texts, tensions that help to explain why Hegel was never able to develop such a social theory himself. In the earliest Jena writings (discussed in chapter 2) and particularly in the *System of Ethical Life*, Hegel postulates a transition from 'natural ethical life' to 'absolute ethical life' in which the differentiation of society goes hand in hand with the development of human autonomy and individuality. Here, under the influence of classical theories of the *polis*, Hegel develops strong notions of both the normative potential of communicative relations and the primacy of the social. But he is unable to provide a sufficiently precise account of either the distinctions between forms of recognition or the stages of individual development. Honneth argues in chapter 3 that this more detailed account is precisely what Hegel's later *Realphilosophie* provides. Unfortunately, however, this gain in analytical and psychological clarity also obscures some of the crucial insights found in the earlier writings, owing to Hegel's increasing reliance on a 'philosophy of consciousness', that is, the metaphysical framework characteristic of subject-centred philosophy from Descartes to Husserl. In focusing on the struggle for recognition at the level of the formation of individual consciousness, Hegel makes social shifts in patterns of recognition mere stages in the overarching process of Spirit's formation.[19] In Honneth's view, the more interesting earlier notion, according to which individual and societal development mutually constitute each other, never returns in Hegel's oeuvre, and it is for this reason that Honneth does not discuss what is certainly the best-known of Hegel's discussions of the struggle for recognition, namely, the master–slave dialectic of the *Phenomenology of Spirit*. In effect, Honneth concludes that the earlier and later Jena writings *negate* each other, without Hegel ever being able to effect their *Aufhebung* [sublation].

In this connection, Mead represents a significant advance. For Honneth's purposes, what makes him interesting is that he provides an account of the tripartite interrelation between individual identity-formation and social patterns of interaction that is built on a non-speculative, postmetaphysical basis. In his discussion of Mead's intersubjectivist conception of the self, Honneth is in substantial agreement with the work of Hans Joas, Ernst Tugendhat, and Habermas.[20] Honneth develops his own criticism of Mead's narrow reliance on the division of labour as a basis for post-traditional solidarity (discussed above) as well as a careful reconstruction of the important distinction in Mead between two kinds of 'respect' (corresponding to Honneth's notions of 'respect' and 'esteem'). But what is more distinctive about Honneth's reading of Mead is his interpretation of the 'I' as a driving force of historical transformation. Something of the sort is needed to account for the expansion of identity-claims over time and for the emergence of new claims to recognition. Honneth sees Mead's notion of the 'I' as offering a way of explaining how innovation is possible in this domain. On his reading, then, the 'I' is not merely the placeholder for the irretrievable subject of an individual's thought and action but also the pre-conscious source of innovation by which new claims to identity come to be asserted.[21] On the basis of this, Honneth can then argue that historical transformations of social relations (in this case, individualization) are driven by the experiences and struggles of individuals and groups rather than functionalist dynamics.[22]

Aside from suggesting new lines of scholarly research, Honneth's discussions of Hegel and Mead serve three further purposes. First, they provide the raw materials from which Honneth constructs his own position, including the notion of struggles for recognition as a driving force in the development of social structures, the tripartite distinction among patterns of recognition and types of practical relation-to-self, and the ideal of full human flourishing as dependent on the existence of reciprocal relations of recognition. Second, these interpretations serve to forestall easy dismissals of either Hegelian or Meadian ideas on the basis of misassociations or distortions built into prevailing views on these thinkers. Finally, the discussions of Hegel and Mead – along with those of Marx, Sorel, and Sartre – serve to situate Honneth's own position within an often-overlooked tradition of social theory. By reconstructing and revising an alternative to the dominant tradition of modern social philosophy founded by Hobbes and Machiavelli, Honneth is able to undermine the apparent self-evidence of its underlying assumptions – in particular, assumptions about both the self-interested (what Honneth calls 'utilitarian') motives for social conflict and the atomistic character of the state of nature. He thereby opens up the theoretical space for conceiving struggles for recognition as attempts on the part of social actors to establish patterns of reciprocal recognition on which the very possibility of redeeming their claims to identity depends. On Honneth's understanding, that possibility is at the heart of social justice in the fullest sense.[23]

Preface

Without the persistent pressure and keen interest of Jürgen Habermas, the first half of this book, which was submitted as a *Habilitation* to the Department of Philosophy of the University of Frankfurt, would not have reached completion within the necessary time period. I wish to thank him here for six years of cooperation, the significance of which for my own process of intellectual formation he will surely underestimate. As always, my friend Hans Joas has closely followed the development of my ideas from their inception. He will, I hope, know the importance that his advice and criticism has long had for my work. I have received important suggestions on several parts of the manuscript from Peter Dews, Alessandro Ferrara, Hinrich Fink-Eitel, Günter Frankenberg, Christoph Menke, Andreas Wildt, and Lutz Wingert. I owe them all my deepest gratitude, even though not all their ideas have made their way into the book. I wish also to thank Waltraud Pfeiffer and Dirk Mende for technical help with the completion of the manuscript. Finally, I consider myself to have been most fortunate in having had Joel Anderson as translator of the English edition. He has the rare ability of understanding the intentions of the author sometimes better than the author himself. I am grateful to him for all his commitment.

A. H.

Frankfurt am Main

Introduction

In the present volume, I attempt to develop, on the basis of Hegel's model of a 'struggle for recognition', the foundations for a social theory with normative content. The intention to undertake this project arose in connection with the conclusions I reached in *The Critique of Power*: any attempt to integrate the social-theoretical insights of Foucault's historical work within the framework of a theory of communicative action has to rely on a concept of morally motivated struggle. And there is no better source of inspiration for developing such a concept than Hegel's early, 'Jena' writings, with their notion of a comprehensive 'struggle for recognition'.[1]

The systematic reconstruction of the Hegelian line of argumentation, which constitutes the first third of the book, leads to a distinction between three forms of recognition, each of which contains a potential motivation for social conflict. This review of the young Hegel's theoretical model also makes clear, however, that the validity of his thoughts hinges, in part, on Idealist assumptions about reason that can no longer be maintained under conditions of postmetaphysical thinking.

The second, theoretical part of the book thus starts from the attempt to develop an empirical version of the Hegelian idea by drawing on the social psychology of G. H. Mead. In this way, an intersubjectivist concept of the person emerges, in which the possibility of an undistorted relation to oneself proves to be dependent on three forms of recognition: love, rights, and esteem. In order to remove the merely historical character of this hypothesis, I attempt to justify, in the empirically supported reconstruction found in the subsequent two chapters, the distinction between the various forms of relations of recognition on the basis of the relevant phenomena. As the results of this investigation show, there are – corresponding to the three forms of recognition – three forms of experiences of disrespect, each of which can generate motives that contribute, in turn, to the emergence of social conflicts.[2]

As a consequence of this second step of the investigation, the idea of a critical social theory begins to take shape, according to which processes of societal change are to be explained with reference to the normative claims that are structurally inherent in relations of mutual recognition. In the final part of the book, I go on to explore, in three directions, the perspectives opened up by this basic idea. First, the historical thread is taken up again, in order to examine where, since Hegel, comparable approaches are to be found. From that point, insights into the historical significance of experiences of disrespect become possible, insights which can be generalized to such an extent that the moral logic of social conflicts becomes evident. Because such a model can only be developed into a critical framework of interpretation for processes of historical development once its normative point of reference has been clarified, I conclude by sketching a conception of ethical life, developed in terms of a theory of recognition, that might accomplish this task. Admittedly, these various suggestions cannot claim to represent anything more than a first attempt to clarify what is involved in the conception under consideration. They are meant to indicate the theoretical directions in which I will have to work further, should my considerations prove tenable.

Although current works of feminist political philosophy often lead in a direction that intersects with the aims of a theory of recognition,[3] I have had to postpone the idea of a critical encounter with this discussion. It would not only have burst the bounds of my framework of argumentation, it would also have taken me well beyond my current level of expertise. Furthermore, in developing my own proposal for interpreting the young Hegel's theory of recognition, I have also unfortunately been unable to take into consideration the work most recently published on this subject.[4] My impression, however, is that they concentrate on phenomena that would be of only secondary interest to me.

Part I

An Alternative Tradition in Modern Social Theory:

Hegel's Original Idea

In his political philosophy, Hegel set out to remove the character of a mere 'ought' from the Kantian idea of individual autonomy by developing a theory that represented it as a historically effective element of social reality, and he consistently understood the solution to the problem thus posed to involve the attempt to mediate between the modern doctrine of freedom and the ancient conception of politics, between morality and ethical life [Sittlichkeit].[1] But it is only in the years that he spent in Jena as a young philosophy lecturer that he worked out the theoretical means for accomplishing this task, an approach whose inner principle pointed beyond the institutional horizon of his day and stood in a critical relationship to the established form of political rule. At the time, Hegel was convinced that a struggle among subjects for the mutual recognition of their identity generated inner-societal pressure toward the practical, political establishment of institutions that would guarantee freedom. It is individuals' claim to the intersubjective recognition of their identity that is built into social life from the very beginning as a moral tension, transcends the level of social progress institutionalized thus far, and so gradually leads – via the negative path of recurring stages of conflict – to a state of communicatively lived freedom. The young Hegel could develop this conception, which has never really been made fruitful, only because he was able to modify the model of 'social struggle' introduced in the social philosophies of Machiavelli and Hobbes in such a way that conflict among humans could be traced back, not to a motive of self-preservation, but to moral impulses. Only because he had already interpreted struggle specifically as a disturbance and violation of social relations of recognition could he then locate within it the central medium of the human spirit's [Geist] process of ethical development.

Within Hegel's oeuvre, of course, the programme thus outlined never made it beyond the level of mere sketches and proposals. Already in the *Phenomenology of Spirit*, the completion of which brought to a close Hegel's period in Jena, the conceptual model of a 'struggle for recognition' had lost its central position within Hegel's theory.

Nonetheless, in the writings that have survived from the period before the final system had been worked out,[2] this model is so clearly recognizable in its theoretical principles that the premises for an independent social theory can be reconstructed from them.

1

The Struggle for Self-preservation: On the Foundation of Modern Social Philosophy

Modern social philosophy entered the history of thought at the moment in which social life had come to be characterized as fundamentally a condition of struggle for self-preservation. Machiavelli's political writings paved the way for this conception, according to which individual subjects and political communities alike oppose one another in a state of constant competition over interests. In the work of Thomas Hobbes, this competition ultimately became the chief foundation for a contractualist justification of the sovereignty of the state. This new model for representing the 'struggle for self-preservation' could only emerge after central components of the political doctrine found in antiquity, accepted until well into the Middle Ages, lost their enormous power to convince.[1] From the Classical politics of Aristotle to the medieval Christian doctrine of natural law, human beings were conceived of fundamentally as entities capable of life in community, as a *zoon politikon*, as beings who had to rely on the social framework of a political community for the realization of their inner nature. Only in the ethical community of the *polis* or *civitas* – whose intersubjectively shared virtues sharply distinguished them from the merely functional nexus formed by economic activities – could the social character of human nature genuinely develop. Starting from this teleological conception of human beings, the traditional doctrine of politics set itself the theoretical task of defining the ethical order of virtuous conduct within which individuals' practical, indeed pedagogical, development could take the most appropriate course. Thus, political science was always an inquiry into the appropriate institutions and laws as well as a doctrine of the good and just life.

But the accelerated transformation of social structures that began in the late Middle Ages and reached its high point in the Renaissance not only brought these two elements of Classical politics into doubt. It robbed them, in principle, of all intellectual vitality. For, as a result of the introduction of new commercial methods, the development of publishing and manufacturing, and finally the newly acquired independence of principalities and trading cities, the sphere of political and economic activity had so outgrown the protective framework of traditional morals that it could no longer sensibly be studied solely as a normative order of virtuous conduct. It comes as no surprise, then, that the theoretical transformation of Classical political philosophy into modern social theory was prepared precisely where those changes in the social structure had already occurred with such clarity. In his political treatises, written as a frustrated diplomat of his native city of Florence, Niccolò Machiavelli departed radically and unceremoniously from traditional philosophical anthropology by introducing a conception of humans as egocentric beings with regard only for their own benefit.[2] In his various reflections on the question of how a political community could prudently maintain and expand its power, Machiavelli set in place a socio-ontological foundation that amounts to the assumption of a permanent state of hostile competition between subjects. Since human beings, driven by endless ambition to continue inventing new strategies for success-oriented action, are mutually aware of the egocentricity of their interests, they ceaselessly face each other in a stance of fearful mistrust.[3] Machiavelli takes it to be self-evident that this unconstrained web of strategic interactions constitutes the raw state of nature, and it is to this perpetual struggle for self-preservation that the central categories of Machiavelli's comparative historical analyses are tailored. This can be seen from the fact that these categories represent nothing other than the structural presuppositions for the successful exercise of power. Even in the places where he still makes use of the basic metaphysical concepts of Roman historiography and speaks, for example, of *'virtu'* and *'fortuna'*, he means only to refer to marginal historical conditions, which, from the perspective of political actors, prove to be practically unharnessable resources for their strategic, power-oriented calculations.[4] For Machiavelli, the ultimate point of reference throughout all his historical investigations remains the question of how a given ruler can adroitly influence this uninterrupted conflict among human beings to his own advantage. It was in his writings, then – including his account of societal development – that the idea of the realm of social action consisting in a permanent struggle among subjects for the preservation of their physical identity first established itself, although it still lacked any theoretical justification.

The mere 120 years that separate Thomas Hobbes from Machiavelli were enough to give this same fundamental ontological conviction the mature form of a scientifically founded hypothesis. Compared to Machiavelli, Hobbes not only has the advantage of the historical and political experience of the development of the modern state apparatus and a further expansion of trade. He could also already find support for his theoretical endeavours in the model of the natural sciences, which meanwhile had attained general credence as a result of Galileo's successful research methodology and Descartes's epistemology.[5] Within the framework of the ambitious project of investigating the 'laws of civil life' in order to provide a scientific basis for all future politics, the same presuppositions about human nature that Machiavelli had taken over in a methodologically uncritical manner from his everyday observations assume the form of scientific assertions about the singular nature of human beings. For Hobbes – who thinks of human beings, mechanistically, as something like self-propelled automatons – what is distinctive about humans is their exceptional ability to concern themselves with their future welfare.[6] As soon as one human being encounters another, however, this anticipatory behaviour generates a form of preventive power-escalation that is born in suspicion. Since both subjects must remain mutually alien and inscrutable in their intentions, each is forced into a prospective expansion of its potential for power, in order to be able to defend itself in the future against possible attacks from the other.

On the basis of this anti-Aristotelian core of his philosophical anthropology, Hobbes then develops, in the second part of his project, the fictitious state among humans that he sought to characterize with the easily misunderstood title 'nature'. As Günther Buck has been able to show convincingly,[7] the doctrine of the state of nature is not intended to present the social point of departure for human socialization in methodological abstraction from all of history. Rather, it is meant to provide a representation of the general state among humans that would, in theory, hold if every political institution regulating social life were now hypothetically removed. Since a stance of preventive power-escalation is supposed to be constitutive for the individual nature of humans, the social relations resulting from such a subtraction would possess the character of a war of all against all. In the third part of his project, Hobbes ultimately uses this theoretically constituted situation to lay a philosophical foundation for his own construction of the sovereignty of the state. The obviously negative consequences of a perpetual situation of struggle among human beings, of permanent fear, and of mutual distrust are supposed to prove that the contractually regulated submission of all subjects to a sovereign ruling power is the only reasonable outcome of an instrumentally rational weighing of interests.[8] In Hobbes's theory, the crucial justification for the social contract lies simply in the fact that it alone can put an end to the war of all against all, a war that subjects wage for their own individual self-preservation.

For Hobbes, as for Machiavelli, this socio-ontological premise – which they share despite all differences of scholarly intent and execution – has the same consequences for the fundamental concept of state action. Since both make subjects' struggle for self-preservation the final point of reference of their theoretical analyses, they must, concomitantly, also consider the ultimate purpose of political practice to be the attempt, over and over again, to bring a halt to this ever-threatening conflict. In the case of Machiavelli, this outcome becomes visible in the radicalness, relative to the political and philosophical tradition, with which he releases the sovereign's exercise of power from all normative bonds and duties.[9] In the case of Thomas Hobbes's theory of the state, the same outcome manifests itself in the fact that he ultimately sacrificed the liberal content of the social contract for the sake of the authoritarian form of its realization.[10]

And it was precisely this tendency of modern social philosophy to reduce the activity of the state to the instrumentally rational establishment of power that the young Hegel opposed in his political philosophy. The exceptional, even unique place of his Jena writings, however, stems from the fact that he appropriated this Hobbesian conceptual model of interpersonal struggle in order to realize his critical intentions.

2

Crime and Ethical Life: Hegel's Intersubjectivist Innovation

By the time Hegel took up the model of social struggle that Machiavelli and Hobbes had each independently implemented, the theoretical context was entirely changed. In his 1802 essay on 'The Scientific Way of Treating Natural Law', in which he outlined a plan for his future works on practical and political philosophy, the hundred years of intellectual development that separate him from Hobbes are already expressed in a shift to a completely different set of questions. Under the influence of Hölderlin's philosophy of unification [*Vereinigungsphilosophie*], he had come to question the individualistic presuppositions of Kant's moral theory, a theory which had determined the horizon of his thinking until well into his years in Frankfurt.[1] At the same time, his reading of Plato and Aristotle had familiarized him with a current within political philosophy that ascribed a much greater role to the intersubjectivity of public life than did comparable approaches of his time.[2] And finally, as a result of his study of British political economy, he had also already come to the sobering insight that any future organization of society would inevitably have to rely on a sphere of market-mediated production and distribution, in which subjects could only be included in society on the basis of the negative freedom guaranteed by formal rights.[3]

By the start of the century, these newly acquired impressions and orientations had gradually matured within Hegel's thought into the conviction that, for the foundation of a philosophical science of society, it would first be necessary to break the grip that atomistic misconceptions had on the whole tradition of modern natural law. This raised, in a fundamental way, a number of theoretical problems for which the long essay on natural law suggests a first approach to a solution.

Despite all the differences between the two conceptions of modern natural law that he distinguishes in his text, Hegel sees them as marked by the same fundamental error. Both the 'empirical' and 'formal' treatments of natural law categorically presuppose the 'being of the individual' to be 'the primary and the supreme thing'.[4] In this context, Hegel labels all those approaches to natural law 'empirical' that start out from a fictitious or anthropological characterization of human nature and then, on the basis of this and with the help of further assumptions, propose a rational organization of collective life within society. The atomistic premises of theories of this type are reflected in the fact that they always conceive of the purportedly 'natural' form of human behaviour exclusively as the isolated acts of solitary individuals, to which forms of community-formation must then be added as a further thought, as if externally.[5] The approaches within the natural law tradition that Hegel terms 'formal' proceed in principle no differently since, instead of starting from a characterization of human nature, they start from a transcendental concept of practical reason. In such theories, represented above all by Kant and Fichte, the atomistic premises are evident in the fact that ethical acts cannot be thought of except as resulting from the exercise of reason, purified of all of the empirical inclinations and needs of human nature. Here, too, human nature is understood as an aggregate of egocentric (or, as Hegel puts it, 'unethical') drives, which subjects must first learn to suppress before they can attain ethical attitudes, that is, attitudes conducive to community.[6] Thus, both approaches remain trapped within the basic concepts of an atomism that presupposes, as something like a natural basis for human socialization, the existence of subjects who are isolated from each other. A condition of ethical unification among people can, however, no longer be seen as developing organically out of this fact of nature, but has to be added externally, as 'something other and alien'.[7] The consequence of this, according to Hegel, is that within modern natural law, a 'community of human beings' can only be conceptualized on the abstract model of a 'unified many',[8] that is, as a cluster of single subjects, and thus not on the model of an ethical unity.

But what concerned Hegel in his political philosophy was the possibility of theoretically explicating just such an ethical totality. As far back as the period in which, together with Schelling and Hölderlin, he drew up the programmatic text that has gone down in intellectual history as 'The Earliest Systematic Programme of German Idealism',[9] one can find in Hegel's thought the idea that a reconciled society could be properly understood only as an ethically integrated community of free citizens. In the meantime, of course, this intuition of his youth had outgrown the aesthetic framework within which it had originated and, as a result of his confrontation with the Classical doctrine of the state, had found in the *polis* a political and institutional model. In the essay on natural law, whenever Hegel speaks, in a normative sense, of the ethical totality of a society, he has in mind the relations within the city-states of antiquity. What he admires about them is the romantically transfigured circumstance that, in publicly practised customs, members of the community could also witness the intersubjective expression of their own particularity. And down to the details of the account of the Estates, his text reproduces the theory in which Plato and Aristotle had presented the institutional constitution of those city-states.

Already at this point, however, Hegel distils from the concrete ideal that he enthusiastically believed he had found in the idea of the *polis* the general features of an ideal community. Indeed, he does this so clearly that one gains at least a rough sense of the conception of ethical totality that he employs in the text. First, the singularity of such a society could be seen, by analogy with an organism, in the 'lively unity' of 'universal and individual freedom'.[10] What this means is that public life would have to be regarded not as the result of the mutual restriction of private spheres of liberty, but rather the other way around, namely, as the opportunity for the fulfilment of every single individual's freedom. Second, Hegel views the mores and customs that come to be employed communicatively within a social community as the social medium through which the integration of universal and individual freedom is to occur. He chose the concept '*Sitte*' ['mores' or 'customs'] quite intentionally, in order to be able to make clear that neither laws prescribed by the state nor the moral convictions of isolated subjects but only attitudes that are actually acted out intersubjectively can provide a sound basis for the exercise of that extended freedom.[11] For this reason, the public 'system of legislation' is always intended to express only the 'living customs' actually 'present in the nation', as the text has it.[12] Third and lastly, Hegel takes a decisive step beyond Plato and Aristotle by including, within the institutional organization of absolute ethical life, a sphere that he provisionally labels 'the system of property and law'. This is linked to the intent to show that individuals' market-mediated activities and interests – which later come to be gathered under the title 'civil society' – comprise a 'negative' though still constitutive 'zone' of the 'ethical' [*sittlich*] whole.[13] A further example in the text of Hegel's attempt to render his societal ideal realistic can be found in his departure from the Classical doctrine of the state, through the initial introduction of the unfree Estate as a class of producing and trading citizens.

Insofar as the foregoing discussion adequately describes the framework within which Hegel attempted, in Jena, to reappropriate the societal ideal of his youth, it also outlined the main problem that will confront him from now on. If indeed it turned out that modern social philosophy is not in a position to account for such a higher-level form of social community owing to the fact that it remains trapped within atomistic premises, then the first implication of this for political theory is that a new and different system of basic concepts must be developed. Hegel thus faces the question of what these categorial tools must be like, if they are to make it possible to explain philosophically the development of an organization of society whose ethical cohesion would lie in a form of solidarity based on the recognition of the individual freedom of all citizens. During the Jena years, Hegel's work in political philosophy was directed towards finding a solution to the systematic problems that this question generates. The various proposals that he developed within the context of the emerging system of the logic of the human spirit have their common roots in this enterprise, and they all refer back to it.

In his essay on the different theories of natural law, however, Hegel has not yet developed a solution to this problem, but he has already marked out the rough contours of the route by which he will reach it. His first step in attempting to give the philosophical science of society a new foundation is to replace atomistic basic concepts with categories that are geared to the social nexus between subjects. In a now famous passage, Hegel quotes Aristotle as follows: 'The nation [*Volk*] comes by nature before the individual. If the individual in isolation is not anything self-sufficient, he must be related to the whole nation in one unity, just as other parts are to their whole'.[14] In the context in which this quotation occurs, Hegel merely wants to say that every philosophical theory of society must proceed not from the acts of isolated subjects but rather from the framework of ethical bonds, within which subjects always already move. Thus, contrary to atomistic theories of society, one is to assume, as a kind of natural basis for human socialization, a situation in which elementary forms of intersubjective coexistence are always present. In so doing, Hegel is quite clearly taking his lead from the Aristotelian notion that there is, inherent in human nature, a substratum of links to community, links that fully unfold only in the context of the *polis*.[15]

What is crucial for everything that follows, however, is the second step, in which Hegel has to show how he can explain the transition from such a state of 'natural ethical life' to the form of societal organization that he previously defined as a relationship of ethical totality. In the theories of natural law criticized by Hegel, the theoretical position thus delineated is occupied either by the model of an original social contract or by various assumptions about the civilizing effects of practical reason. They are each supposed to explain how the overcoming of human 'nature' can bring about an orderly condition of collective social life. But for Hegel there is no need to appeal to such external hypotheses, for the simple reason that he has already presupposed the existence of intersubjective obligations as a quasi-natural precondition for every process of human socialization. What he has to explain, then, is not the genesis of mechanisms of community-formation in general, but rather the reorganization and expansion of embryonic forms of community into more encompassing relations of social interaction. In order to address the issue this raises, Hegel begins by appealing once again to Aristotelian ontology, from which he borrows the idea that this transition must have the form of a teleological process in which an original substance gradually reaches its full development. At the same time, however, he emphasizes so decisively the negative, agonistic character of this teleological process that one can easily detect in his reflections the basic thought that he works out, with the help of the concept of recognition, in repeated proposals in the subsequent years. Hegel sets out to conceptualize the path by which 'ethical nature attains its true right'[16] as a process of recurring negations, by which the ethical relations of society are to be successively freed from their remaining one-sidedness and particularities. As he puts it, the 'existence of difference' is what allows ethical life to move beyond its natural initial stage and, in a series of rectifications of destroyed equilibria, ultimately leads to a unity of the universal and the particular. Put positively, this means that the history of human spirit is to be understood as a conflictual process in which the 'moral' potential inherent in natural ethical life (as something 'enclosed and not yet unfolded'[17]) is gradually generalized. In the same passage, Hegel speaks of the 'budding of ethical life' as 'the emerging progressive supersession of the negative or subjective'.[18]

What remains completely unclear with regard to this basic conception, however, is what these undeveloped potentials of ethical life must be like, if they are to be already inherent, as an existing difference, in the initial structures of social ways of life. And left equally open in the text is the question of the proposed shape of this process of recurring negations by which these same ethical potentials could develop in the direction of universal validity.

For Hegel, the solution to these two problems is further complicated by the need to describe the normative content of the first stage of socialization in such a way that a process can arise involving both a growth of community ties and, at the same time, an increase in individual freedom. For only if the world-historical course of the 'budding of ethical life' can be conceived as an interpenetration of socialization and individuation can one assume that the organic coherence of the resulting form of society lies in the intersubjective recognition of the particularity of all individuals. In the early Jena years, however, Hegel does not yet have the suitable means for solving the problems generated by this difficult task. He is able to find a satisfactory answer only after, in the course of reinterpreting Fichte's theory of recognition, he has also given the Hobbesian concept of struggle a new meaning.[19]

In the beginning of his Jena period, just as previously in Frankfurt, Hegel always referred to Fichte only critically. As we have seen, Hegel considered him to be the central representative of the 'formal' approach within the natural law tradition, which was unable to provide a theoretical account of a 'genuinely free community of living relations'.[20] But in the *System of Ethical Life* – written in 1802, immediately after the completion of the natural law essay – Hegel treats Fichte's theory positively, drawing on it in order better to describe the internal structure of those forms of ethical relations that he wished to presuppose as a fundamental 'first' of human socialization. In his essay, 'The Foundations of Natural Law', Fichte had conceived of recognition as the 'reciprocal effect' [*Wechselwirkung*] between individuals that underlies legal relations: by both mutually requiring one another to act freely and limiting their own sphere of action to the other's advantage, subjects form a common consciousness which then attains objective validity in legal relations.[21] Hegel first removes the transcendental implications from Fichte's model and then applies it directly to various different forms of reciprocal action among individuals. He thus projects onto the intersubjective process of mutual recognition communicative forms of life, which he had heretofore described, following Aristotle, merely as various forms of ethical life. He now sees a society's ethical relations as representing forms of practical intersubjectivity in which the movement of recognition guarantees the complementary agreement and thus the necessary mutuality of opposed subjects. The structure of any of these relationships of mutual recognition is always the same for Hegel: to the degree that a subject knows itself to be recognized by another subject with regard to certain of its [the subject's] abilities and qualities and is thereby reconciled with the other, a subject always also comes to know its own distinctive identity and

thereby comes to be opposed once again to the other as something
particular. But in this logic of the recognition relationship, Hegel also
detects an implicit inner dynamic, which allows him to take a second
step beyond Fichte's initial model. Since, within the framework of an
ethically established relationship of mutual recognition, subjects are
always learning something more about their particular identity, and
since, in each case, it is a new dimension of their selves that they see
confirmed thereby, they must once again leave, by means of conflict,
the stage of ethical life they have reached, in order to achieve the
recognition of a more demanding form of their individuality. In this
sense, the movement of recognition that forms the basis of an ethical
relationship between subjects consists in a process of alternating stages
of both reconciliation and conflict. It is not hard to see that Hegel
thereby infuses the Aristotelian concept of an ethical form of life with
a moral potential that no longer arises merely out of the fundamental
nature of human beings but rather out of a particular kind of relationship between them. Thus, the coordinates of his political philosophy
shift from a teleological concept of nature to a concept of the social, in
which an internal tension is contained constitutively.

By thus using a theory of conflict to make Fichte's model of recognition more dynamic, Hegel gains not only the possibility of providing a first determination of the inner potential of human ethical life
but also the opportunity to make its 'negative' course of development
more concrete. The path that takes him there consists in a reinterpretation of the model of an original struggle of all against all, with
which Thomas Hobbes (drawing on Machiavelli) had opened the
history of modern social philosophy.[22] If the reason why subjects have
to move out of ethical relationships in which they find themselves is
that they believe their particular identity to be insufficiently recognized, then the resulting struggle cannot be a confrontation purely
over self-preservation. Rather, the conflict that breaks out between
subjects represents, from the outset, something ethical, insofar as it is
directed towards the intersubjective recognition of dimensions of human individuality. It is not the case, therefore, that a contract among
individuals puts an end to the precarious state of a struggle for survival of all against all. Rather, inversely, this struggle leads, as a moral
medium, from an underdeveloped state of ethical life to a more mature level of ethical relations. With this reinterpretation of the Hobbesian model, Hegel introduces a virtually epoch-making new version
of the conception of social struggle, according to which practical conflict between subjects can be understood as an ethical moment in
a movement occurring within a collective social life.[23] This newly

created conception of the social thereby includes, from the start, not only a field of moral tensions but also the social medium by which they are settled through conflict.

It is only in the Jena writings, however, that the basic theoretical idea resulting from this innovative coupling of Hobbesian and Fichtean themes gradually takes shape. In the *System of Ethical Life*, the first in this series of writings, this newly acquired model first becomes evident in the construction of the argument, which represents, as it were, a mirror image of the model of the state in *Leviathan*. Instead of starting from a struggle of all against all, Hegel begins his philosophical account with elementary forms of interpersonal recognition, which he presents collectively under the heading 'natural ethical life'. And it is not until these initial relations of recognition are injured by various kinds of struggle – grouped together as an intermediate stage of 'crime' – that a state of social integration emerges that can be conceptualized formally as an organic relationship of pure ethical life. For methodological reasons, Hegel attempted (following Schelling) to give his text a very schematic form of presentation.[24] But if, subsequently, one peels this form away from the substance of the argument, the individual steps of a social-theoretical model become clearly visible.

Hegel initially describes the process by which the first social relations are established in terms of the release of subjects from their natural determinations. This growth of 'individuality' occurs in two stages of mutual recognition, which differ from each other in the dimensions of personal identity that receive practical confirmation. In the relationship between 'parents and children', which represents 'the universal reciprocal action and formative education of human beings', subjects recognize each other reciprocally as living, emotionally needy beings. Here, the component of individual personality recognized by others is 'practical feeling', that is, the dependence of individuals on vitally essential care and goods. The 'labour' of raising children, which for Hegel constitutes the inner determination of the family, is directed towards the formation of the child's 'inner negativity' and independence, so that, as a result, 'the unification of feeling' must be 'superseded'.[25] Hegel then follows this (now superseded) form of recognition with a second stage, still under the heading 'natural ethical life', of contractually regulated relations of exchange among property owners. The path leading to this new social relationship is described as a process of legal universalization. The practical relations to the world that subjects had in the first stage are then wrenched from their merely particular conditions of validity and transformed into universal, contractually established legal claims. From now on, subjects mutually recognize each other as bearers of legitimate claims to possession, thereby constituting each other as property owners. In the act of exchange, they relate to each other as 'persons' who are accorded the 'formal' right to respond to all offered transactions with 'yes' or 'no'. To this extent, the recognition that single individuals receive here in the form of a legal title represents the negatively determined freedom 'to be the opposite of oneself with respect to some specific characteristic'.[26]

The formulations with which Hegel chooses to portray this second stage suffice to make clear why he considered this still to be a 'natural' form of ethical life as well. The establishment of legal relations actually creates a social situation that is itself still marked by the 'principle of singularity', from which only relations of absolute ethical life are completely free. For, in a type of societal organization characterized by legal forms of recognition, subjects are constitutively integrated only via negative liberties, that is, merely on the basis of their ability to negate social offers. By this point, of course, the socializing movement of recognition has already broken through the particularistic constraints placed on it in the first stage by affective family ties. But initially, progress in social universalization is paid for with an emptying and formalizing of the aspects of the individual subject that receive intersubjective confirmation. Within society, the individual is not yet, as Hegel says, posited as a 'totality' and thus not yet as a 'whole that reconstructs itself out of difference'.[27]

What sets the *System of Ethical Life* apart is the fact that Hegel counterposes the two 'natural' forms of recognition (as a whole) to various kinds of struggle, which he summarizes in a separate chapter. Whereas the social-philosophical proposals of the following years are constructed in such a way that the struggle for recognition leads from one stage of ethical life to the next, here there is only one single stage of various different struggles between the two stages of elementary and absolute ethical life. It is difficult to see what theoretical reasons may have moved Hegel to this unconventional model, a model that is not particularly plausible either in terms of social history or of developmental logic. In part, of course, these reasons are generated by the methodological restrictions that accompany the schematic application of Schelling's epistemology. But they are also, in part, the result of the direct opposition to Hobbes, which may have provoked him to depict the 'natural' state of conflict-free ethical life in a unified manner. In any case, Hegel does not yet use his model of struggle here to theorize the transition between the individual stages already distinguished within the movement of recognition. Rather, he follows them with a single stage of different struggles, whose collective effect consists in continually interrupting already established processes of mutual recognition with new conflicts. What primarily interests Hegel is the internal course of the struggle resulting from these disruptions of social life, and his analysis of this is based on interpretating acts of destruction as expressions of 'crime'.

For Hegel, the various acts of destruction that he distinguishes, in his intermediate chapter, represent different forms of crime.[28] He connects criminal acts with the previous stage of ethical life by characterizing each type as a form of the negative exercise of abstract freedom, specifically, the abstract freedom that subjects had already been granted in juridified relations of recognition. The claim that the form of law, on the one hand, and criminal acts, on the other, are dependent on each other becomes theoretically comprehensible once one also takes into account the conception of 'crime' already contained in Hegel's early theological writings. There, he had conceived of criminal acts as actions that are tied to the social precondition of legal relations, in the sense that they stem directly from the indeterminacy of a form of individual freedom that is merely legal. In a criminal act, subjects make destructive use of the fact that, as the bearer of rights to liberty, they are integrated only negatively into the collective life of society.[29] In the context of the new text, however, Hegel made no further use of the other side of the theoretical determinations that he had developed in his earlier writings for characterizing crime. Excluded here is the motivational consideration that the act of a criminal represents something like a reaction-formation vis-à-vis the abstractness and one-sidedness structurally inherent in legal relations as such. Owing to the lack of this affirmative component, the *System of Ethical Life* leaves unanswered the question as to which motives provide the impulse for criminal acts. There are only a few places in the argument where one can find comments suggesting an answer along the original lines. 'Natural annihilation', for instance, is said to be directed against the 'abstraction of the cultured', and Hegel speaks elsewhere of crime in general as an 'opposition to opposition'.[30] If one pulls such formulations together and connects them with the older conception, one begins to suspect that Hegel traces the emergence of crime to conditions of incomplete recognition. The criminal's inner motive then consists in the experience of not being recognized, at the established stage of mutual recognition, in a satisfactory way.

This far-reaching theory is further supported by the fact that it enables one to decipher the logic upon which Hegel based his account of the different species of crime. The order in which he presents the individual types of destructive behaviour makes sense when one keeps in mind that the point of the enterprise lies in tracing crime back to incomplete forms of recognition. Hegel introduces into his account the idea of a still fully pointless act of destruction. In acts of 'natural devastation' or 'annihilation', as he calls them, individuals react aimlessly to the experience of the 'abstraction' of already established ethical life. It is unclear whether this is to be taken as meaning that elementary forms of disrespect here constitute the occasion for destructive acts. Moreover, such acts of blind destruction are, in Hegel's sense, not really crimes at all, since they lack the social precondition of legally recognized freedom.

In the stricter sense, crime only emerges with the kind of negative action that Hegel introduces in the second stage. In robbing another person, a subject wilfully violates the universal form of recognition that had already developed with the establishment of legal relations. Although Hegel refuses to say anything about the motives for this type of destructive act, the context of his argument suggests that they may lie in the experience of abstract legal recognition itself. This is supported not only by the activist character of formulations in which Hegel speaks of the 'injury to the law' as well as of the 'goal of robbing',[31] but also by his portrayal of the progression of the conflict situation that emerges with the act of predatory crime. The crime of robbery initially only restricts a subject in its right to its own property. But at the same time, the subject is also attacked in such a way that it is injured, in its entirety, as a 'person', as Hegel puts it. Since we are still operating here at the stage of natural ethical life – where the abstractness of law 'does not yet have its reality and support in something itself universal',[32] and thus lacks the executive power found in state authority – every subject must defend its rights by itself and, hence, each subject's entire identity is threatened by theft.[33]

The affected subject's only appropriate response to this injury to its own person is to defend itself actively against its assailant. This 'repercussion' of the crime for its perpetrator – in the form of the injured person's resistance – is the first sequence of actions that Hegel explicitly calls a 'struggle'. What emerges is a struggle of 'person' against 'person', that is, between two rights-bearing subjects, a struggle for the recognition of each party's different claim: on the one hand, the conflict-generating claim to the unrestricted development of that subject's subjectivity; on the other hand, the reactive claim to social respect for property rights. Hegel considers the outcome of the struggle unleashed by the collision of these two claims to be a foregone conclusion, in that only one of the two divided parties can refer the threat

itionally back to itself as a personality, because only the in-
ubject struggles, in resisting, for the integrity of its whole per-
hereas the criminal is actually merely trying to accomplish
someuing in his or her own particular interest. Therefore, as Hegel
quickly concludes, it is the first, attacked subject that 'must gain the
upper hand' in the struggle, because it 'makes this personal injury a
matter of its entire personality'.[34]

Hegel follows this social conflict, which starts with a theft and ends
with the 'coercion' of the criminal, with a third and final stage of
negation, namely, the struggle for honour. With regard to its starting
conditions alone, this case of conflict represents the most demanding
form of intersubjective diremption [*Entzweiung*]. This conflict is based
not on a violation of an individual assertion of rights, but rather on a
violation of the integrity of the person as a whole. Admittedly, Hegel
once again leaves the particular motives behind this conflict-generating
crime indeterminate here. The reasons, in each case, why a person sets
about destroying the framework of an existing relationship of recognition by injuring or insulting the integrity of another subject remain
unclear. At this point, however, the reference to a totality is presupposed for both participants in the conflict, in the sense that each is
fighting for the 'entirety' of his or her individual existence. This can be
understood to mean that the intention behind the criminal's insulting
act is to demonstrate one's own integrity publicly and thereby make
an appeal for the recognition of that integrity, but then the criminal's
insulting act would, for its part, have its roots in a prior experience of
being insufficiently recognized as an individuated personality.

In any case, the two opposing parties in the emerging conflict both
have the same goal, namely, to provide evidence for the 'integrity' of
his or her own person. Following the usage of his day, Hegel traces
this mutually pursued intention back to a need for 'honour'. This is
initially to be understood as a type of attitude towards oneself, as it
is phrased in the text, through which 'the singular detail becomes
something personal and whole'.[35] 'Honour', then, is the stance I take
towards myself when I identify positively with all my traits and peculiarities. Apparently, then, the only reason that a struggle for 'honour'
would occur is because the possibility of such an affirmative relation-
to-self is dependent, for its part, on the confirming recognition of other
subjects. Individuals can only identify completely with themselves to
the degree to which their peculiarities and traits meet with the approval and support of their partners to interaction. 'Honour' is thus
used to characterize an affirmative relation-to-self that is structurally
tied to the presupposition that each individual particularity receives

intersubjective recognition. For this reason, both subjects i
gle are pursuing the same goal, namely, the re-establishm
honour – which has been injured for different reasons in
by attempting to convince the other that their own personali
recognition. But they are only able to do this, Hegel further asserts, by
demonstrating to each other that they are prepared to risk their lives.
Only by being prepared to die do I publicly show that my individual
goals and characteristics are more significant to me than my physical
survival. In this way, Hegel lets the social conflict resulting from insult turn into a life-and-death struggle, a struggle which always occurs outside the sphere of legally backed claims, since 'the whole [of
a person] is at stake'.[36]

However unclear this account may be on the whole, it offers, for
the first time, a more precise overview of Hegel's theoretical aims in
the intermediate chapter on 'crime'. The fact that, in the progression
of the three stages of social conflict, the identity claims of the subjects
involved gradually expand rules out the possibility of granting a merely
negative significance to the acts of destruction that Hegel describes.
Taken together, the various different conflicts seem rather to comprise
precisely the process that prepares the way for the transition from
natural to absolute ethical life by equipping individuals with the
necessary characteristics and insights. Hegel not only wants to describe
how social structures of elementary recognition are destroyed by
the negative manifestation of freedom; he also wants to show, beyond
this, that it is only via such acts of destruction that ethically more
mature relations of recognition can be formed at all, relations that
represent a precondition for the actual development of a 'community
of free citizens'.[37] Here, one can analytically distinguish two aspects of
intersubjective action as the dimensions along which Hegel ascribes to
social conflicts something like a moral-practical potential for learning.
On the one hand, it is apparently via each new provocation thrust
upon them by various crimes that subjects come to know more about
their own, distinctive identity. This is the developmental dimension
that Hegel seeks to mark linguistically with the transition from 'person'
to 'whole person'. As in the earlier section on 'natural ethical life', the
term 'person' here designates individuals who draw their identity
primarily from the intersubjective recognition of their status as legally
competent agents, whereas the term 'whole person', by contrast, refers
to individuals who gain their identity above all from the intersubjective
recognition of their 'particularity'. On the other hand, however, the
route by which subjects gain greater autonomy is also supposed to
be the path to greater knowledge of their mutual dependence. This is

the developmental dimension that Hegel seeks to make clear by letting the struggle for honour, in the end, change imperceptibly from a conflict between single subjects into a confrontation between social communities. Ultimately, after they have taken on the challenges posed by different crimes, individuals no longer oppose each other as egocentric actors, but as 'members of a whole'.[38]

When these two dimensions are considered together and as a unity, then one begins to see the formative process with which Hegel aims to explain the transition from natural to absolute ethical life. His model is guided by the conviction that it is only with the destruction of legal forms of recognition that a consciousness emerges of the moment within intersubjective relationships that can serve as the foundation for an ethical community. For, by violating first the rights and then the honour of persons, the criminal makes the dependence of individuals on the community a matter of common knowledge. To this extent, the social conflicts that shattered natural ethical life prepare subjects to mutually recognize one another as persons who are dependent on each other and yet also completely individuated.

In the course of his argument, however, Hegel continues to treat this third stage of social interaction, which is supposed to lead to relations of qualitative recognition among the members of a society, merely as an implicit presupposition. In his account of 'absolute ethical life', which follows the crime chapter, the intersubjective foundation of a future community is said to be a specific relationship among subjects, for which the category of 'mutual intuition' emerges here. The individual 'intuits himself as himself in every other individual'.[39] As the appropriation of Schelling's term 'intuition' [*Anschauung*] suggests, Hegel surely intends this formulation to designate a form of reciprocal relations between subjects that goes beyond merely cognitive recognition. Such patterns of recognition, extending even into the sphere of the affective (for which the category of 'solidarity' would seem to be the most likely label),[40] are apparently supposed to provide the communicative basis upon which individuals, who have been isolated from each other by legal relations, can be reunited within the context of an ethical community. In the remaining parts of the *System of Ethical Life*, however, Hegel does not pursue the fruitful line of thought thus outlined. At this point, in fact, the thread of the argument drawing specifically on a theory of recognition breaks off entirely, and the text limits itself, from here on, to an account of the organizational elements that are supposed to characterize political relations in 'absolute ethical life'. As a result, however, the difficulties and problems that Hegel's reconstructive analysis had already failed to address at the previous stages remain open at the end of the text.

Among the unclarities that characterize the *System of Ethical Life* as a whole, the first question to be asked is to what degree the history of ethical life is, in fact, to be reconstructed here in terms of the guiding idea of the development of relationships of recognition. Admittedly, one might object to this reading on the grounds that the text's Aristotelian frame of reference is not at all sufficiently differentiated conceptually to be able to adequately distinguish various forms of intersubjective recognition. In many places, however, the argumentation does suggest a distinction between three forms of recognition, differing from each other with regard to the 'how' as well as the 'what' of practical confirmation: in the affective relationship of recognition found in the family, human individuals are recognized as concrete creatures of need; in the cognitive-formal relationship of recognition found in law, they are recognized as abstract legal persons; and finally, in the emotionally enlightened relationship of recognition found in the State, they are recognized as concrete universals, that is, as subjects who are socialized in their particularity. If, furthermore, in each of the relations of recognition, the institution is more clearly distinguished from the mode, the stage theory that Hegel had in mind can be summarized in the schema shown in figure 1.

In such a stage theory of social recognition, different modes of recognition correspond to different concepts of the person in such a way that a sequence emerges of ever more demanding media of recognition. In the *System of Ethical Life*, however, the corresponding distinctions are too evidently lacking for the certain presence of such a theory

	Object of Recognition		
	individual (concrete needs)	person (formal autonomy)	subject (individual particularity)
Mode of Recognition:			
intuition (affective):	family (love)		
concept (cognitive):		civil society (law)	
intellectual intuition (affect that has become rational):			State (solidarity)

Figure 1

to be unambiguously assumed. Even if it were possible to extract a sufficiently clear distinction of three modes of recognition from Hegel's application of Schelling's model of knowledge, the text would still be obviously missing the complementary concepts of a theory of subjectivity, with which one could also effect such a differentiation with regard to what it is about a person that gets recognized.

The second difficulty that the *System of Ethical Life* fails to consider arises from the question as to the status of 'crime' within the history of ethical life. There is good reason to believe that Hegel granted criminal acts a constructive role in the formative process of ethical life because they were able to unleash the conflicts that, for the first time, would make subjects aware of underlying relations of recognition. If this were the case, however, then the moment of 'struggle' within the movement of recognition would be granted not only a negative, transitional function but also a positive (that is, consciousness-forming) function. Along the diagonal axis (in figure 1) that points in the direction of increasing 'universalization', this moment of 'struggle' would then represent, in each case, the practical conditions of possibility for the transition to the next stage in social relations of recognition. Against this reading, however, it must be pointed out that Hegel's theory leaves the various crimes too unmotivated for them to be able to assume this sort of systematic position in his argumentation. If within this theoretical construct social conflicts were, in fact, supposed to take on the central role of clarifying the reciprocity of specific recognition rules, then it would have been necessary to explicate its internal structure more precisely, both in theoretical and in categorial terms. Thus, in the *System of Ethical Life*, the social-philosophical model that Hegel develops in Jena in order to explain the history of human ethical life is evident only in outline. He is still lacking the crucial means that would put him in a position to provide a more determinate version of his mediation of Fichte and Hobbes.

It becomes possible for Hegel to take such a step towards greater precision once he begins to replace the Aristotelian framework guiding his political philosophy with a new frame of reference. Up to this point, he has drawn his conception of 'ethical life' from a philosophical world of ideas for which the ontological reference to a natural order – however it was conceived – was central. For this reason, he could describe ethical relations among people only as gradations of an underlying natural essence, so that their cognitive and moral qualities had to remain peculiarly indeterminate. In the 'First Philosophy of Spirit', written in 1803/4, however, which stems from the proposal for a system of speculative philosophy once labelled '*Realphilosophie, I*',[41] the concept of 'nature' has already lost its overarching, ontological meaning. Hegel no longer uses it to designate the constitution of reality as a whole, but only of the realm of reality that is opposed to spirit as its other – that is, prehuman, physical nature. Of course, at the same time that the concept of nature was thus restricted, the category of 'spirit' or that of 'consciousness' increasingly took over the task of characterizing exactly that structural principle according to which the social lifeworld is demarcated from natural reality. Here, for the first time, the sphere of ethical life is thus freed up for the categorial definitions and distinctions that are taken from the process of Spirit's reflection.[42] The place occupied by Aristotelian natural teleology, which still had a complete hold on the *System of Ethical Life*, gradually comes to be taken by a philosophical theory of consciousness.

Admittedly, in this process of conceptual transformation, which already points in the direction of the final system, the fragments from 1803/4 have only the status of an intermediate stage. Here, Hegel still clings to the formal structure of his original approach, both in the sense that the ethical relations associated with the State continue to form the central point of reference for the reconstructive analysis and in the sense that the category of consciousness merely serves the explication of forms of ethical life.[43] But even by itself, the turn to categories of the philosophy of consciousness is enough to give the model of a 'struggle for recognition' a markedly altered formulation. Hegel can no longer conceive of the emergence of a State community as the agonistic development of elementary structures of an original, 'natural' form of ethical life, but must instead consider it directly to be the process by which Spirit is formed. This process occurs via the sequence of the mediating instances of language, tool, and family goods, through the use of which consciousness gradually learns to comprehend itself as an 'immediate unity of singularity and universality',[44] and accordingly reaches an understanding of itself as 'totality'. In this new context, 'recognition' refers to the cognitive step taken by a consciousness that has already developed 'ideally' into a totality, at the moment in which it 'perceives itself – in another such totality, consciousness – to be the totality it is'.[45] And the reason why this experience of perceiving oneself in others has to lead to a conflict or struggle is that it is only by mutually violating each other's subjective claims that individuals can come to know whether or not, in them, the respective others also re-identify themselves as a 'totality':

> But this, that my totality as the totality of a single [consciousness] is precisely this totality subsisting, on its own account, in the other

consciousness, whether it is recognized and respected, this I cannot know except through the appearance of the actions of the other against my totality; and likewise the other must equally appear to me as a totality, as I do to him.[46]

As this shows, Hegel has improved the theoretical clarity of his derivation of the struggle for recognition quite a bit, in comparison with the earlier text from the Jena period. The turn to philosophy of consciousness now allows him unambiguously to locate the motives for initiating a conflict in the interior of the human spirit, which is supposed to be constructed in such a way that for its complete realization it presupposes knowledge of its recognition by others, which can only be acquired through conflict. Individuals can feel sure that they are recognized by their partners to interaction only by experiencing the practical reaction with which the others respond to a targeted, even provocative challenge.[47] On the other hand, it is clear that the social function that the struggle thus initiated is to have in the context of the process of ethical formation remains basically unchanged in the new theoretical context. Indeed, as in the *System of Ethical Life*, conflict represents a sort of mechanism of social integration into community, which forces subjects to cognize each other mutually in such a way that their individual consciousness of totality has ultimately become interwoven, together with that of everyone else, into a 'universal' consciousness. As in the earlier text, this now 'absolute' consciousness finally provides Hegel with the intellectual basis for a future, ideal community: produced by mutual recognition as a medium of social universalization, 'the spirit of a people' is formed, and to that extent the 'living substance' of its ethics is formed as well.[48]

Despite these rough points of agreement in outcome, however, there can be no mistake as to the serious difference between the two fragmentary texts at the level of fundamentals. Both texts do, of course, conceive of the struggle for recognition as a social process that leads to increasing integration into community, in the sense of a decentralization of individual forms of consciousness. But only the earlier text – that is to say, only the *System of Ethical Life* – attaches to this struggle the further significance of being, at the same time, a medium of individualization, of increasing ego-competence. This surprising contrast becomes comprehensible in systematic terms when one considers more closely the points of conceptual divergence to which the different approaches must necessarily give rise. As has been shown, the change in human interactive relations described in the *System of Ethical Life* is a change with a direction. From the start, owing to the text's Aristotelian frame of reference, the foregoing reconstructive analysis has centred on the normatively substantive relationships of communication out of which individuals must be differentiated before they can understand each other to be individuated subjects. Taken together, however, both the emancipation of individual subjects and their growing communalization among each other should be initiated and driven on by the struggle for recognition, which, to the degree to which it gradually makes them aware of their subjective claims, simultaneously allows a rational feeling for their intersubjective similarities to emerge. But Hegel must distance himself from the complex task thus formulated as soon as he replaces the Aristotelian frame of reference with a theory of consciousness as the basis for his political philosophy. Because the object domain of his reconstructive analysis is now no longer composed primarily out of forms of social interaction – that is, of 'ethical relations' – but consists rather in stages of the self-mediation of individual consciousness, communicative relations between subjects can no longer be conceived as something that in principle precedes individuals.

Whereas Hegel's philosophical investigations had, until this point, proceeded from the elementary system of relationships associated with communicative action, here (in the fragments of 1803/4) the analysis begins with the theoretical and practical confrontation of individuals with their environment. The intellectual formative process resulting from this confrontation – the further development of which takes the form of Spirit's reflection on the mediations that it has already intuitively accomplished – allows, first, a consciousness of totality to emerge in the individual subject, which leads, second, to the stage of universalization or decentralization of ego-perspectives that accompanies the struggle for recognition. To this extent, the conflict between subjects has lost the second dimension of significance that it had in the *System of Ethical Life*. For it no longer represents a medium for consciousness-formation of individuals as well but is left instead only with the function of being a medium of social universalization, that is, of integration into community. Because Hegel gives up, along with the Aristotelianism of his early Jena writings, the notion of an original intersubjectivity of human life, he can no longer conceive the process of individualization in terms of the agonistic release of individuals from already existing communicative relations. In fact, his political theory of ethical life completely loses the character of a 'history of society', of an analysis of directional changes in social relations, and gradually takes on the form of an analysis of the education [*Bildung*] of the individual for society.

If these considerations are correct, Hegel paid for the theoretical gains of his turn to the philosophy of consciousness by sacrificing his strong intersubjectivism. By making the conceptual modification first introduced in the proposed system of 1803/4, Hegel does create, for the first time, the theoretical possibility for conceptually distinguishing more precisely between the individual stages of individual consciousness-formation. At the same time, this generates the opportunity for differentiating various concepts of the person that his approach had been lacking. But the benefit thus obtained, in terms of a theory of subjectivity, comes at the expense of a communication-theoretical alternative, which was in fact also implicit in the reference to Aristotle. The turn to the philosophy of consciousness allows Hegel to completely lose sight of the idea of an original intersubjectivity of humankind and blocks the way to the completely different solution that would have consisted in making the necessary distinctions between various degrees of personal autonomy within the framework of a theory of intersubjectivity. But the categorial advantages and the theoretical losses that this cognitive step generates for Hegel's idea of a 'struggle for recognition' can only be adequately assessed in connection with the text in which this conceptual reorientation comes to a provisional conclusion. Already in the 1803/4 draft of his *Realphilosophie* – the last text before the *Phenomenology of Spirit* – Hegel analysed the formative process of Spirit entirely within the framework of the newly acquired paradigm of the philosophy of consciousness. Despite the fact that virtually all echoes of the *System of Ethical Life* have disappeared from this text, never again in the later political philosophy is the 'struggle for recognition' given such a strong, systematic position as here.

3

The Struggle for Recognition: On the Social Theory in Hegel's Jena Realphilosophie

Although, up to this point, the philosophy of consciousness had played only a limited role in Hegel's work, in the *Realphilosophie* it comes to define both the architectonics and the methodology of the whole. What enabled Hegel to develop this first complete statement of his philosophy as a unified system was his clearer understanding of the theoretical presuppositions of the concept of 'Spirit' [*Geist*]. Under the renewed influence of Fichte, he came to view the defining feature of Spirit as the ability to be 'both itself and the other to itself': Spirit is characterized by self-differentiation, in the sense that Spirit is able to make itself an other to itself and, from there, to return to itself. Once he views this achievement not as a single act but as the form of movement found in processes, Hegel has the unified principle in terms of which he can make sense of the structure of reality: the constant developmental law underlying all occurrences is this double movement of externalization and return, and it is in the permanent repetition of this movement that Spirit realizes itself in stages. But since this developmental process is, in itself, a process of reflection – and thus takes place in the form of ideational differentiations – philosophical analysis only needs to reconstruct this process with sufficient care in order to reach its systematic goal. Indeed, as soon as it has methodically reconstructed all the steps of this developmental process, philosophy will have reached the final point at which Spirit has completely differentiated itself and, to this extent, attained 'absolute' knowledge of itself. Thus, already at this point, the structure of the entire Hegelian project is modelled on the process of the realization of Spirit, just as it will be in the final system. If not in its execution then certainly in its idea, Hegel's theory already includes the three major components of

logic, philosophy of nature, and philosophy of Spirit, in which Spirit
is portrayed, in sequence, first in its inner constitution as such, then in
its externalization in the objectivity of nature, and finally in its return
into the sphere of its own subjectivity.

Of course, in working out the details of his entire project in terms
of the philosophy of consciousness, Hegel also altered that part of the
project that had previously been completely occupied with the analysis of ethical life. The sections collected under the title 'Philosophy of
Spirit' now have to depict the entire formative process that Spirit must
complete after having returned to itself, by its own reflection, from its
externalization in nature. Because of this, these sections can no longer
restrict themselves to the explication of the structure of ethical relations. Rather, the third part of the system now includes, in addition,
the final formative step in which Spirit gains insight into its own inner
constitution with the help of 'art, religion, and science'. To this extent,
it is also no longer the ethical relations belonging to the State but
rather these three media of knowledge that provide the highest, 'absolute' point of reference for Hegel's account of the formative process
of Spirit within the sphere of human consciousness. In general, the
development of the stages of this process can therefore be assessed in
terms of the contribution that individual forms of consciousness are
able to make to the development of 'art, religion, and science'. The
theory of ethical life thus also loses the central function that it had
previously fulfilled as an overarching frame of reference for his
philosophy of Spirit. The constitution of human consciousness is now
no longer integrated as a constitutive dimension into the process of
the development of ethical social relations. Matters are, rather, just the
other way around: social and political forms of human interaction now
represent mere transitional stages in the process of the consciousness-
formation that produces the three media of Spirit's self-knowledge.

Nowhere is this decline in the role of the theory of ethical life clearer
than in the modifications that Hegel made in the internal organization
of his philosophy of Spirit. Its new organizing principle is basically the
result of a compromise between the intentions of the old conception
in terms of a 'theory of society' and the requirements set by the new
framework of the philosophy of consciousness. Thus, in terms of his
categories, Hegel retains his original intention of reconstructing the
formation of Spirit within the sphere of human consciousness up to
the point at which, in the ethical relations belonging to the State, the
institutional structures of a successful form of social integration into
community begin to emerge. There is no other way to explain his
choice once again of the concept of 'constitution' as the title for the

final section of his systematic account, a concept which (as in the *System of Ethical Life*) designates a constellation of political institutions. As befits the matter in hand, however, Hegel no longer lets the process of Spirit's realization be consummated in the establishment of State relations, but rather presents it as completed only with the advent of the forms of knowledge in which Spirit 'comes to an intuition of itself as itself'.[1] For this reason, the old title 'Constitution' now actually means something quite different compared with the earlier texts, because it subsumes under itself everything that later, in the usage of the *Encyclopedia*, will be called 'absolute Spirit'. And it is not until this more appropriate title is put in the place of the one that Hegel had used previously (solely for purposes of establishing theoretical continuity) that the other two labels used in the text for stages of Spirit's formation also become intelligible.

The chapter in which Hegel now begins his reconstruction – and which thus takes the place previously reserved for the section on 'natural ethical life' – carries the title 'Subjective Spirit', a term added by the editors of the lecture manuscripts on the basis of the system found in the *Encyclopedia*. By contrast, the second chapter – which, together with the account of the social reality of Spirit, forms the bridge between the entry stage and the sphere of the 'absolute' – carries Hegel's own title of 'Actual Spirit'. With regard to Hegel's original intent, both titles are, in a number of respects, questionable.[2] Taken together, however, and supplemented by the appropriate title for the third chapter, they do nonetheless reveal Hegel's basic systematic intentions in organizing his 'philosophy of Spirit' as he does: the process of Spirit's realization, which plays itself out within the sphere of human consciousness, is to be presented here as a series of stages that emerge via a method of observing first the relationship of individual subjects to themselves, then the institutional relations of subjects among themselves, and finally the reflexive relations of socialized subjects to the world as a whole. This stage structure, however, which is already suggested by the chapter divisions ('subjective', 'actual', and 'absolute'), may lead one to overlook the particular construction that distinguishes the 'Jena Lectures on the Philosophy of Spirit' from all later texts. In these lectures, Hegel once again includes the socio-structural model of the struggle for recognition into the first formative stage in such a way that it can become the driving force, not of the emergence of absolute Spirit, but certainly of the development of an ethical community.

In the first part of his philosophical analysis, Hegel's method involves reconstructing the formative process of subjective Spirit by

gradually extending it to include more and more of the necessary
conditions for individual consciousness's experience of itself. The
outcome of this reconstructive process is supposed to indicate which
crucial experiences a subject must, on the whole, have had before it
can view itself as a person with 'rights' and, to that extent, can participate in the institutional life of a society, that is, in 'actual Spirit'.[3] For
the cognitive side of this formative process, Hegel first appeals to a
series of stages leading, by way of the faculty of the imagination, from
intuition to the capacity for the linguistic representation of things. In
making its way along this path, individual consciousness learns to
comprehend itself as the 'negative' force that independently generates
the order within reality, thereby making itself into an 'object'
[*Gegenstand*]. On the other hand, experiences of this kind still do not
suffice, for they can only teach the subject that it is able to produce the
world categorially, not that it is able to do so practically, with regard
to the world's content. To this extent, the formative process needs to
be extended with regard to precisely this dimension of practical experience, through which intelligence gains 'the consciousness of its
own activity, that is, as its own positing of content or making itself its
own content'.[4] The subject's full experience of itself, as found in the
consciousness of intersubjectively obligatory rights, is only possible
on the presupposition that individuals can learn to conceive of
themselves as the subjects of practical productions as well. Hence, it
is the movement of self-objectification that forms the second side of
the formative process of subjective spirit that Hegel examines. This
movement is constructed in the form of a series of stages moving
toward the realization of the individual will. Drawn via Fichte from
the intellectual movement of *Sturm und Drang*, the concept of the 'will'
represents, for the Hegel of the *Realphilosophie*, the key to the whole
field of the subject's practical relation to the world.[5] Up to this point,
subjective Spirit has only been given as 'intelligence', since it has been
considered merely with regard to its cognitive relation to reality. It
only becomes the will, according to Hegel, when it leaves the horizon
of merely theoretical experience behind and gains practical access to
the world. Here, the plan or intention that the concept of the 'will' is
supposed to designate consists in more than the urge towards self-
objectification. Rather, what this term emphasizes is the character of
decisiveness that accompanies the intention to experience oneself
as oneself in encountering an object of one's action: 'That which wills
[*das Wollende*] wills, that is, it wants to posit itself, to make itself, as
itself, its own object'.[6] For Hegel, the formative process of the will
is thus composed of forms of self-experience that stem, in turn, from

the decisive intent to realize its own intentions practically and 'objectively' [*gegenständlich*]. Once again, the division of stages results from the anticipation of the 'completeness' of a legal person's self-consciousness, from which the organization of the development of theoretical consciousness had already been derived.

Hegel has the practical side of the individual formative process begin with the subject's instrumental experience of itself. He sees this as inherent in the internal connection of labour, tools, and products. In contrast to animals, the human Spirit does not respond to 'feelings of lack' (the sensing of unsatisfied needs) by directly consuming objects. In the case of the human Spirit, this 'mere satisfaction of desires' is replaced by the act – 'reflected in itself' – of labour, which delays the process of satisfying drives in that it produces objects whose consumption is not bound to any situation but is possible in the future. The activity of labour is always accompanied by a 'division of the I beset by drives',[7] because it requires forms of motivation and discipline that can only be acquired by interrupting the immediate satisfaction of needs. The energies that one releases and that flow into labour are of course assisted by 'tools', energy-saving devices that reflect generalized experiences of working with objects. Hegel then considers a 'work' [*Werk*] to be the result of labour activity mediated by the use of tools. It is in relation to a work that the subject first discovers not only that it is able to constitute reality categorially, but also 'that the content as such is via it'.[8] In this sense, in experiencing the product of its instrumental action, intelligence gains precisely the 'consciousness of its doings' that necessarily remained inaccessible to it, as long as it related to the world only cognitively. The moment in which intelligence becomes aware of its ability to produce objects practically occurs when it has before its eyes, in a work, the product of its own activity. The type of practical activity that reflects the labour product back to intelligence as an independent accomplishment is, however, restricted in character, for it can only come about under the compulsion of self-discipline. In encountering the result of its labour activity, subjective Spirit experiences itself as a being who is capable of activity due to self-constraint. Hegel thus also speaks of labour, in summary, as an experience of something 'making itself into a thing'.[9]

If these formulations are given the strong reading suggested by the ontological concept of 'thing' [*Ding*], then it is not difficult to see why Hegel had to consider the will's first, instrumental stage of experience incomplete. Because, in the course of its labour, subjective Spirit becomes acquainted with itself only as an active 'thing' – that is, as a being that gains its capacity for action only by adapting to natural

causality – such an experience is far from sufficient for the development of a consciousness of itself as a legal person. For acquiring that
sort of self-understanding would require, in addition, at least that it
learn to comprehend itself as an intersubjective being existing alongside persons with competing claims. Hence, if the constitution of individual consciousness of right is to be explained, the formative process
of subjective Spirit needs to be extended along a further dimension of
the practical relation to the world. It is this that Hegel now seeks to
find in an initial form of mutual recognition.

The full extent to which Hegel has subjugated his thought to the
monological premises of the philosophy of consciousness becomes
evident in the difficulties that he has in introducing this new, intersubjective dimension of the 'will'. Methodologically, the transition to
intersubjective forms of the realization of the will no doubt serves to
introduce the dimension of experience whose absence is precisely what
had left subjective Spirit's instrumental experience of itself incomplete.
In keeping with his self-understanding, however, which is already
that of the philosophy of consciousness, Hegel apparently feels forced
to portray this transition not as the outcome of a methodological
operation but as a material stage in the formative process of Spirit.
The task with which Hegel further burdens himself is solved in the
text with the help of the bizarre, strictly misogynistic construction of
'cunning' as a female characteristic. With the replacement of tools by
machines, subjective consciousness becomes 'cunning', because it
knows how to harness – passively, as it were – natural forces for its
own purposes in dealing with nature. The ability, however, to let 'the
activity of the other carry one' belongs exclusively to the female psy-
che. For that reason, with the emergence of 'cunning', the will is supposed to have 'divided itself' into the 'two extremes' of male and
female and, from that point on, is relieved of its 'solitary existence'.[10]
Although this 'deduction' of the female interaction partner is subsequently bracketed from the argumentative course of the account, there
remains the theoretical result that Hegel here extends subjective Spirit's
sphere of actualization to include the relationship between the sexes.
And in systematic terms, the motivation for such an extension can
only be seen in the fact that the sexual relationship between men and
women is supposed to introduce an additional condition for the constitution of the self-consciousness of a legal person.

As to the advantage that gender relations have over instrumental
activity, specifically with regard to experiential content, Hegel rightly
sees this to lie in the reciprocity of knowing oneself in another.
In relationships of sexual interaction both subjects can recognize

[*wiedererkennen*] themselves in their partner, due to their mutual desire to be desired. With regard to the act as well as the result of labour, the ego is always given to itself only as a reified subject of action but, in encountering the desire extended to it by the other, it experiences itself to be the same vital, desiring subjectivity that it desires of the other. Sexuality thus represents the first form of the unification of opposing subjects: 'Each one is identical to the other precisely owing to that in virtue of which each is opposed to the other; the other, that through which the other exists for one, is oneself'.[11] This reciprocal experience of knowing-oneself-in-the-other develops into a relationship of genuine love only to the degree that it can become intersubjectively shared knowledge on the part of both. For only when each subject has also seen that 'the other knows itself likewise in its other' can it possess the certain 'trust' that 'the other . . . is for me'. In order to designate a similar relation of knowing oneself in the other, Hegel now makes use, for the first time, of the concept of 'recognition': in love relationships, he writes in a marginal remark, it is the 'uncultivated natural self' that is 'recognized'.[12]

As in the *System of Ethical Life*, Hegel conceives of love as a relationship of mutual recognition, in which natural individuality is first confirmed. Here, this definition admittedly acquires, even more clearly than before, the particular sense (based on the theory of subjectivity) according to which the volitional subject is able to experience itself for the first time as a needy, desiring subject only after having had the experience of being loved. If one generalizes this second thesis systematically, one arrives at the theoretical premise that the development of a subject's personal identity presupposes, in principle, certain types of recognition from other subjects. For the superiority of interpersonal relationships over instrumental acts was apparently to consist in the fact that relationships give both interlocutors the opportunity to experience themselves, in encountering their partner to communication, to be the kind of person that they, from their perspective, recognize the other as being. The line of thought entailed by Hegel's argument here represents a significant step beyond the mere claim, found in theories of socialization, that the formation of the subject's identity is supposed to be necessarily tied to the experience of intersubjective recognition. His idea leads to the further conclusion that an individual that does not recognize its partner to interaction to be a certain type of person is also unable to experience itself completely or without restriction as that type of person. The implication of this for the relationship of recognition can only be that an obligation to reciprocity is, to a certain extent, built into such relations, an obligation that requires but does not force subjects to recognize one another in a certain way: if I do not recognize my partner to interaction as a certain type of person, his reactions cannot give me the sense that I am recognized as the same type of person, since I thereby deny him precisely the characteristics and capacities with regard to which I want to feel myself affirmed by him.

But for the moment, such a conclusion – with which one could show that the relationship of recognition implicitly makes reciprocal claims on subjects – is of little interest to Hegel. The aspect of 'love' that occupies him is primarily the particular function that must be attached to it in the formative process of a legal person's self-consciousness. In the passage referred to in the marginal note on 'recognition', we find the programmatic statement that love is 'the element . . . of ethical life – though not yet ethical life itself'. It represents, Hegel elaborates, 'only the suggestion of it', the 'suggestion of the ideal in the actual'.[13] Hence, in both formulations, love's significance for the individual formative process is fixed only negatively, by determining its distance from the societal relations of ethical life. In this way, Hegel apparently hopes to work against the misconception to which he succumbed in his youth, when he was still trying to construe the affective nexus of a society as a whole in terms of quasi-erotic relationships of love. That is why, already in the *System of Ethical Life*, the position that the early theological writings had given to love as a force of social integration was replaced by the more abstract – as it were, rational – feeling of solidarity. If, however, the two above-mentioned formulations from the *Realphilosophie* are put in positive terms, they provide significant insights into the function that love, as a relationship of recognition, is supposed to have in the subject's formative process. In our context, to speak of 'love' as an 'element' of ethical life can only mean that, for every subject, the experience of being loved constitutes a necessary precondition for participation in the public life of a community. This thesis becomes plausible when it is understood as a claim about the emotional conditions for successful ego-development: only the feeling of having the particular nature of one's urges fundamentally recognized and affirmed can allow one to develop the degree of basic self-confidence that renders one capable of participating, with equal rights, in political will-formation.[14] In this context, the fact that Hegel describes 'love', further, as a 'suggestion' of ethical life could mean that he views it as the primary experiential context in which human beings are able to acquire a sense for the possibility of the unification of mutually opposed subjects. Without the feeling of being loved, it would be impossible for the idea of an ethical community ever to acquire what one might call inner-psychic representation. But this second thesis is itself not entirely free from the overtones of the original mistake of equating social bonds and sexual love. Thus, in continuing his investigation, Hegel will have to be intent to distinguish clearly enough between the form of integration corresponding to ethical community, on the one hand, and the emotional relationship between men and women, on the other.

With regard to the recognition relationship of love – that is, with regard to the first stage of formation, in which the individual will can experience itself to be vital subjectivity – Hegel claims that there are two further ways in which its internal experiential potential can increase. As we have seen, in the stabilization of the erotic relationship into love, the reciprocal relation of knowing oneself in the other has already developed into a shared piece of knowledge. Once again, via the cooperative activity found in the institutionalized relationship of marriage, this intersubjectively shared knowledge now takes on a reflexive form, because it reaches actuality in an objective [gegenständlich] 'third': just as individual labour found a medium in tools, marital love finds in 'family property' a medium in which it can be seen to be the 'permanent, ongoing possibility of their existence'.[15] Of course, family possessions have in common with tools the limitation of being merely a dead, emotionless, and thus inadequate expression of the experiential content that is supposed to be incorporated in them: 'But this object does not yet have the element of love in it; love is in the extremes instead . . . Love is not yet the object'.[16] In order to be able to witness without restriction their own love in an external medium, the loving pair must therefore take the further step of mutual objectification. In fact, it is only with the birth of offspring that love becomes a 'knowing that knows' [erkennende Erkennen] in that, from that point on, the couple has the child before their eyes as bodily proof of their mutual knowledge of the inclinations of the other. Here, Hegel is entirely a classical theoretician of the bourgeois family,[17] viewing the child as the highest embodiment of the love between men and women: 'In the child, they see love; [it is] their self-conscious unity as self-conscious'.[18]

Of course, for Hegel, none of these various forms of the development of love represents, in itself, an experiential context that could enable subjective Spirit to learn to conceive of itself as a legal person. What the love relationship does admit is the maturation of preliminary relations of mutual recognition that constitute a necessary precondition for every further development of identity, in that they reaffirm the individual in his particular nature of his urges and thereby grant him an indispensable degree of basic self-confidence. But within a framework

of interaction as narrowly constrained as that of the family, nothing
has yet been accomplished in terms of teaching subjects about the role
that intersubjectively guaranteed rights must take on in the social life-
nexus of a society. From the perspective of the question as to the
constitutive conditions for legal personhood, the recognition relationship of love itself turns out to be an incomplete field of experience. For
within the loving relationship to family members, subjective Spirit
remains undisturbed by the kind of conflicts that would force it to
reflect upon socially encompassing, universal norms for the regulation
of social intercourse. Without an awareness of such generalized norms
of interaction, however, subjective Spirit will not learn to conceive of
itself as a person with intersubjectively recognized rights. As a result,
Hegel is again forced to extend the subject's formative process along
a further dimension of practical reference to the world. It is to this end
that, in the context of his *Realphilosophie*, Hegel once again takes up the
means of theory-construction found in the 'struggle for recognition'.

What makes this reappropriation of the familiar model especially
significant is clearly the fact that, for the first time, Hegel introduces
it directly as a critique of Hobbes's account of the state of nature. Up
to this point, the critical implications of the account of the 'struggle
for recognition' for Hobbes's conception of human nature could be
deduced only indirectly from the way in which it is situated in the
construction of the *System of Ethical Life*. Here, however, Hegel asserts
the premises of this communications-theoretic model of the struggle
more directly in confrontation with the notion of an original state of
a 'war of all against all'. In the text, the transition to the entire problematic of a state of nature coincides with the methodological step in
which the individual will's sphere of realization is to be extended
along an additional dimension. Since the subject was not yet able to
experience itself to be a person with rights within the recognition
relationship of the family, Hegel relocates the subject theoretically into
a social environment that appears, externally at least, to be the situation described in accounts of the state of nature. At this point in his
argumentation, however, he is more prudent than before, in that he
no longer tries to base the advent of this new volitional sphere on an
act of Spirit itself, but represents it simply as a mere methodological
operation. The single family totality is now placed (analytically, as it
were) beside a series of just such family identities so as to give rise to
a first state of collective social life. Insofar as each of these coexistent
families 'take possession of a piece of land'[19] as part of its economic
holdings, it necessarily excludes the others from the use of common
land. For this reason, the plurality of different families brings with it

the emergent social relations of competition that seem, at first glance, to correspond to the relations described in the tradition of natural law:

> This relation is what is usually referred to as the *state of nature*, the free, indifferent being of individuals toward one another. And natural law should answer the question as to what rights and obligations the individuals have toward one another, in accordance with this relation.[20]

Hegel thus takes up the doctrine of the state of nature initially because the model it contains seems to provide an appropriate depiction of the original social situation that he intends to introduce into his system as an additional experiential domain of the individual will. Indeed, he even goes one step further and approvingly quotes Hobbes's famous formulation, in order to clearly identify the task necessarily facing subjects, given the threatening situation of mutual competition: 'Their [Individuals'] only relationship, however, lies in superseding this relationship: *exeundum e statu naturae* [to leave the state of nature]'.[21] Only after following the Hobbesian account to this decisive point does Hegel develop, in a second step, a theoretical counter-critique that nearly coincides, in argumentative substance, with the ideas already found in the essay on natural law. As in the earlier text, his central objection here consists in the fact that Hobbes himself is not in a position to grasp the transition to the social contract as a practically necessary occurrence under the artificial circumstances of the state of nature. Everyone who starts from the methodological fiction of a state of nature among human beings is confronted fundamentally with the same problem: how, in a social situation marked by relations of mutual competition, do individuals arrive at an idea of intersubjective 'rights and duties'? The answers that various natural law traditions have given to this question all have, for Hegel, the same negative feature. The 'determination of right' is always, as it were, 'imported' from the outside, in that the act of making the contract is posited either as a demand of prudence (Hobbes) or as a postulate of morality (Kant, Fichte). It is typical of philosophical solutions of this kind that the transition to the social contract is something that happens 'within me'. '[I]t is the movement of my thought',[22] by which the necessity of forming a contract enters the situational structure termed the 'state of nature'. Against this, Hegel wishes to show that the emergence of the social contract – and, thereby, of legal relations – represents a practical event that necessarily follows from the initial social situation of the state of nature itself. This is to be a matter, as it were, no longer of theoretical but of empirical necessity, with which the formation of the contract comes about within this situational structure of mutual competition. In order to be able to make this plausible, one clearly needs a completely different description of what occurs between human beings under the artificial conditions of the state of nature:

> Law [*Recht*] is the *relation* of persons, in their conduct, to others, the universal element of their free being or the determination, the limitation of their empty freedom. It is not up to me to think up or bring about this relation or limitation for myself; rather, the subject-matter [*Gegenstand*] is itself this creation of law in general, that is, the *recognizing* relation.[23]

The last sentence already provides some indication of how Hegel imagines the frame of reference for such a description, in terms of which what goes on in the state of nature could be grasped in a way that differs from traditional theoretical approaches. His line of thought can be understood as follows: in order to show, as against the dominant intellectual tradition, that subjects can, on their own, reach a conflict resolution based on law (as formulated in the social contract) even under conditions of hostile competition, theoretical attention must be shifted to the intersubjective social relations that always already guarantee a minimal normative consensus in advance; for it is only in these pre-contractual relations of mutual recognition – which underlie even relations of social competition – that the moral potential evidenced in individuals' willingness to reciprocally restrict their own spheres of liberty can be anchored. In light of this, the social-ontological frame of reference within which this description of the situation was undertaken needs to be extended categorially so as to include a further dimension of social life: with regard to the social circumstances characterizing the state of nature, one must necessarily consider the additional fact that subjects must, in some way, have already recognized each other even before the conflict. Accordingly, the sentence in which Hegel had referred to the 'recognizing relation' is followed immediately by the virtually programmatic assertion that:

> In recognition, the self ceases to be this individual. It exists by right in recognition, that is, no longer in its immediate existence. The one who is recognized is recognized as immediately counting as such, through his *being* – but this being is itself generated from the concept. It is recognized being [*anerkanntes Sein*]. Man is necessarily recognized and necessarily gives recognition. This necessity is his own, not that of our thinking in contrast to the content. As recognizing, man is himself this movement, and this movement itself is what supersedes his natural state: he is recognition.[24]

This is how Hegel explicates what it means to integrate the obligation of mutual recognition into the state of nature as a social fact. For the moment, his crucial argument here is merely that all human coexistence presupposes a kind of basic mutual affirmation between subjects, since otherwise no form of being-together whatsoever could ever come into existence. Insofar as this mutual affirmation always already entails a certain degree of individual self-restraint, there is here a preliminary, still implicit form of legal consciousness. But then the transition to the social contract is to be understood as something that subjects accomplish in practice, at the moment in which they become conscious of their prior relationship of recognition and elevate it explicitly to an intersubjectively shared legal relation. In light of this line of thought, one can now also see why Hegel could have come up with the idea of analysing this new experiential stage of the individual will by means of an immanent critique of the natural law tradition. If it can, in fact, be shown that the social relations found in the state of nature lead – of their own accord, as it were – to the intersubjective generation of a social contract, then the experiential process by which subjects learn to comprehend themselves to be legal persons would thereby be captured as well. To a certain extent, the immanent critique of the doctrine of the state of nature would then coincide with the analysis of the constitution of legal persons. A corrected, accurate description of the acts carried out under conditions of hostile competition would in fact represent precisely the formative process in which individuals learn to see themselves as being fitted out with intersubjectively accepted rights. Thus, having outlined his theoretical intentions with sufficient clarity, Hegel is now compelled to provide this alternative description of the state of nature. In the text, this takes the form of an account in which conflicts over the unilateral seizure of possessions are interpreted not as 'struggles for self-assertion' but as 'struggles for recognition'.

Consistent with this, Hegel even explicates the starting-point of this conflict – which is supposed to be characteristic for the fictional state of nature in general – in a manner that differs from what is usually found in the tradition going back to Hobbes. In Hegel's account, a family's exclusive seizure of property appears from the start as a grave disturbance of the collective social life. He can arrive at this interpretation because he makes use of a method of presentation in which the conflict-generating incident is grasped only one-sidedly, from the point of view taken by the passively participating subjects. For, seen from their perspective, such an act of directly taking possession reveals itself to be an event that excludes them from an existing context of interaction and relegates them, accordingly, to the position of isolated individuals, of individuals who are merely 'for themselves'. The passively participating individual is 'a being-for-himself, because he is not for the other, because he is excluded by the other from Being [*Sein*]'.[25] Crucial to this opening image is the fact that Hegel derives the reaction-formation of excluded subjects from a motivational situation whose core is formed by the disappointment of positive expectations vis-à-vis the partner to interaction. Unlike in Hobbes's depiction, the individual here reacts to the seizure of property not with the fear of having his survival subsequently threatened but rather with the feeling of being ignored by his social counterpart. Built into the structure of human interaction there is a normative expectation that one will meet with the recognition of others, or at least an implicit assumption that one will be given positive consideration in the plans of others. As a result, the act of aggression with which the excluded subject subsequently responds to the seizure of property is put in completely different light, compared with Hobbes's account of the state of nature. The reason why the socially ignored individuals attempt, in response, to damage the others' possessions is not because they want to satisfy their passions, but rather in order to make the others take notice of them. Hegel interprets the destructive reaction of the excluded party as an act whose real aim is to win back the attention of the other:

> The excluded party spoils the other's possession, by introducing his excluded being-for-himself into it, his 'mine'. He ruins something in it – an annihilation like that of desire – in order to give himself his sense of self, yet not his empty sense of self but rather his self positing itself within another, in the knowing of another.[26]

Hegel puts this even more succinctly in the next sentence, in which he asserts that the excluded subject's practical resistance is directed 'not at the negative aspect, the thing, but rather the self-knowledge of the other'.[27]

Having thus reconstructed the course of the conflict from the perspective of the propertyless party, Hegel then goes on in the next step of his account to do the same from the point of view of the propertied party. On the part of the attacked subject, the experience of having its possessions destroyed generates a certain normative irritation. For in light of the other's aggressive reaction, the attacked subject realizes, in retrospect, that in this social context its own action (that is, the original seizure of property) necessarily acquires a meaning quite different from the one it originally ascribed to the action. In acting, the property-seizing subject had initially been occupied only with itself. It carried out the act of seizure, egocentrically conscious solely of expanding its economic holdings by one additional object. The counter-reaction of its partners to interaction brings home, for the first time, the fact that in acting it related indirectly to its social environment as well, by excluding others from the use of the object. In this sense, the other is constitutively included in the propertied subject's self-perception as well, since the other has enabled it to decentre its initially egocentric way of looking at things. The property-seizing individual 'becomes aware that he has done something altogether different from what he intended. His intention [*Meinen*] was the pure relating of his Being to himself, his uninhibited being-for-himself'.[28]

At the same time, of course, to the degree to which its action-orientation has been decentralized, the attacked subject realizes that the other's attack was aimed not at the possessions in question but at itself as a human person. It learns to see the destructive act as an attempt by the other to provoke a reaction on its part. The initial property seizure has thus ultimately grown into a situation of conflict in which two parties stand opposed as enemies, both of them aware of their social dependence on the other:

> Thus angered, the two parties stand opposed to one another, and now the second is the insulter, and the first is the insulted; for in taking possession, the first intended nothing toward the other. The second, however, did insult, since he intended the first: what he annihilated was not the specific form of the thing but the form of the other's labour or activity.[29]

This attempt to represent the original situation of the state of nature from the performative perspective of the participating subjects leads to a preliminary conclusion, which already suggests a radical criticism of Hobbes's theory: if the social meaning of the conflict can only be adequately understood by ascribing to both parties knowledge of their dependence on the other, then the antagonized subjects cannot be conceived as isolated beings acting only egocentrically. Rather, in their own action-orientation, both subjects have already positively taken the other into account, before they became engaged in hostilities. Both must, in fact, already have accepted the other in advance as a partner to interaction upon whom they are willing to allow their own activity to be dependent. In the case of the propertyless subject, this prior affirmation is apparent in the disappointment with which it reacts to the other's inconsiderate seizure of property. In the case of the propertied subject, by contrast, the same prior affirmation is evidenced in the readiness with which it takes over the other's definition of the situation as its own action-interpretation. Both parties have, simply in virtue of the propositional content of their respective action-orientations, already mutually recognized each other, even if this social accord may not be thematically present to them.

Hegel can, therefore, correctly conclude that the conflict in the state of nature presupposes an implicit agreement between subjects, one that consists in the affirmation of each other as partners to interaction:

> The supersession of the exclusion has already occurred; both parties are outside themselves, both are one knowledge [*ein Wissen*], are objects for themselves. Each is conscious of himself in the other – as one who is negated [*aufgehoben*], to be sure – but, at the same time, positivity is on the side of each. . . . Each is outside himself.[30]

In contrast to this unthematized presupposition of their interaction, however, both parties knowingly find themselves initially in a situation of direct opposition. Hegel defines the intersubjective relationship between the divided subjects following the destruction of the object of possession as a relation of 'inequality': whereas the initially excluded subject has re-established itself in the other's consciousness by destroying the other's alien property and has thereby acquired an intersubjectively reinforced understanding of itself, the other must feel robbed of just this knowledge, since its own reading of the situation did not receive intersubjective approval. Having just been forced to give its partner to interaction attention and confirmation, this subject now lacks any possibility of safeguarding its individual will via the recognition of another. In order to explain what practical course this asymmetrical constellation of relations is to take, Hegel briefly summarizes the underlying implication of his argumentation once more. It belongs to the 'actuality' of a being-for-itself to be 'recognized by the other, to count as absolute for him'.[31] Given that the attacked subject presently lacks any experience of being confirmed by its counterpart, it can only regain an intersubjectively authenticated understanding of itself by attempting to do what its partner to interaction did to it. It must set out 'no longer to establish its existence but rather its knowledge of itself, that is, to become recognized'.[32] But unlike its partner, the attacked subject needs to do more than just remind the other of itself, so to speak, through an act of provocation. Rather, it must provide evidence that it was insulted by the hostile destruction of property not for the sake of the possessions *per se* but due to the misinterpretation of its intentions. It can, however, convince the other of this only by demonstrating, via its willingness to enter a struggle for life and death, that the legitimacy of its claims matters more to it than physical existence. For this reason, Hegel considers the continuation of this intermediate stage of the conflicts within the state of nature to be a struggle, into which the attacked subject forces its partner to interaction, in order to demonstrate to the other the unconditionality of its will and thereby to prove that it is a person worthy of recognition:

> In order to count as absolute, however, it must present itself as absolute, as will, that is, as something for which what counts is no longer its existence (which it had as a possession) but rather its known being-for-itself, whose being has the significance of self-knowledge and in this way comes into existence. Such presentation, however, is the self-executed negation [*Aufhebung*] of the existence that belongs to it. . . . To itself as consciousness, what it seems to intend is the death of an other; but what it intends is its own death – suicide, in that it exposes itself to danger.[33]

This life-and-death struggle, into which the insulted subject drags the other by means of a death-threat, acquires a special position within Hegel's reconstruction. It marks the experiential stage within the individual formative process, in which subjects finally learn to understand themselves as persons endowed with 'rights'. Strangely, however, Hegel provides anything but a satisfying answer to the crucial question as to what the particular qualities of experience are supposed to be that give this struggle such practical and moral force. The cursory, concluding part of his account of subjective Spirit's constitution is limited to the apodictic assertion that, in the situation of reciprocal death-threats, the implicit (indeed, already achieved) recognition necessarily gives rise to an intersubjectively acknowledged legal relation. In experiencing the finitude of life, the formative process of the individual will – which has already made its way through the stages of the use of tools and of love – has arrived at its definitive end. Because both subjects have 'seen the other as pure Self' in the struggle for life and death, they both possess 'a knowledge of the will',[34] in which, as a matter of principle, the other has been taken into consideration as a person endowed with rights. This single suggestion is all that is to be found in this passage, in which Hegel forges a constitutive link between the intersubjective emergence of legal relations and the experience of death. For this reason, there is still the need for an additional, stronger interpretation, in order to turn this provocative suggestion into an argumentatively plausible line of thought.

A first reading of this sort emerges from the thesis, developed by Andreas Wildt, that Hegel is speaking here of a 'life-and-death struggle' only in a metaphorical sense. On this view, what is meant by these drastic metaphors are those moments of existential 'threat' in which a subject is forced to realize that a meaningful life is only possible 'in the context of the recognition of rights and duties'.[35] What this suggested reading shares with a second interpretive approach is the fact that it starts out from the monological situation of a subject confronted with its own life. Alexandre Kojève has provided the most impressive development of the thesis that, with the idea of a 'life-and-death struggle', Hegel anticipated existentialist lines of thought, because in it the possibility of individual freedom is tied to the condition of an anticipatory certainty of one's own death.[36] On a third, intersubjectivist interpretation, by contrast, it is not one's own death but the possible death of one's interaction partner that occupies the centre of attention.[37] For Hegel's statements can also be understood as asserting that it is only with the anticipation of the finitude of the other that subjects become conscious of the existential common ground on the basis of which they learn to view each other reciprocally as vulnerable and threatened beings.

Admittedly, neither this proposed interpretation nor, certainly, Kojève's explain why it is that the anticipation of one's own or the other's death is supposed to lead to the recognition, in particular, of the claim to individual rights. In the text, however, Hegel clearly takes this for granted without really trying to justify it: through the reciprocal perception of their mortality, the subjects in the struggle discover that they have already recognized each other insofar as their fundamental rights are concerned and have thereby already implicitly created the social basis for an intersubjectively binding legal relationship. For the explanation of this subsequent discovery, however, the reference to the existential dimension of death seems to be completely unnecessary. For it is the mere fact of the morally decisive resistance to its interaction partner that actually makes the attacking subject aware that the other had come to the situation harbouring normative expectations in just the way that it itself had vis-à-vis the other. That alone, and not the way in which the other asserts its individual rights, is what allows subjects to perceive each other as morally vulnerable persons and, thereby, to mutually affirm each other in their fundamental claims to integrity. In this sense, it is the social experience of realizing that one's interaction partner is vulnerable to moral injury – and not the existential realization that the other is mortal – that can bring to consciousness that layer of prior relations of recognition, the normative core of which acquires, in legal relations, an intersubjectively binding form. But in making the encounter with death a precondition of intersubjectively established awareness of the legitimacy of individual rights, Hegel went well beyond the bounds of the matter to be explained. The fact that there would have been an appropriate place in his construction for this reference to the finitude of individuals will become apparent in the theoretical difficulties generated by the transition to the form of recognition beyond law.

With these relatively few indications as to the ultimate course of the life-threatening struggle, Hegel considers the task that he set himself in the chapter on subjective Spirit's formative process to be completed. Since, from this point on, the individual will is able to comprehend itself on the basis of the reactions of every other individual as a person endowed with rights, it is capable of participating in the universal sphere where the reproduction of social life can occur. Of course, the fact that Hegel sees the individual formative process coming to an end here must not mislead one into thinking this sphere of the universal is supposed to be something alien or superordinate to subjects. Hegel rather conceives of the 'spiritual actuality' of society, the 'universal will', as an all-embracing medium capable of reproducing itself only through the intersubjective practice of mutual recognition. The sphere of 'being recognized' is formed through the accumulation of the outcomes of all individual formative processes taken together and is kept alive, in turn, only by the continually new development of individuals into legal persons. Indeed, in what follows, Hegel takes a crucial step beyond this rather static model in that he again includes, in his account of social reality, subjects' striving for recognition as a productive force for change. The struggle for recognition not only contributes to the reproduction of the spiritual [*geistig*] element of civil society (as a constitutive element of every formative process) but also (as a source of normative pressure towards legal development) innovatively influences the inner form it takes.

The theoretical framework in which the further determination of the struggle for recognition is developed results from the specific task that Hegel sets himself in the chapter that follows the analysis of 'subjective Spirit'. There, in accordance with the logic of presentation governing his entire project, Hegel has to reconstruct the formative process of Spirit at the new stage that is reached with the entrance of the individual will into social reality. But insofar as the sphere of society is supposed to be constituted exclusively by legal relations and these relations have, up to this point, remained utterly undetermined, the real challenge for him now is to comprehend the construction of social reality as a process of the realization of law. For social life, legal relations thus represent a sort of intersubjective basis, because they obligate every subject to treat all others according to their legitimate claims. Unlike love, law represents, for Hegel, a form of mutual recognition that structurally rules out a restriction to the particular realm of close social relations. It is therefore only with the establishment of the 'legal person' that a society has the minimum of communicative agreement – or 'universal will' – that allows for the collective reproduction of its central institutions. For only when all members of society mutually respect their legitimate claims can they relate to each other socially in the conflict-free manner necessary for the cooperative completion of societal tasks. For this, of course, the mere principle of legal relations thus far considered does not provide an adequate foundation, since, as such, it leaves completely undecided what rights the subject actually has. At the point of intersection associated with 'being abstractly recognized', in which the individual formative processes of all members of society eventually converge, it is open, to a certain extent, in which respect and to what degree legal persons have to recognize each other reciprocally.[38] For this reason, in the second chapter of his 'Philosophy of Spirit', he reconstructs the development of social reality as a formative process, through which the substantive meaning of these abstract relations of legal recognition gradually expands. For Hegel, civil society represents an institutional system that results from the accumulation of new forms of the concretization of legal relations.

This task is easily handled, so long as one is only talking about the explication of those individual rights-claims that follow directly from the integration of subjective Spirit into the sphere of 'being recognized'. Since, initially, the human individual can be defined abstractly as an 'enjoying and working' being,[39] it is beyond doubt for Hegel that the process of forming the institutions of society commences with the legal generalization of these two traits. What this means for the individual's 'desire' is that it gains the 'right to make its appearance',[40] that is, to be transformed into a claim based on need, that the individual can legitimately expect to see met. On the other hand, this implies that the individual activity of labouring is turned into a form of social activity that no longer serves, in a clear and visible manner, one's own needs but rather, 'abstractly', the needs of others. The transformation of needs into legitimate consumer interests requires the separation of the labour process from the direct purpose of the satisfaction of needs: 'Each satisfies the needs of many, and the satisfaction of one's own many particular needs is the labour of many others'.[41] Obviously, in order for the abstractly produced goods to be able to find their way to the needs anonymously directed at them, a further concretization of legal recognition must be presupposed. The subjects must have mutually recognized the legitimacy of the property that they have produced through labour and thereby become property-owners for each other, so that an appropriate portion of their legitimate wealth can be exchanged for a product of their choice. Hegel sees in exchange the prototype for reciprocal action among legal persons. Exchange value represents for him the Spiritual embodiment of the agreement between the participating subjects: 'What is universal is value; the movement, as perceptible, is the exchange. This same universality is mediation as conscious movement. Property is thus an immediate having, mediated through being-recognized, or: its existence is spiritual essence'.[42]

Hegel still considers the institutions of property and exchange – which, taken together, constitute the functional preconditions for the system of social labour – also to be the direct results of an organization of the basic human relations to reality in terms of relations of legal recognition. This sphere of the 'immediacy of being recognized' is not completely abandoned before the introduction of 'contract'. There, the consciousness of the reciprocity of action orientations already implicit in exchange acquires the reflexive form of linguistically mediated knowledge. In contracts, actual acts of exchange are replaced by the mutually articulated obligation to do something in the future: 'It is an exchange of declarations, no longer an exchange of objects – but it counts as much as the object itself. For both parties, the will of the other counts as such. Will has returned into its concept'.[43]

In this sense, the introduction of contractual relations is accompanied by a broadening of the concrete meaning of the institutionalized form of recognition. For it is in terms of the specific capacity to bind itself to the moral content of its performative expressions that the legal subject finds confirmation as a contractual partner: 'The recognition of my personhood, in the contract, allows *me* to count as existing, my word to count for the performance. That is: the I, my bare will, is not separated from my existence; they are equal'.[44] For Hegel, of course, this new stage in the concretization of legal recognition also brings with it, as usual, the correlate possibility of violating the law. As in the earlier texts, Hegel assumes there to be a structural link between contractual relations and the breaking of the law. This time, however, he sees this as lying in the fact that the contract presents the subject with an opportunity for subsequently breaking its word, since the contract opens up a temporal gap between the formal assurance and the actual completion of the deed. It is 'the indifference to existence and to time'[45] that makes contractual relations particularly vulnerable to the risk that the law will be broken.

Hegel interprets breach of contract as a separation of the 'individual and shared wills', without considering the possibility that it might be a matter of deliberate deception: 'I can unilaterally break the contract, since my individual will counts as such – not merely insofar as it is shared, but rather the shared will is shared only insofar as my individual will counts. . . . Actually asserting the difference, I thus break the contract.'[46] The appropriate reaction to a subject pulling out of a contractual relationship in this egocentric manner is the application of means of legitimate force. By such means, societies constituted by legal relations attempt to compel those who have broken their word to subsequently fulfil their contractually incurred obligations. Hegel unhesitatingly derives the legitimacy of this use of force from the normative content of the rules guaranteeing the reciprocity of recognition at the stage reached thus far: unless the subject accepts the obligations stemming from its consent to the contract, it violates the rules of recognition to which it owes its status as a legal person in the first place. In this sense, the application of force is the final means by which the delinquent subject can be prevented from falling out of society's network of interaction:

> My word must count, not on the moral grounds that I ought to be at one with myself and not change my inner disposition or conviction (for I can change these). But my will exists only as recognized. I not only contradict myself, but also the fact that my will is recognized; my word cannot be relied upon, that is, my will is merely mine [*mein*], mere opinion [*Meinung*]. . . . I am compelled to be a person.[47]

With the introduction of this legal coercion of the contract-breaker, the course of the conflict takes a direction that allows Hegel to assume that there is also a struggle for recognition within the stage of legal relations. To reach this crucial conclusion, one need take only the further step of defining the application of legal force as something that, in turn, necessarily generates in the subject a sense of being disrespected. Hegel develops a theory of this sort by attempting to draw a motivational link between having to endure legal coercion and committing a crime. According to him, for anyone who knows himself as a legal subject to be socially sure of his claims, the experience of legal compulsion necessarily represents an injury to one's own personhood. Since the individual breaking the contract can already comprehend itself as a subject with this sort of guarantees, it reacts accordingly with a feeling of indignation. This feeling can, however, find suitable expression only in an act of transgression. Hegel is so confident of the deduction thus outlined that he believes he can put aside, with a single word, all attempts to explain crime in terms of a motive other than that of social disrespect:

> The inner source of crime is the coercive force of the law; exigency and so forth are external causes, belonging to animal need, but crime as such is directed against the person as such and his knowledge of it, for the criminal is intelligence. His inner justification is the coercion, the opposition to his individual will to power, to counting as something, to be recognized. Like Herostratus, he wants to be something, not exactly famous, but that he exercise his will in defiance of the universal will.[48]

The interpretation of crime found in these sentences, in terms of a theory of recognition, not only explains why Hegel is able to proceed from a revival of the struggle for recognition within the legal sphere; it also fills the theoretical gap left in the 'System of Ethical Life' by the lack of the requisite account of the motivation for crime. Crime represents the deliberate injury of 'universal recognition [*Anerkanntsein*]'. It is committed in full awareness, on the part of the one committing the crime, of the fact that 'he is injuring a person, something that is recognized in itself [*an sich*]'.[49] The motivational cause for such an act lies in the feeling of not having the particularity of one's 'own will' recognized in the application of legal coercion. In this sense, what occurs (as part of the advanced stage of law) in the case of crime is the same as what occurred (as part of the conditions for the individual formative process) in the case of the struggle for life and death. By means of an act of provocation, a subject attempts to induce either a single other or the united others to respect the aspect of its own expectations not yet recognized by current forms of interaction. In the first case, that of the individual formative process, the layer of personhood not yet recognized was comprised of those claims aimed at acquiring autonomous control over the means for the reproduction of one's own life. Accordingly, the successful establishment of recognition was also accompanied by progress in terms of socialization, because each individual could know itself to be both an autonomous legal person and a social member of a community based on law. In the second case, by contrast – that of the formative process of the 'universal will' – the layer of the not-yet-recognized is apparently supposed to consist in those claims related to the realization of individual aspirations under conditions of equal rights and duties. It is in this still rather vague sense that one can understand the statement at least that the goal of crime is the assertion of the 'individual will'. But Hegel further

complicates the task of understanding his intended meaning by tying
the experience of having one's individual uniqueness disregarded to
the conditions for the application of legal coercion. For what is it
supposed to mean that a subject must feel injured, with regard to its
claim to realize its own will, in being legitimately forced to fulfil its
contractually agreed duties?

As is not difficult to see, the answer to this question also prejudges
the manner in which the role of the struggle for recognition within the
legal relationship is to be interpreted. Hegel conceives of the formative process of the 'universal will', and thereby the constitution of
society, as a process in which the meaning of legal recognition is
gradually made more concrete. Here, as in the *System of Ethical Life*,
crime necessarily acquires the catalysing function of a moral provocation, by which the 'universal will' of the united legal subjects are led
to a further step of differentiation. But again, what this step will involve in detail can only be determined on the basis of the normative
expectations with which, in the cryptic form of crime, the disrespected
subject appeals to society. For this reason, an answer to the question
as to what role the struggle for recognition acquires at the level of
social reality will not be forthcoming until the interpretive difficulties
generated by Hegel's thesis about the 'inner source of crime' have
been resolved.

There are two possibilities for reinterpreting Hegel's not only terse
but vague remarks in such a way that they give rise to an objectively
consistent hypothesis with regard to the problem outlined. First, one
can understand the specific disrespect experienced, as a result of legal
compulsion, by the reneging subject in terms of an abstraction from
the concrete conditions of the individual case. The 'individual will'
would then lack social recognition because the application of the legal
norms institutionalized together with contractual relations proceeds in
such an abstract fashion that the context-specific, individual motive
for breaking the contract is not taken into consideration. On this first
interpretation, the injurious quality of legal coercion is a matter of the
false formalism of an approach to the application of norms, in which
it is presumed that one can disregard the particular circumstances of
a concrete situation. And correspondingly, what the united legal subjects would have to have learned in response to the criminal's provocation would have to consist in an increase in context-sensitivity in
the application of legal norms. On the other hand, however, one can
also understand the disrespect said to be linked to the exercise of legal
coercion in the sense of an abstraction from the material conditions for
the realization of individuals' intentions.[50] In this case, the 'individual

will' would lack social recognition because the legal norms institutionalized together with contractual relations are so abstractly constituted that the individual opportunities for the realization of legally guaranteed freedoms are not taken into consideration. On this second interpretation, therefore, the injurious quality of legal coercion is a matter of the formalism, not of the application of norms, but of the content of the legal norms themselves. And what is to be learned as a result of the criminal's moral provocation would thus have to consist in the extension of legal norms along the dimension of substantive equality of opportunity.

The decision as to which of these two possible interpretations more accurately represents Hegel's intention crucially depends, of course, on how his argument itself proceeds. For once it is known what the next step in the concretization of legal relations is supposed to consist in, the motivational cause for the crime should become clear in retrospect, and it should thereby become possible to determine the type of social disrespect involved. Surprisingly, however, Hegel considers the only innovation brought about by the moral provocation of the crime to be the institutional restructuring of the law from a formally organized into a State-organized relationship, that is, a transition from natural to positive law. There is no mention in his analysis, however, of progress that would affect the content or structure of legal recognition. Hegel construes the transition to a state-based legal system quite schematically, as Kant had already done in his *Rechtslehre*,[51] with the help of the bridge concept of 'punishment'. Because crime represents an individualistic act of injury to the universal will, the universal will's reaction must, conversely, be aimed at re-establishing its intersubjective power over the breakaway individual. But this 'inversion of the injured universal recognition [*Anerkanntsein*]'[52] must take the form of the punishment of the criminal, by which his act is avenged in such a way that the destroyed relationship of legal recognition is ultimately re-established. With the exacting of punishment, the moral norms that have underlain social life, up to this point, only as a spiritual element enter the world of external appearance. Hence, in the execution of the punishment, the united legal subjects look upon their shared normative intuitions for the first time in the objective form of a law. This, in turn, represents the very embodiment of all the negative regulations, under threat of state sanctions, formally governing legal relations between subjects. In this development, to repeat, progress is reflected only at the level of legal relations: under pressure from the crime, the legal norms take on the character of publicly controlled regulatory laws, thereby acquiring the additional sanctionary force of the state, but without being further concretized or differentiated with regard to their moral content. But if the innovation in legal relations that is practically effected by the criminal were to be limited to this single, institutional dimension, the actual appeal his act made would thereby escape social consideration. For the act's hidden but decisive goal must, in any case – and thus independent of how it is to be interpreted in detail – be considered to be the overcoming of legal formalism, the injurious effect of which is certainly not neutralized by the mere creation of state sanctions. Thus, crime is to be traced back to the feeling of disrespect, the normative causes of which cannot really be eliminated by the legal innovations that it is supposed to be able to bring about forcibly. For that to happen, changes would have to be made that would correct the mistake found in forms of law that are either too abstract in their usage or too formalist in their content. In this respect, the further course of Hegel's text not only fails to provide any indication of which of the two possible readings might contain the most appropriate interpretation of crime; his analysis also fails to live up to its own standards, since it originally set out to interpret into the criminal's deed a radical demand for legal recognition that it ultimately cannot integrate into the framework of legal relations. Hegel allows the struggle for recognition – which he again conceives of, at the level of the universal will, as the driving force of the formative process – to generate moral demands, for which he is unable to indicate the adequate forms of their legal redemption. For this reason, the fertile idea contained in the suggestion that the development of legal relations is itself once again subject to the normative pressure of a struggle for recognition must remain, within the entirety of the text, merely suggestive.

One could, of course, criticize this thesis by noting that Hegel viewed the recognition of the 'individual will' as having its proper place only within the ethical relations of the State. Indeed, in the *System of Ethical Life*, the subject's claim to have the individual particularity of its life respected was not to be satisfied already in the sphere of law but was rather to be confirmed only in the sphere of the spirit of the nation [*Volksgeist*] represented by the State. The earlier text's theoretical justification for this must still hold, as far as the substance of the ideas goes, for the *Realphilosophie* as well. Since the law represents a relation of mutual recognition through which every person, as bearer of the same claims, experiences equal respect, it precisely cannot serve as a medium for the respect of every individual's particular life-history. Instead, this (to a certain extent) individualized form of recognition presupposes, in addition to cognitive achievement, an element of emotional concern, which makes it possible to experience the life of the other as a risky attempt at individual self-realization. If we read this thesis into the chapter on 'Actual Spirit', it becomes at least a bit clearer why Hegel cannot allow the criminal's implicit demand to be met within legal relations: respect for the 'will' of the individual person, as it is demanded by the criminal deed, can only be realized completely in a relationship of recognition that, unlike the one based on law, is supported by feelings of social concern. This does still leave unresolved the question of why Hegel did not also theoretically pursue these forms of the concretization of legal relations, which could have mitigated – from within, as it were – the original formalism of legal relations by taking the particular situation of individuals better into account. In this way, he would have had to take notice not only of new, social contents of the law but also of more context-sensitive forms of the application of law. But this thesis makes it probable that Hegel did not overlook the problem entirely but rather believed that it could only be appropriately solved at another point in his study.

According to what has been said until now, this other point would have to be found where Hegel begins to explicate the integration of societal life within the sphere of ethical life. For, as the *System of Ethical Life* demonstrated, it is only within this institutional framework that the sort of mutual recognition can develop by which the subject's 'individual will' is socially confirmed. Admittedly, the consciousness-theoretic architectonics guiding the *Realphilosophie* accord this same sphere a position that is entirely different from the one it had occupied as part of the Aristotelian scheme of the earlier text. This now no longer refers to the apex of the spiritual clustering of all potentials of societal life but rather that particular stage of the formative process in which Spirit begins to return to its own medium. Under the heading 'Actual Spirit', Hegel follows Spirit's externalization into the objectivity of social reality up to the threshold at which, together with the emergence of the legislative power, institutions of the State have been developed. For him, the condition of legal recognition, that is, the spiritual element of social life, has thereby freed itself from all remainders of the subjective faculty of choice [*Willkür*] to such a degree that it has come to realize itself fully. This thus provides the point of departure for the new stage of the formative process, in which Spirit can return from social objectivity to its own medium. In keeping with his original premises, however, Hegel conceptualizes the first step of Spirit's return into itself as something that Spirit can only complete by once more effecting a presentation of itself within the formative stage from which it last departed. And it is precisely this self-reflection of Spirit within the medium of a well-formed legal reality that constitutes, for him, the process of the formation of the State and thereby of ethical life.

If the construction of the ethical sphere is conceived in terms of such a model of the self-reflection of Spirit, this cannot but have an influence on the notions that are developed out of the social relationships within that sphere. The reference back to the *System of Ethical Life* brings with it the expectation that, in the *Realphilosophie*, Hegel will explicate in greater detail the notion of an ideal community and, with it, the particular mode in which the intersubjective recognition of the biographical uniqueness of all subjects is to occur. In this theoretically extended context, a more precise description will have to be found for the form of reciprocal respect that was only vaguely defined in the earlier text by the concept 'intellectual intuition'. This expectation is further supported by the fact that, in the *Realphilosophie*, the formative processes of 'subjective' and 'actual' Spirit were basically already conceived as stages, in each of which a new potential for relations of reciprocal recognition would unfold in the formation of structures. To a large extent, Spirit's experience at the first stage of formation can be understood as a gradual realization of love relations, while that of the second stage of formation could only be interpreted as an agonistic realization of legal relations. Were Hegel to take such expectations into account, he would have to conceptualize the ethical sphere of the State as an intersubjective relationship in which members of society could know themselves to be reconciled with each other precisely to the degree to which their uniqueness would be reciprocally recognized. The respect of each and every person for the biographical particularity of every other would constitute, as it were, the habitual underpinnings of a society's common mores [*Sitten*]. Just such a conception of ethical life, however, is now a thought that Hegel can no longer entertain. It eludes his account quite fundamentally, because he conceives the organization of the ethical sphere on the pattern of a self-manifestation of Spirit. In this regard, the consciousness-theoretic architectonics ultimately do prevail over the 'recognition-theoretic' substance of the work: Hegel gives in to the pressure to project into the organization of the ethical community the hierarchical schema of the whole and its parts, in terms of which he had already laid out the constitution of the ethical community in Spirit's act of reflection upon its own moments of externalization.

A conception of ethical life in terms of a theory of recognition proceeds from the premise that the social integration of a political community can only fully succeed to the degree to which it is supported, on the part of members of society, by cultural customs that

have to do with the way in which they deal with each other reciprocally. For this reason, the basic concepts with which the ethical preconditions for such community-formation are described must be
tailored to the normative characteristics of communicative relations.
The concept of 'recognition' represents a particularly suitable instrument, since this makes it possible to distinguish systematically between
forms of social interaction with regard to the pattern of respect for
another person that it entails. Hegel, to whom such a conception owes
its existence in the first place, admittedly structures his own theory of
ethical life, in the *Realphilosophie*, in completely different conceptual
terms. The categories with which he operates refer not to interactive
relations among members of society but rather only and always to
their relations to the superordinate instance of the State. As has already been said, for Hegel the State here represents the institutional
embodiment of the act of reflection by which Spirit presents itself once
again at the previously abandoned stage of the actuality of right. But
if the State is to act in Spirit's place, it must take the interactive relations maintained at an equal level by subjects within the legal sphere
and turn them into moments of its own objectification. Accordingly,
the construction of the ethical sphere occurs as a process in which
all elements of social life are transformed into components of an
overarching State. This generates a relationship of asymmetrical dependence between the State and its members similar to the one that
holds fundamentally between Spirit and the products of its manifestation. In the State, the universal will is to collect itself into 'a unity',[53]
into the point of a single instance of power that must, in turn, relate
to its bearers – to legal persons, that is – the way it relates to figures
of its Spiritual production. Therefore, Hegel can do nothing but depict
the sphere of ethical life on the basis of the positive relationship that
socialized subjects have, *not* among each other, but rather with the
State (as the embodiment of Spirit). In his approach, it is cultural
customs of this authoritarian type that unexpectedly take on the role
that should actually have been played, within the 'recognition-theoretic' conception of ethical life, by specific and highly demanding forms
of mutual recognition.

Against the grain of his own argumentation, Hegel was driven by
his use of motifs from the philosophy of consciousness for the construction of the State to this 'substantialistic' model of ethical life,[54] the
consequences of which are reflected at every level of his analysis. To
begin with, Hegel no longer traces the founding of the State back to
an intersubjective conflict, as was the case with the emergence of legal
relations, but rather explains it by means of the tyrannical rule of

charismatic leaders. Because it is only in the face of their singular
executive power that one has a premonition of the 'absolute will' of
Spirit, they are also the only ones in a position to forcibly bring about
the social obedience that must precede the development of State power.
The subjectivity of Spirit can only be reflected in the singularity of
individual heroes, who in turn offer an advance image of the mono-
lithic authority of the State: 'In this way all States were established,
through the noble force of great men; not by physical strength, for the
many are physically stronger than one . . . This is what is preeminent
in the great man: to know, to express the absolute will. All flock to his
banner. He is their god'.[55]

And it is in the context of this line of thought that one finds one of
the very few passages in Hegel's oeuvre in which he makes a positive
reference to Machiavelli's political thought. Because he has, in the
meantime, come to think of the State in terms of the model of self-
realizing Spirit and must accordingly conceive of the founding of the
State as an act of one-sided subjugation – thus moving, in general, a
good bit closer to the founding generation of modern social philosophy – Hegel can now repress all the doubts of an advocate of the
theory of recognition and accord the 'principle' unrestricted rever-
ence: 'It is in this grand sense that Machiavelli's *The Prince* is written:
that in the constituting of the State, in general, what is called treach-
ery, deceit, cruelty, etc. carries no sense of evil but rather a sense of
that which is reconciled with itself'.[56] The same reasons that Hegel
introduced, in the first step of his analysis, to explain the emergence
of the State are the very ones he appeals to, in the next step, for the
purpose of justifying the monarchical form of organization of the State.
Since the subjectivity of Spirit – which the State is to represent institutionally – can be depicted within society only as a singular person,
the representative branches of government must be headed by an
hereditary monarch. Hegel is incapable of conceiving of the mode of
political will-formation in terms of anything other than constitutional
monarchy, because his consciousness-theoretic construction of the State
requires an ultimate accumulation of all power in the hands of a single
individual: 'The free universal is the point of individuality. This individuality, so free of the knowledge shared by all, is not constituted
by them. As the extreme pole of government – thus as an immediate,
natural individuality – it is the hereditary monarch. He is the firm,
immediate knot of the whole'.[57]

Nowhere, finally, does it become clearer to what extent Hegel has
purged the sphere of ethical life of all intersubjectivity than in that
part of his analysis in which he is concerned with the role of the

ethically educated [*sittlich gebildet*] citizen. Here, we find the concepts '*bourgeois*' and '*citoyen*' introduced as labels for the two roles that one must fill once the political community has been established over and above legal relations. In the first role, one has 'the individual as one's end' and follows one's private interests within the legally regulated framework of market exchange. In the second, by contrast, one has 'the universal as such as one's end',[58] and participates actively in the concerns of political will-formation. Whereas Hegel deduces the status of the *bourgeois* (the purposively rational subject capable of forming contracts) directly from intersubjective relations of legal recognition, he sees the status of the citizen as defined solely in relation to the superordinate universal of the State. Unlike legal subjects, *citoyens* are no longer conceived as social persons who owe their capacities and qualities to successful interaction with individuals who can, in the same way, know themselves to be *citoyens*. Rather, the self-consciousness of the citizen is constituted in the reflexive relationship of the lone subject to that part of itself in which the idea of the ethical whole is objectively represented. Thus, the ethical relationship

> is the movement of [the individual] educated for obedience toward the community. Underlying all is this existent essence. The second [element] is trust, which enters here, that is, that the individual likewise knows his Self therein, as his essence, although he may not conceive or understand how he is sustained in it, through what connections and arrangements.[59]

Naturally, this definition only puts the concluding seal on the negative findings to which we were already led anyway, in going through the *Realphilosophie*'s chapter on ethical life. Hegel does not – as one actually would have expected – conceive of the State's realm of action as the locus of the realization of those recognition relationships in which the individual generates respect for his biographical uniqueness. The reason why he is not in a position to do so is that he views the ethical sphere on the whole as a form of objectivation of Spirit's self-reflection, so that the place of intersubjective relations has to be taken throughout by relationships between a subject and its moments of externalization. Ethical life has become, in short, a form of monologically self-developing Spirit and no longer constitutes a particularly demanding form of intersubjectivity. Earlier, of course, Hegel wanted to understand the constitution of both the legal person and social reality as stages of a formative process that Spirit completed in the form of a movement of externalization and return. But that did nothing to keep him, within the framework of the philosophy of consciousness, from making the relationships of interaction between subjects so strong that they had to become media of those formative processes. Thus, in the *Realphilosophie*, as in the *System of Ethical Life* before, Hegel could once again portray the construction of the social world as an ethical learning process leading, via various stages of a struggle, to ever more demanding relationships of reciprocal recognition. Had he consistently carried the logic of this process into the constitution of ethical community, that would have opened up the form of social interaction in which each person, in his or her individual particularity, can reckon with a feeling of recognition based on solidarity. In addition, this would have made it possible to situate the experience of death – the emotional significance of which for the encounter with the other had certainly not escaped Hegel's notice – within a more suitable context than intersubjective relationships centred on conflicts over individual rights. But this step – the logical turn to a conception of ethical life based on the theory of recognition – is not a step that Hegel ever took. In the end, the programme of the philosophy of consciousness gained the upper hand, within Hegel's thought, over all intersubjectivist insights to such an extent that ultimately, in the final stage of the formative process, even its substantive content had to be conceived completely according to the pattern of a self-relation of Spirit. For this reason, however, two issues remain equally unresolved up until the end of the *Realphilosophie*: the fate of the 'individual will', to which Hegel himself referred in his interpretation of 'crime' and the prospects for the vision of a 'genuinely free community', from which he had, after all, once taken his point of departure in the Jena writings. For the solution to both problems, one would need to assume the sort of intersubjectivist concept of 'ethical life' that, after Hegel's transition to a philosophy of consciousness is virtually completed, is no longer available to him.

Hegel never returned to the extraordinary programme that he had pursued in ever new and always fragmentary versions in the Jena writings. Already in the theoretical text with which, drawing on the *Realphilosophie*, he concluded his work in Jena and set the course for his future creative work, one finds a systematic approach robbed of the decisive point. The *Phenomenology of Spirit* allots to the struggle for recognition – once the moral force that drove the process of Spirit's socialization through each of its stages – the sole function of the formation of self-consciousness. Thus reduced to the single meaning represented in the dialectic of lordship and bondage, the struggle between subjects fighting for recognition then comes to be linked so closely to the experience of the practical acknowledgement of one's labour that its own particular logic disappears almost entirely from view.[60] In this sense, the new (and, methodologically speaking, certainly superior) conception found in the *Phenomenology of Spirit* represents, in effect, a fundamental turning-point in the course of Hegel's thought. As a result, the possibility of returning to the most compelling of his earlier intuitions, the still incomplete model of the 'struggle for recognition', is blocked. Accordingly, in the large works that were to follow, one finds only traces of the programme pursued in Jena. But neither the intersubjectivist concept of human identity, nor the distinction of various media of recognition (with the accompanying differentiation of recognition relations), nor, certainly, the idea of a historically productive role for moral struggle – none of these ever again acquires a systematic function within Hegel's political philosophy.

Part II

A Systematic Renewal:

The Structure of Social Relations of Recognition

Hegel's original plan – to provide a philosophical reconstruction of the organization of individual ethical communities as a sequence of stages involving a struggle for recognition – never made it past the half-way point. Before he could develop even an outline of the idea that emerged from his intersubjectivist reinterpretation of Hobbes's doctrine of the state of nature, he sacrificed it for the sake of trying to erect a system based on the philosophy of consciousness, thus leaving the original project unfinished. Today, however, the fact that Hegel's early theory of recognition was destined to remain a fragment is his least of the obstacles to reappropriating the systematic content of the theory. Of far greater significance are the difficulties stemming from the fact that the approach's central line of thought is tainted by metaphysical premises that can no longer be easily reconciled with contemporary thought.

Part I of our investigation did nevertheless show that, in his Jena writings, the young Hegel (well ahead of the spirit of the age) pursued a programme that sounds almost materialist. He set out to reconstruct the ethical formation of the human species as a process in which, via stages of conflict, a moral potential that is structurally inherent in communicative relations between subjects comes to be realized. Of course, within his thought, this construction is still subject to the taken-for-granted presupposition that the conflict under examination is defined by an objective movement of reason that brings to fruition either (in Aristotelian terms) the social nature of human beings or (in terms of the philosophy of consciousness) the self-relation of Spirit. Hegel did not conceive of this formative process – which he described in terms of a movement of recognition mediated by the experience of struggle – as an inner-worldly process occurring under contingent conditions of human socialization. This saved him from having to supply arguments for the strong assertions made about the concrete qualities of historically situated agents. Instead, however lively – indeed, praxis-oriented – his constructions in the Jena writings may be, they still owe a large part of their plausibility to the metaphysical background certainty provided by an overarching event of reason [*Vernunftgeschehen*].

But with the advent of the intellectual movement that set out to dis-
mantle the theoretical presuppositions of German Idealism in order to
advance to an empirically grounded, detranscendentalized concept
of reason, this metaphysical backing for Hegel's philosophy became
dated, and in losing the foundation for the Idealist concept of Spirit,
it also lost the privilege that had previously shielded it from being
tested against empirical reality.[1] Henceforth, the process set in motion
by the first generation of Hegel's students – by Feuerbach, Marx, and
Kierkegaard, with their critique of 'idealism about reason' – could no
longer be stopped by any counter-movement. Gradually, in the course
of the ensuing debate, new aspects of the human spirit's finitude had
to be revealed, aspects from which Hegel had been able to abstract in
his conception of reason. And, concomitantly, every later attempt to
revive his philosophical theory was obliged to make contact with the
empirical sciences in order, from the outset, to avoid falling back into
metaphysics. In this way, the history of post-Hegelian thought has
generated theoretical premises that ought not to be contradicted by
any updating reconstruction of his work today. For this reason, if the
motivation for drawing on Hegel's original model of a 'struggle for
recognition' is to be found neither in the intention to develop a normative theory of institutions,[2] nor solely in the goal of constructing a
moral conception extended in terms of the theory of subjectivity,[3] but
rather in a social theory with normative content, then this entails three
fundamental tasks, resulting from the shifts in theoretical context since
Hegel:

1. Hegel's model starts from the speculative thesis that the formation of the practical self presupposes mutual recognition between
subjects. Not until both individuals see themselves confirmed by the
other as independent can they mutually reach an understanding of
themselves as autonomously acting, individuated selves. For Hegel,
this thesis has to be the point of departure, since it discloses, as it
were, the basic structural feature of the societal subject-matter with
which he is concerned in his theory of ethical life. But his thoughts
remain bound by presuppositions of the metaphysical tradition, because instead of viewing intersubjective relationships as empirical
events within the social world, he builds them up into a formative
process between singular intelligences. For an approach that aims to
reappropriate Hegel's model as a stimulus for a normatively substantive theory of society, a merely speculative foundation is not sufficient. Hence, what is needed, in the first place, is a reconstruction of
his initial thesis in the light of empirical social psychology.

2. The second thesis (and the first that is constitutive for Hegel's conceptual model) asserts, on the basis of intersubjectivist premises, the existence of various forms of reciprocal recognition, which are to be distinguished according to the level of autonomy they make possible for an agent. Both the *System of Ethical Life* and the *Realphilosophie* contained at least a tendency to assume – with regard to 'love', 'law' [*Recht*], and 'ethical life' – a sequence of recognition relations, in the context of which individuals reciprocally confirm each other to an increasing degree as autonomous and individuated persons. For Hegel, a systematic compartmentalization of forms of recognition is necessary, since it is only with their help that he can develop the categorial framework he needs for a theory capable of explaining the formative process of ethical life as a stage sequence of intersubjective relationships. His proposed distinctions remain bound to metaphysical presuppositions, however, insofar as they represent a mere extension of relationships that have been constructed purely conceptually to cover empirical reality. Today, before one can draw on this typology as part of an updating reconstruction, an empirically supported phenomenology is thus needed, one that allows Hegel's theoretical proposal to be tested and, if necessary, corrected.

3. Finally, Hegel's conceptual model finds its completion in the third thesis, according to which the sequence of forms of recognition follows the logic of a formative process that is mediated by the stages of a moral struggle. In the course of their identity-formation and at their current stage of integration into community, subjects are, as it were, transcendentally required to enter into an intersubjective conflict, the outcome of which is the recognition of claims to autonomy previously not socially affirmed. There are two equally strong assertions flowing into this thesis of Hegel's, which began to emerge only in outline in the writings discussed above: first, that successful ego-development presupposes a certain sequence of forms of reciprocal recognition and, second, that subjects are informed of the absence of this recognition by experiencing disrespect in such a way that they see themselves obliged to engage in a 'struggle for recognition'. Both hypotheses are bound to the premises of the metaphysical tradition by their commitment to the teleological framework of a developmental theory that allows the ontogenetic process of identity-formation to flow directly into the formation of societal structures. For anyone attempting to reappropriate Hegel's conceptual model today under altered theoretical conditions, this tangled complex of highly speculative claims represents the greatest challenge. This challenge is only to be met by submitting the individual hypotheses to separate tests. The questions are to be addressed

as to, first, whether Hegel's assumption that stages of recognition move in a certain direction can withstand empirical doubts; second, whether these forms of reciprocal recognition can be mapped onto corresponding experiences of social disrespect; and, finally, whether there is historical or sociological evidence for the claim that such forms of disrespect have actually served as a source of motivation for social confrontations. The answers to these questions amount to an explication, at least in broad strokes, of the moral logic of social conflicts. This is impossible, however, without first taking up, once again, the historical thread that ran through Part I. For Hegel relegated the experience of social struggle to the speculative horizon of an Idealist theory of reason to such an extent that it was only the historical-materialist turn of his successors that could give this experience a place in historical reality.

In Part II of this study, I shall be attempting to solve only the first two of the three large issues posed by the attempt to render Hegel's theoretical model relevant again under conditions of postmetaphysical thinking. In Part III, I shall turn to the difficult questions raised by the third complex of problems and suggest a number of possible avenues to be pursued by social philosophy. One of the theories that forms a bridge between Hegel's original insight and our intellectual situation can be found in the social psychology of George Herbert Mead. Because his writings allow for a translation of Hegel's theory of intersubjectivity into a postmetaphysical language, they can prepare the way for the project undertaken here.

4

Recognition and Socialization: Mead's Naturalistic Transformation of Hegel's Idea

Nowhere is the idea that human subjects owe their identity to the experience of intersubjective recognition more thoroughly developed on the basis of naturalistic presuppositions than in the social psychology of George Herbert Mead.[1] Even today, his writings contain the most suitable means for reconstructing the intersubjectivist intuitions of the young Hegel within a postmetaphysical framework. Mead clearly has more in common with the Hegel of the Jena period than just the idea of a social genesis of ego-identity. And the agreement between their political-philosophical approaches is not limited to their criticisms of the atomism of social contract theory. Mead's unsystematic social psychology, recorded largely in the form of lecture transcriptions, exhibits parallels with Hegel's early work even with regard to the core issue that interests us here: Mead also aims to make the struggle for recognition the point of reference for a theoretical construction in terms of which the moral development of society is to be explained.[2]

Mead arrives at the premises of his theory of intersubjectivity by way of a detour through an epistemological examination of the subject-matter of psychology. From the start, his interest in psychological research was set by the need to develop a non-speculative solution to the problems of German Idealism. Mead shared with many philosophers of his time the hope that empirical psychology could contribute to improving our knowledge of the specific cognitive faculties of human beings.[3] What soon comes to be the focus of his attention is the foundational theoretical problem of how psychological research is to gain access to its specific subject-matter, namely, the psychical. He expected the answer to this question to contribute to a full explanation of human subjectivity, one that would be able to accommodate the insights of German Idealism. In attempting to resolve these issues, Mead begins by taking up the basic pragmatist idea, inherited from Peirce via Dewey, that it is precisely in the situations in which actions are problematized during their performance that humans make cognitive gains. For individual subjects, a world of psychological experiences can only emerge at the moment in which they encounter such difficulties in carrying out a preconceived plan of action that their interpretation of the situation, which had heretofore been objectively reliable, is robbed of its validity and comes to be separated from the rest of reality as a merely subjective notion. The 'psychical' represents, as it were, the experience that one has of oneself whenever one is prevented by a problem that emerges in practice from carrying out the action in the usual way. So, psychology gains access to its field of study from the perspective of an actor who is aware of his or her subjectivity because he or she is forced – under pressure from an action-problem that needs to be solved – to rework creatively his or her interpretation of the situation:

> [The subject-matter of functionalist psychology is] that phase of experience within which we are immediately conscious of conflicting impulses which rob the object of its character as object-stimulus, leaving us in this respect in an attitude of subjectivity; but during which a new object-stimulus appears due to the reconstructive activity which is identified with the subject 'I' as distinct from the object 'me'.[4]

Mead immediately raises the objection against himself that such a 'definition of the psychical' cannot supply the requisite proof for the accessibility of the subjective world. In the moment at which the instrumental action is disrupted, an actor does, in fact, become conscious of the subjective character of his or her current interpretation of the situation. But his or her attention is not at all directed primarily towards the problem-solving activity of its own self, but rather 'toward the sharper definition of the objects which constitute the stimulation'.[5] Because instrumental actions only require that a subject creatively adapt, in cases of disturbances, to a mistakenly assessed reality, they are not the appropriate model for the desired explanation of the psychical. In order to be able to supply psychology with the same perspective from which the actor becomes conscious of his or her subjectivity, one needs to focus on a type of action in which it is functional for agents to reflect on their own subjective conduct at the moment of the disturbance. Mead turns to this other – and, for his explanatory aims, more suitable – type of action at the point at which he begins to extend the Darwinian model of an organism relating to its environment to include a social dimension: as soon as we imagine an interaction between several organisms, we have in mind an action-event that functionally requires all participants to reflect, in moments of crisis, upon their own reactive conduct. For the purposes of psychology, human interactive behaviour represents a particularly appropriate starting-point, since it forces subjects to become conscious of their own subjectivity as problems emerge:

> A man's reaction toward weather conditions has no influence upon the weather itself. It is of importance for the success of his conduct that he should be conscious not of his own attitudes, of his own habits of response, but of the signs of rain or fair weather. Successful social conduct brings one into a field within which a consciousness of one's own attitudes helps toward the control of the conduct of others.[6]

For Mead, this functionalist principle frames the methodology within which he pursues his research interests from this point on: by taking the perspective that actors take when their dealings with their partners to interaction are jeopardized, psychology can gain insight into the mechanisms by which a consciousness of one's own subjectivity emerges. Of course, in order to complete this task, one must first answer the far more fundamental question as to how a subject is able to arrive at a consciousness of the social meaning of its behavioural expressions at all. For in order to be in a position to 'control the conduct of others', an actor must already have some sense of what his or her own conduct means for each other interaction partner in the shared action-situation. Compared to the development of self-consciousness, the emergence of knowledge of the meaning of one's behavioural reactions is the more primary phenomenon. Thus, to begin with, social psychology must clarify the mechanism by which a consciousness of the meaning of social actions could emerge in human interaction. Mead's explanation takes its point of departure from the observation that one possesses knowledge of the intersubjective meaning of one's actions only if one is capable of generating the same reaction in oneself that one's behavioural expressions stimulated in the other: I can become aware of what my gesture signifies for the other only by producing the other's reply in myself. For Mead, however, this ability to provoke in oneself the reaction produced in the other is tied to the evolutionary precondition for a new form of human communication. As both Herder and, later, Gehlen saw, in contrast to all non-vocal means of reaching agreement, vocal gestures are the first to have the special quality of affecting both the agent and his or her interaction partner in the same way at the same instant: 'While one feels but imperfectly the value of his own facial expression or bodily attitude for another, his ear reveals to him his own vocal gesture in the same form that it assumes to his neighbor'.[7] Whenever one influences one's partners to interaction by means of a vocal gesture, one can simultaneously trigger the other's reaction in oneself, since one hears one's own utterance as a stimulus coming from the outside. But, as a result, the vocal gesture – to which one can respond just like any other hearer – comes to have the same meaning to oneself as it has for one's addressees.

With both ontogenetic and species-historical processes in mind, Mead draws conclusions from this communications-theoretic insight for the question as to the conditions under which human consciousness emerges. The development of the consciousness of oneself is connected to the development of consciousness of meaning in the sense that, in the individual experiential process, the latter prepares the way for the former: the ability to call up in oneself the meaning that one's action has for others also opens up the possibility for one to view oneself as a social object of the actions of one's partner to interaction. In perceiving my own vocal gesture and reacting to myself as my counterpart does, I take on a decentred perspective, from which I can form an image of myself and thereby come to a consciousness of my identity:

> Certainly the fact that the human animal can stimulate himself as he stimulates others and can respond to his stimulations as he responds to the stimulations of others, places in his conduct the form of a social object out of which may arise a 'me' to which can be referred so-called subjective experiences.[8]

The concept of the 'me' that Mead uses here to characterize the result of this original relation-to-self is supposed to make it terminologically clear that individuals can only become conscious of themselves in the object-position. For the self that one catches sight of in reacting to oneself is always what one's interaction partner sees as his or her partner to interaction perceived, and never the current agent of one's own behavioural expressions. Mead thus distinguishes the 'me' – which, since it only reflects the other's image of me, only preserves my momentary activity as something already past – from the 'I', which represents the unregimented source of all my current actions. The concept of the 'I' is meant to designate the instance of human personhood that is responsible for the creative response to action-problems but that can never, as such, be glimpsed. In its spontaneous activity, of course, this 'I' not only precedes the consciousness that one has of oneself, from the point of view of one's partner to interaction, but also constantly refers back to the behavioural expressions contained consciously within the 'me' and comments on them. In the individual's personality, there is a relationship between the 'I' and the 'me' comparable to the relationship between two partners to dialogue:

> The 'I' ... never can exist as an object in consciousness, but the very conversational character of our inner experience, the very process of replying to one's own talk, implies an 'I' behind the scenes who answers to the gestures, the symbols, that arise in consciousness.... The self-conscious, actual self in social intercourse is the objective 'me' or 'me's' with the process of response continually going on and implying a fictitious 'I' always out of sight of himself.[9]

In suggesting that there are several 'me's' formed in the subject's ongoing 'process of response', Mead already reveals the direction that his investigation of the development of human identity will subsequently take. Thus far, his studies – still largely related to questions about the foundations of psychology – enabled him to develop an intersubjectivistic conception of human self-consciousness: a subject can only acquire a consciousness of itself to the extent to which it learns to perceive its own action from the symbolically represented second-person perspective. This thesis constitutes a first step towards a naturalistic justification of Hegel's theory of recognition insofar as it can indicate the psychological mechanism that makes the development of self-consciousness dependent upon the existence of a second subject: without the experience of having an interaction partner react, one would not be in a position to influence oneself – with the help of utterances that one can perceive oneself – so as to learn to understand one's reactions as something produced by one's own person. Like Hegel, but with the tools of empirical science, Mead inverts the relationship between the ego and the social world and asserts the primacy of the perception of the other to the development of self-consciousness:

> Such a 'me' is not then an early formation, which is then projected and ejected into the bodies of other people to give them the breadth of human life. It is rather an importation from the field of social objects into an amorphous, unorganized field of what we call inner experience. Through the organization of this object, the self, this material is itself organized and brought under the control of the individual in the form of so-called consciousness.[10]

Of course, with regard to his theory of recognition, the Hegel of the Jena period was pursuing a more comprehensive goal than that of explaining the possibility of self-consciousness. Indeed, even the concept of 'recognition' quite clearly signals that he was concerned less with the relations of cognitive interaction by which a subject acquires a consciousness of itself than with those forms of practical affirmation by which it gains a normative understanding of itself as a certain kind of person. In the context of the writings in which he works out his model of the 'struggle for recognition', Hegel is interested above all in the intersubjective conditions for a *practical* relation-to-self. The development of an *epistemic* self-relation, by contrast, represents a necessary though insufficient condition, on the basis of which the identity of the practical ego can constitute itself.[11] Mead's theory contains the means for a naturalistic translation of this core of Hegel's theory of recognition as well. For after having advanced to an intersubjective conception of self-consciousness, his writings also move in the direction of an investigation of the practical relation-to-self. Soon after the completion of his early articles, which focused on the issue of self-consciousness, Mead turned to the issue of the subject's moral and practical identity-formation. For Mead, the topic arises out of the attempt to extend the conceptual distinction between the 'I' and the 'me' to cover the normative dimension of individual development.

Up to this point, Mead had used the category of the 'me' to designate the cognitive image that one forms of oneself as soon as one has learned to perceive oneself from the second-person perspective. He arrives at a new stage in the development of his social psychology once he integrates the aspect of moral norms into the observation of the interactive relationship. For this raises the question as to how the self-image established in the 'me' must be constituted if, with regard to the reactions of one's partners to interaction, one is no longer dealing merely with cognitive predictions about behaviour but rather with normative expectations. The first suggestion of this expanded formulation of the issue is to be found already in the final essay in a series of articles on the explanation of self-consciousness. At one point there, he briefly sketches the mechanism by which a child learns the elementary forms of moral judgement: 'Thus the child can think about his conduct as good or bad only as he reacts to his own acts in the remembered words of his parents'.[12] In this case, the behavioural reactions with which a subject (in the role of its interaction partner) attempts to influence itself contain the normative expectations of its personal environment. Accordingly, however, the 'me' to which the subject turns, from the second-person perspective, can no longer represent a neutral

instance of cognitively overcoming a problem but must r̥
body a moral instance of intersubjective conflict-resolution.
extension of social reaction to include normative action-cont
'me' is transformed from a cognitive into a practical self-i
one's own person. By putting itself in the normative point of ..̣w of
its interaction partner, the other subject takes over the partner's moral
values and applies them to its practical relation to itself.

In a further step, Mead quickly makes this basic thought the starting-
point for an explanation of human identity-formation. The idea guiding
him here is that of a gradual generalization of the 'me' in the course
of the child's social development. If it is the case that the mechanism
of personality formation consists in one's learning to conceive of oneself from the normative perspective of one's neighbour, then the frame
of reference for one's practical self-image must gradually expand along
with the circle of partners to interaction. In his lectures on social
psychology, published posthumously in *Mind, Self, and Society*,[13] Mead
initially portrays this general direction of development, as is well
known, by referring to two phases of children's playful activities. In
the stage of role-taking 'play', the child communicates with himself or
herself by imitating the behaviour of a concrete partner to interaction,
in order then to react in a complementary manner in his or her own
action. By contrast, the second stage – that of the competitive 'game'
– requires the maturing child to represent the action-expectations of
all of his or her playmates, in order to be able to perceive his or her
own role within the functionally organized action-context. The distinction between the two stages can be seen in the different degrees of
generality of the normative action-expectations that the child must
anticipate in each case: in the first case, it is the concrete pattern of
conduct of a significant other that has to be integrated into the child's
own action as controlling normative expectations, whereas in the second case it is the socially generalized patterns of conduct of a whole
group. For this reason, in the transition from 'play' to 'game', the
social norms of action of the generalized other make their way into
the practical self-image of the maturing child:

> The fundamental difference between the game and play is that in the
> [former] the child must have the attitude of all the others involved in
> that game. The attitudes of the other players which the participant as-
> sumes organize into a sort of unit, and it is that organization that con-
> trols the response of the individual. The illustration used was of a person
> playing baseball. Each one of his own acts is determined by his assump-
> tion of the action of the others who are playing the game. We get then
> an 'other' which is the organization of the attitudes of those involved in
> the same process.[14]

From the concrete illustrative material supplied by the shift in children's playing behaviour, Mead distils a developmental mechanism that is supposed to underlie the human socialization process as a whole. The conceptual link between the narrower and broader explanatory scope is the category of the 'generalized other': just as children develop, in the transition to the 'game', the capacity to orient their conduct towards rules that they derive from a synthesis of the perspectives of all the players, the process of socialization *per se* involves the internalization of norms of action that result from a generalization of the action-expectations of all members of society. In learning to generalize internally an ever-larger number of interaction partners to such an extent that a sense of social norms of action is acquired, the subject gains the abstract ability to participate in the norm-governed interactions. For those internalized norms tell one both what one can expect from others and what one is legitimately obliged to do for them. What this means for the earlier question as to how the 'me' changes in this process of social development is that individuals learn to conceive of themselves, from the perspective of a generalized other, as members of a society organized in terms of the division of labour:

> This getting of the broad activities of any given social whole or organized society as such within the experiential field of any one of the individuals involved or included in that whole is, in other words, the essential basis and prerequisite of the fullest development of that individual's self: only in so far as he takes the attitudes of the organized social group to which he belongs toward the organized, co-operative social activity or set of such activities in which that group as such is engaged, does he develop a complete self or possess the sort of complete self he has developed.[15]

If it is the case that one becomes a socially accepted member of one's community by learning to appropriate the social norms of the 'generalized other', then it makes sense to use the concept of 'recognition' for this intersubjective relationship: to the extent that growing children recognize their interaction partners by way of an internalization of their normative attitudes, they can know themselves to be members of their social context of cooperation. The idea of speaking here of a relationship of mutual recognition is Mead's own: 'It is that self which is able to maintain itself in the community, that is recognized in the community in so far as it recognizes the others'.[16] In this context, however, Mead works this out in a way that has much more in common with what Hegel had in mind than the mere parallels with regard to the concept of 'recognition' might suggest. Like Hegel, he

too conceives the self-understanding of a person who l
view himself or herself from the perspective of the gene
as the self-understanding of a legal person. With the appi
the social norms regulating the cooperative nexus of the c
maturing individuals not only realize what obligations the}
à-vis members of society; they also become aware of the 1
are accorded to them in such a way that they can legitimatu,y count
on certain demands of theirs being respected. Rights are, as it were, the
individual claims about which I can be sure that the generalized other
would meet them. Insofar as this is the case, such rights can be said
to be socially granted only to the extent to which a subject can conceive of itself as a fully accepted member of its community. For this
reason, rights play an especially significant role in the formative process of the practical ego:

> If one is maintaining his property in the community, it is of primary
> importance that he is a member of that community, for it is his taking
> of the attitude of the others that guarantees to him the recognition of his
> own rights.... It gives him his position, gives him the dignity of being
> a member in the community.[17]

It is no coincidence that Mead speaks at this point of the 'dignity'
one is granted as soon as one is recognized, through the granting of
rights, as a member of the community. For, implicit in the term is the
systematic assertion that the experience of recognition corresponds to
a mode of practical relation-to-self in which one can be sure of the
social value of one's identity. The general concept that Mead selects
for designating this consciousness of one's own worth is that of 'self-
respect'. He means it to refer to the positive attitude towards oneself
that one is capable of taking if one is recognized by the members
of one's community as being a particular kind of person. The degree
of self-respect is in turn dependent on the level of individualization of
the traits or abilities in terms of which one is affirmed by one's partners in interaction. Since 'rights' are something that allows every human
being to feel recognized with regard to characteristics that he or she
shares with every other member of the community, Mead considers
them to be a solid, though only very general, basis for self-respect:

> It is interesting to go back into one's inner consciousness and pick out
> what it is that we are apt to depend upon in maintaining our self-
> respect. There are, of course, profound and solid foundations. One does
> keep his word, meet his obligations. And that provides a basis for self-
> respect. But those are characters which obtain in most of the members

of the community with whom we have to do. We all fall down at certain points, but on the whole we always are people of our words. We do belong to the community and our self-respect depends on our recognition of ourselves as such self-respecting individuals.[18]

Up to this point, one can still understand Mead's reconstruction of practical identity-formation as a more precise social-psychological version of the young Hegel's theory of recognition. Of course, *Mind, Self, and Society* nowhere mentions the sort of stage of mutual recognition that Hegel tried to characterize with the romantic concept of 'love'. That may also be the reason why, in working out the details of his theory, Mead leaves out the fundamental form of self-respect associated with the development of a feeling of trust in one's own abilities.[19] But with regard to the relationship of recognition that Hegel introduced under the heading of 'law' [*Recht*] as a second stage in his developmental model, the conception of the 'generalized other' represents not only a theoretical amendment but also a substantive deepening. Recognizing one another as legal persons means that both subjects control their own action by integrating into it the community's will, as that is embodied in the intersubjectively recognized norms of their society. For, once partners to interaction all take on the normative perspective of the 'generalized other', they know – reciprocally – what obligations they have to each other. Accordingly, they can also both conceive of themselves as bearers of individual claims, claims that the other knows he or she is normatively obliged to meet. At the individual level, the experience of being recognized as a legal person by the members of one's community ensures that one can develop a positive attitude towards oneself. For in realizing that they are obliged to respect one's rights, they ascribe to one the quality of morally responsible agency. However, because one necessarily shares the capacities thus entailed with all of one's fellow citizens, one cannot yet, as a legal person, relate positively to those of one's characteristics that precisely distinguish one from one's partners in interaction. For that, a form of mutual recognition is needed in which each individual is affirmed not only as a member of his or her community but just as much as a biographically individuated subject. Mead also agrees with Hegel that insofar as legal relations of recognition are unable to give a positive expression to the individual differences between citizens of a community, they are still incomplete.

Of course, Mead departs from this shared frame of reference as soon as he begins to consider the creative potential of the 'I' in his discussion of identity-formation. In Hegelian terms, this thematic extension can be understood as involving the subsequent attribution, to the movement of recognition, of the psychological force that explains its inner dynamic. Up to this point, Mead has been considering the development of a subject's practical relation-to-self only from the standpoint of what changes occur within the individual subject's 'me' during the process of maturation, as the subject comes into contact with an ever-expanding circle of partners to interaction. He has temporarily excluded from his analysis the 'I', namely, the instance of spontaneous reaction-formation that cannot as such be grasped cognitively. But a complete explanation of what occurs in the formative process of moral subjects would have to include, along with the aspect of the normative control of one's conduct, some consideration of the creative deviations with which, in our everyday action, we ordinarily react to social obligations:

> Over against the 'me' is the 'I'. The individual not only has rights, but he has duties; he is not only a citizen, a member of the community, but he is one who reacts to this community and in his reactions to it, as we have seen in the conversation of gestures, changes it. The 'I' is the response of the individual to the attitude of the community as this appears in his own experience. His response to that organized attitude in turn changes it.[20]

The practical spontaneity that marks our action in everyday life is to be traced back to the achievements of an 'I' that, as in the case of cognitive self-relation, is opposed to the 'me' as an unconscious force. Whereas the latter harbours the social norms in terms of which one controls one's conduct in accordance with society's expectations, the former is the collection site for all the inner impulses expressed in involuntary reactions to social challenges. As with the 'I' of self-knowledge, however, the 'I' of practical identity-formation is not something that can be grasped directly. For we can only know that portion of what is going on in our spontaneous action-expressions that can be perceived as a departure from normatively requisite patterns of behaviour. This is why, for good reasons, the concept of the 'I' found in *Mind, Self, and Society* has something unclear and ambiguous about it. What it stands for is the sudden experience of a surge of inner impulses, and it is never immediately clear whether they stem from pre-social drives, the creative imagination, or the moral sensibility of one's own self. As Mead says, drawing on William James, he wants this conception to call attention to a reservoir of psychical energies that supply every subject with a plurality of untapped possibilities for identity-formation:

⌐ possibilities in our nature, those sorts of energy which William James took so much pleasure in indicating, are possibilities of the self that lie beyond our own immediate presentation. We do not know just what they are. They are in a certain sense the most fascinating contents that we can contemplate, so far as we can get hold of them.[21]

If this creative reaction-potential of the 'I' is conceived of as the psychological counterpart to the 'me', then it quickly becomes apparent that, in the process of identity-formation, the mere internalization of the perspective of the 'generalized other' cannot be the end of the matter. Rather, one constantly senses urges within, stemming from demands that are incompatible with the intersubjectively recognized norms of one's social environment, so that one has to put one's own 'me' into doubt. For Mead, this inner friction between the 'I' and the 'me' represents the outline of the conflict that is supposed to be able to explain moral development of both individuals and society. As the representative of the community, the 'me' embodies the conventional norms that one must constantly try to expand, in order to give social expression to the impulsiveness and creativity of one's 'I'. Mead thus introduces into the practical relation-to-self a tension between the internalized collective will and the claims of individuation, a tension that has to lead to a moral conflict between the subject and the subject's social environment. For in order to be able to put into action the demands surging within, one needs, in principle, the approval of all other members of society, since their collective will controls one's own action as an internalized norm. The existence of the 'me' forces one to fight, in the interest of one's 'I', for new forms of social recognition.

Mead initially explicates the structure of such moral conflicts by making use of examples related to inner demands whose satisfaction presupposes the extension of individual rights. The choice of this point of departure is supported by an implicit distinction, although it is not immediately clear whether this is supposed to be a distinction among stages or dimensions of identity-formation. From the outside, the demands of the 'I' can be distinguished on the basis of whether the context in which they are to be met is that of individual autonomy or personal self-realization. In the first case, it is a matter of the 'freedom from given laws', whereas in the second, it is a matter of the 'realization of the self'. For the moment, what is of interest is not yet this distinction *per se* but only the fact that Mead's explanation starts from the former class of 'I'-demands. He thus has in mind situations in which a subject senses inner impulses to act in a way that is hampered by the rigid norms of society. What Mead views as specific to these cases is that they allow the individual involved actively to resolve his or her moral conflict only by carrying out a particular form of idealization: if one is to realize the demands of one's 'I', one must be able to anticipate a community in which one is entitled to have those desires satisfied. This becomes unavoidable because by questioning intersubjectively accepted norms one eliminates the internal conversation partner to whom one had previously been able to justify one's action. Thus, what comes to take the place of the 'generalized other' of the existing community is that of a future society, in which one's individual claims would, prospectively, be accepted. In this sense, the practical aspiration to greater freedom of action already entails the counterfactual supposition of the expanded recognition of rights:

> The demand is freedom from conventions, from given laws. Of course, such a situation is only possible where the individual appeals, so to speak, from a narrow and restricted community to a larger one, that is, larger in the logical sense of having rights which are not so restricted. One appeals from fixed conventions which no longer have any meaning to a community in which the rights shall be publicly recognized, and one appeals to others on the assumption that there is a group of organized others that answer to one's own appeal – even if the appeal be made to posterity.[22]

One is capable of 'asserting' oneself, as Mead says – that is, of defending the demands of the 'I' vis-à-vis one's societal environment – only if, instead of taking the perspective of the existing collective will, one can take the perspective of an expanded community of rights. The ideal 'me' thus erected provides one, in spite of the break with the community, with the intersubjective recognition without which one cannot maintain a sense of personal identity. But because the impulsiveness of the 'I' cannot be stilled, it introduces an element of normative idealization into all social practices. In defending their spontaneously experienced demands, subjects have no option but to secure acceptance, again and again, from a counterfactually posited community that grants them greater freedom, as compared to the established relations of recognition. For Mead, it is the movement stemming from the enormous number of these moral deviations – which blanket the social life-process, as it were, with a network of normative ideals – that constitutes the developmental process of society: 'That is the way, of course, in which society gets ahead, by just such interactions as those in which some person thinks a thing out. We are continually changing our social system in some respects, and we are able to do that intelligently because we can think'.[23]

This thesis holds the theoretical key to a conception of societal development that, in a surprising way, provides a social-psychological basis for the Hegelian idea of a 'struggle for recognition'. Mead forges a systematic link between the unceasing urges of the 'I' and the social life-process by drawing together the multitude of moral deviations into a single historical force: in every historical epoch, individual, particular anticipations of expanded recognition relations accumulate into a system of normative demands, and this, consequently, forces societal development as a whole to adapt to the process of progressive individuation. And since subjects can defend the claims of their 'I' – even after social reforms have been carried out – only by anticipating yet another community that guarantees greater freedoms, the result is a chain of normative ideals pointing in the direction of increasing personal autonomy. Under the pressure of this collectively anticipated pattern of development, so to speak, the process of civilization follows, as Mead puts it, a tendency toward the 'liberation of individuality':

> One difference between primitive human society and civilized human society is that in primitive human society the individual self is much more completely determined, with regard to his thinking and his behaviour, by the general pattern of the organized social activity carried on by the particular social group to which he belongs, than he is in civilized human society. In other words, primitive human society offers much less scope for individuality – for original, unique, or creative thinking and behaviour on the part of the individual self within it or belonging to it – than does civilized human society; and indeed the evolution of civilized human society from primitive human society has largely depended upon or resulted from a progressive social liberation of the individual self and his conduct, with the modifications and elaborations of the human social process which have followed from and been made possible by that liberation.[24]

Like Hegel in his treatment of the formative process of the 'collective will', Mead views the moral development of societies as a process in which the meaning of legal recognition is gradually broadened. Both thinkers agree that, historically, the potential for individuality is only unleashed via an increase in legally enforced freedoms. Like Hegel, Mead considers the motor of these directed changes to be a struggle in which subjects continually strive to expand the range of their intersubjectively guaranteed rights and, in so doing, to raise the level of their personal autonomy. For both thinkers, then, the historical liberation of individuality occurs in the form of a long-term struggle for recognition. But, unlike Hegel, Mead can offer an explanation for this developmental process, one that reveals its motivational basis. The forces that propel the 'movement of recognition' each time anew represent the uncontrollable levels of the 'I', which can only express themselves freely and without coercion if they meet with the approval of the 'generalized other'. Because subjects are forced, under pressure from their 'I', to constantly loosen the constraints on the norms embodied in the 'generalized other', they are, to a certain extent, psychologically required to do what they can to expand legal recognition relations. The social praxis resulting from the collective effort to 'enrich the community' in this way is what can be called, within Mead's social psychology, the 'struggle for recognition'.

Mead's lack of hesitation in drawing conclusions of this type for a theory of society becomes visible at those points in his lectures in which he speaks of social upheavals of past ages. His examples usually refer to historical situations in which normatively broadened concepts of the social community became the motivational core of social movements. The 'struggle for recognition' proceeds from moral ideas in which charismatically endowed personalities were capable of extending the 'generalized other' of their social environment in a manner that fits with the intuitive expectations of their contemporaries. As soon as these intellectual innovations came to influence the consciousness of larger groups, a struggle for the recognition of expanded rights-claims had to emerge, one capable of putting the institutionalized order into question. In illustrating his thesis historically, Mead places particular emphasis on the socially revolutionary influence of Jesus:

> The great characters have been those who, by being what they were in the community, made that community a different one. They have enlarged and enriched the community. Such figures as great religious characters in history have, through their membership, indefinitely increased the possible size of the community itself. Jesus generalized the conception of the community in terms of the family in such a statement as that of the neighbour in the parables. Even the man outside of the community will now take that generalized family attitude toward it, and he makes those that are so brought into relationship with him members of the community to which he belongs, the community of a universal religion.[25]

What this example also shows, however, is that Mead associates two very different processes with the idea of social struggle leading to an expansion of legal recognition relations. In the first sense, the concept captures the process by which all members of a community experience a gain in personal autonomy in virtue of having their rights expanded. The community is 'enlarged' in the internal sense that the measure of individual liberty in that society increases. In the second sense, the same concept also stands for the process by which the rights existing within a given community are extended to an ever-larger circle of persons. In this case – sketched in the example quoted above – the community is 'enlarged' in the social sense that an increasing number of subjects are integrated into the community by being granted those rights. Mead does not sufficiently distinguish between the universalization of social norms and the expansion of individual freedom. And this makes his conception of a society's legal relations – which he, like Hegel, attempts to develop in terms of a theory of recognition – of only limited applicability.

In contrast to Mead, however, the early Hegel not only had the love relationship precede legal relations as a stage of recognition; he also distinguished legal relations from a further relationship of recognition in which subjects are supposed to be affirmed in their individual particularity. In Mead's social psychology, one finds a theoretical parallel to this at the point where he integrates into his framework of analysis the class of 'I'-demands that he had previously tried to put in a separate category of demands. As we have seen, this is to include urges of the 'I', the satisfaction of which presupposes not so much the growth of personal autonomy as opportunities for individual self-realization. Mead does not indicate whether he wants this second class of demands to designate a dimension or a stage of practical identity-formation. In any event, he seems to assume that such appeals can only appear as something distinct after a subject already has some basic sense of being recognized as a member of a community:

> But that is not enough for us, since we want to recognize ourselves in our differences from other persons. We have, of course, a specific economic and social status that enables us to so distinguish ourselves. . . . We may come back to manners of speech and dress, to a capacity for remembering, to this, that, and the other thing – but always to something in which we stand out above people.[26]

Mead reckons with the existence of human impulses that are geared towards distinguishing oneself from all other partners to interaction in order to gain a consciousness of one's individual uniqueness. Since the satisfaction of such impulses is linked to preconditions other than those provided by the extension of legal relations of recognition, Mead tacks on an independent class of 'I'-demands. As he immediately stresses, however, even the urge for self-realization is dependent on a particular sort of recognition: 'Since it is a social self, it is a self that is realized in its relationship to others. It must be recognized by others to have the very values which we want to have belong to it'.[27]

Mead considers self-realization to be a process in which one develops abilities and traits and can convince oneself of their unique value for the surrounding social world, on the basis of the recognizing reactions of one's partners to interaction. For this reason, the type of confirmation on which one depends cannot be the type that one experiences as a bearer of normatively regulated rights and duties. For the characteristics attributed to one as a legal person are precisely those one shares with all other members of one's community. The 'me' of self-realization is not the instance of normative control of behaviour that one acquires by learning to accommodate the moral expectations of an ever-larger circle of partners to interaction. For, from the perspective that one takes towards oneself in internalizing that sort of 'generalized other', one can only understand oneself as a person with the same characteristics of morally responsible agency that all other members of society possess. By contrast, the 'me' of individual self-realization requires that one be able to understand oneself as a unique and irreplaceable person. To this extent, Mead must intend this new instance to be a medium of ethical self-assurance, a medium that contains the value-convictions of a community in light of which subjects can assure themselves of the social significance of their individual capacities.

If individual self-realization turns out to be dependent, in this sense, on the existence of an evaluative 'me', then it would have been up to Mead, in the next step of his study, to examine its development in the individual subject with as much care as he devoted to analysing the development of the moral 'me'. For, to the extent that the maturing child's social circle of partners to interaction is enlarged, the instance of ethical self-confirmation must also go through a process of universalization. The esteem that the child directly experiences, to begin with, in the affectionate attention of concrete others must dissolve into a form of recognition that offers intersubjective confirmation of one's individually chosen way of life. In order to arrive at a 'me' that can provide this sort of ethical support, every individual must learn to generalize the value-convictions of all of his or her interaction partners sufficiently to get an abstract idea of the collective goals of the community. For it is only within the horizon of these commonly shared values that one can conceive oneself as a person who is distinguished from all others in virtue of a contribution to society's life-process that is recognized as unique. Had Mead actually pursued this line of research, he would have quickly run up against the social-philosophical problem that the early Hegel tried to resolve with his concept of ethical life. What Hegel wanted to circumscribe as a third, ethical relationship of mutual recognition can be viewed, from Mead's perspective, as an answer to the question of which counterfactually presupposed addressee one must turn to when one feels that one's particular abilities are not recognized within the intersubjectively established value-system of one's society.[28] The ethical concept of the 'generalized other' that Mead would have arrived at, had he considered the idealizing anticipation of subjects who know themselves to be unrecognized, serves the same purpose as Hegel's conception of ethical life. It identifies a relationship of mutual recognition in which every individual can know himself or herself to be confirmed as a person who is distinct from all others in virtue of his or her particular traits and abilities.

Within the framework of his lectures, however, Mead did not pursue the questions inevitably raised by the process of individual self-realization. In the sections concerned with the relevant class of 'I'-impulses, one finds only a few, rather unsystematic references to how the 'feeling of superiority' appears in everyday life. As a result Mead also could not clarify why the realization of the 'self' necessitates the anticipation of the 'generalized other' inherent in the process of gaining personal autonomy. The question as to the form that reciprocal recognition must take, as soon as one is no longer dealing with the intersubjective establishment of rights but rather with the confirmation of individual particularity, remains beyond the scope of his discussion. There is only one point at which Mead breaks through this general reservedness and reveals a view of the social relationship to which he accorded the possibility of successfully granting individuals recognition for their particular abilities. As an answer to this problem, his proposal, in terms of a model of the functional division of labour, is interesting primarily because of the multitude of difficulties that it reveals:

> If one does have a genuine superiority it is a superiority which rests on the performance of definite functions. One is a good surgeon, a good lawyer, and he can pride himself on his superiority – but it is a superiority which he makes use of. And when he does actually make use of it in the very community to which he belongs it loses that element of egoism which we think of when we think of a person simply pluming himself on his superiority over somebody else.[29]

The solution that Mead envisions here involves linking self-realization to engaging in socially useful work. The degree of recognition accorded to persons who, within the context of the societal division of labour, fulfil their functions 'well' is enough to help them develop a consciousness of their individual particularity. What this implies with regard to the issue of the preconditions for self-respect is that one is capable of fully respecting oneself if one can identify, within the objectively pre-established distribution of functions, the positive contribution that one makes to the reproduction of the community. As is easy to see, Mead here wants to uncouple the intersubjective pre-conditions for self-realization from the contingent value-premises of a particular community. The 'generalized other' upon whose ethical goals I depend in wanting to be assured of social recognition for my chosen way of life is supposed to be replaced by the rules of a functional division of labour, as something more objective. This model fits well with the historical tendency towards individualization, which Mead had asserted at another level, in that it aims to keep to a minimum the influence of collective values on the choice of direction in which one realizes oneself. Because subjects can come to possess a consciousness of their individual particularity simply in knowing that they have reliably fulfilled their work obligations, they are freed of all standard-ized patterns of self-realization, such as those set out in traditional societies, say, in terms of the concept of honour. In sum, therefore, Mead's idea represents a post-traditional answer to the Hegelian prob-lem of ethical life. The relationship of mutual recognition in which subjects can know themselves to be confirmed not only with regard to their moral commonalities but, beyond this, with regard to their par-ticular qualities, is to be found in a transparent system of the func-tional division of labour.

What Mead apparently did not realize, however, is that this model allows the difficulties that it was designed to avoid to reappear at another point. If members of society are to be able to assure themselves of their singularity by reliably and satisfactorily accomplishing the tasks ascribed to them within the division of labour, then one can hardly say that this occurs in independence from the ethical goals of the community. For, in fact, it is the shared conception of the good life that determines the valuableness of individual tasks. In each case, not just the issue of how a job (defined in terms of the division of labour) is to be done 'well' but even the issue of what counts as a socially useful piece of work turns, in each case, on the intersubjectively ob-ligatory values, that is, the ethical [*sittlichen*] convictions that give a society its individual character. Hence, the functional division of labour cannot be viewed as a value-neutral system incorporating the implicit rules according to which one can ascertain – objectively, as it were – one's particular contribution to the community.

Mead is right to assume that one cannot conceive of oneself as a unique and irreplaceable person until one's own manner of self-realization is recognized by all interaction partners to be a positive contribution to the community. Insofar as this is the case, one's practical self-understanding – one's 'me', that is – will be constructed in such a way that it allows one to share with other members of the community not only moral norms but ethical goals as well. Just as one can understand oneself, in light of shared norms of action, as a person possessing certain rights vis-à-vis all others, one can see oneself, in light of shared value-convictions, as a person of unique significance to all. But, for understandable reasons, Mead tries to equate the ethical goals of a post-traditional community so completely with the objective requirements of the functional division of labour that the problem actually challenging him slipped through his fingers unnoticed. What he lost sight of was the issue of how to define the ethical convictions found in a 'generalized other' in such a way that, on the one hand, they are substantive enough to allow any and every individual to become conscious of his or her particular contribution to the societal life-process and yet, on the other hand, they are formal enough not to end up restricting the historically developed latitude for personal self-realization. The moral-cultural conditions under which post-traditional and, in Mead's sense, more highly individualized societies can reproduce themselves also necessarily set normative limits on their ethical values and goals. The intersubjectively obligatory conception of the good life – to which one has, as it were, become ethically accustomed – can only be construed as giving all members of the community the opportunity to determine their way of life for themselves, within the framework of the rights accorded to them. The difficulty, therefore, that Mead broached (only to ignore it again) consists in the task of equipping the 'generalized other' with a 'common good' that puts everyone in the same position to understand his or her value for the community without thereby restricting the autonomous realization of his or her self. For only this sort of democratized form of ethical life would open up the horizon within which subjects with equal rights could mutually recognize their individual particularity by contributing, in their own ways, to the reproduction of the community's identity.

By contrast, the proposed solution found in Mead's model of the functional division of labour is not able to cope theoretically with the problem of the ethical integration of modern societies. The idea of having individuals come to be recognized, with regard to their particular qualities, by engaging in socially useful work is destined to fail in virtue of the fact that the evaluation of the various functional jobs depends, for its part, on the overarching goals of the community. But, however objectivistically reductionist it may be, Mead's conception nevertheless has the advantage of making more clearly apparent the difficulties that also tainted the young Hegel's model that was sketched in Part I. As we saw, in both Mead and Hegel, the idea of a socially influential 'struggle for recognition' is geared towards a highest stage, in which subjects are supposed to receive confirmation as biographically individuated persons. At the point where Mead brought in the model of the functional division of labour for this form of recognition, we found in Hegel's early work the outline of an idea of relationships based on solidarity. 'Solidarity' is, however, only one possible title of the intersubjective relationship that Hegel aimed to designate with the concept of 'reciprocal intuition' ['*wechselseitige Anschauung*']. For Hegel, it represents a synthesis of both preceding types of recognition, since it shares with 'law' [*Recht*] the cognitive point of view associated with universally equal treatment, but shares with 'love' the aspect of emotional attachment and care. Until he succumbed to a substantialistic conception of it, Hegel understood 'ethical life' as the type of social relationship that arises when love has been refined, under the cognitive impress of the law, into universal solidarity among members of a community. Since everyone who has this attitude can respect the other in his or her individual particularity, it is in this attitude that the most advanced form of mutual recognition is realized.

Compared with Mead's proposed solution, however, one can now see that such a formal conception of ethical life cannot, in principle, offer any clue as to why the individuals should experience reciprocal feelings of respect based on solidarity. Without the addition of an orientation to shared goals and values – the sort of thing Mead was pursuing in an objectivistic manner with his idea of a functional division of labour – the concept of solidarity lacks the underpinning of a motivating experiential nexus. In order to be able to offer a stranger the recognition associated with concern (based on solidarity) for his or her way of life, I need to have already had the shock of an experience that taught me that we share, in an existential sense, our exposure to certain dangers. But the issue of what these risks are that have already linked us together is, in turn, a matter of our shared ideas about what constitutes a successful life within our community. The extent to which the social integration of societies is normatively dependent on a shared conception of the good life is a question that lies at the centre of debates between liberalism and communitarianism. We shall return to this discussion indirectly at the end of the book, when we attempt to derive a formal conception of ethical life from the ideas developed by Hegel and Mead.

5

Patterns of Intersubjective Recognition: Love, Rights, and Solidarity

The theoretical resources found in Mead's social psychology made it possible to give Hegel's theory of a 'struggle for recognition' a 'materialist' reformulation. What re-emerged in Mead, in the altered form of an empirical hypothesis, was not only the general premise of the early Hegel – that practical identity-formation presupposes intersubjective recognition – but also postmetaphysical, naturalistic equivalents for the conceptual distinctions among various stages of recognition and even the wide-reaching assertion of a struggle mediating between these stages. Thus, by drawing on Mead's social psychology, it becomes possible to take the idea that the young Hegel outlined in his Jena writings with such brilliant rudimentariness and make it the guiding thread of a social theory with normative content. The intention of this is to explain processes of social change by referring to the normative demands that are, structurally speaking, internal to the relationship of mutual recognition.

The point of departure for a social theory of this sort has to be the basic claim on which the pragmatist Mead and the early Hegel are agreed in principle: the reproduction of social life is governed by the imperative of mutual recognition, because one can develop a practical relation-to-self only when one has learned to view oneself, from the normative perspective of one's partners in interaction, as their social addressee. Admittedly, this general premise has explanatory power only when it includes a dynamic element. The aforementioned imperative, which is anchored in the social life-process, provides the normative pressure that compels individuals to remove constraints on the meaning of mutual recognition, since it is only by doing so that they are able to express socially the continually expanding claims of their subjectivity. To this extent, the species-historical process of individualization presupposes an expansion of the relations of mutual recognition. The developmental hypothesis thus outlined can, however, become a building block for a social theory only to the degree to which it can be linked back to events within social life-practice. It is by way of the morally motivated struggles of social groups – their collective attempt to establish, institutionally and culturally, expanded forms of reciprocal recognition – that the normatively directional change of societies proceeds. In his theory of recognition, Hegel made this shift to a model of conflict in an idealistic manner, whereas Mead made it in a clearly 'materialist' manner. In doing so, both thinkers interpreted social struggle, contrary to the tradition reaching from Machiavelli through Hobbes to Nietzsche, in such a way that social struggle could become a structuring force in the moral development of society. But before I can outline at least a few of the essential features of the social theory I have in mind, two presuppositions must first be systematically clarified, presuppositions that are inherent but not developed in Hegel's and Mead's theories of recognition. First, the three-part division that both authors appear to make among forms of recognition needs a justification that goes beyond what has been said thus far. The extent to which such a distinction actually fits anything in the structure of social relations is something that must be demonstrated – independently of the texts discussed until now – by showing that this way of distinguishing phenomena can be brought into approximate agreement with the results of empirical research. In what follows, this demonstration is to take the form of a phenomenologically oriented typology that aims to describe the three patterns of recognition in such a way that they can be checked empirically against the data from individual sciences. Central here will be evidence for the claim that the various forms of reciprocal recognition can, in fact, be mapped onto different levels of the practical relation-to-self in the way suggested, in vague outline, in Mead's social psychology. On the basis of this typology, one can approach the second task that Hegel and Mead bequeathed to us in failing to clarify a crucial implication of their theoretical ideas. Both thinkers were in fact equally unable to identify accurately the social experiences that would generate the pressure under which struggles for recognition would emerge within the historical process. Neither in Hegel nor in Mead does one find a systematic consideration of those forms of disrespect that, as negative equivalents for the corresponding relations of recognition, could enable social actors to realize that they are being denied recognition. In chapter 6, therefore, the attempt will be made to close this gap in the account by systematically separating different types of denigration and insult. This will link back to the typology of forms of recognition in that forms of disrespect will be distinguished according to which level of a person's intersubjectively acquired relation-to-self they injure or even destroy.[1]

Although Mead has no appropriate replacement for the romantic concept of 'love' to be found in Hegel's writings, his theory ultimately does, like Hegel's, contain a distinction between three forms of mutual recognition: the emotional concern familiar from relationships of love and friendship is distinguished from legal recognition and approval associated with solidarity as particular ways of granting recognition. Already in Hegel, these three patterns of reciprocity are mapped onto particular concepts of the person in the sense that the subjective autonomy of the individual increases with each stage of mutual regard. But not until Mead does the intuition implicit in this acquire the systematic cast of an empirical hypothesis, according to which, in the sequence of the three forms of recognition, the person's relation-to-self gradually becomes increasingly positive. Furthermore, both thinkers – the author of the *Realphilosophie* as well as the American pragmatist – are attempting to locate the different forms of recognition in separate spheres of the reproduction of society. Early in his political philosophy, Hegel distinguishes family, civil society, and State. In Mead, one can discern a tendency to set primary relationships to concrete others apart from legal relations and the sphere of work as two different ways of realizing the generalized other.

One of the things that speaks in favour of the systematic structure inherent in these different three-part divisions is the astonishing manner in which these differentiations are reflected in a number of other social philosophers. Max Scheler, for example, distinguishes 'life-community', 'society', and (based on solidarity) 'community of persons' as three 'essential social units', which, like Hegel and Mead, he associates with developmental stages of human personhood.[2] In Plessner's 'Bounds of Community' – which, to be sure, is heavily dependent on Scheler's social ontology – one finds a distinction, with regard to various degrees of intersubjective trust, between the three spheres of primary bonds, commerce within society, and the community of shared concerns [*Sachgemeinschaft*].[3] But no matter how extensive such a list of historical interconnections among theories might be, it could hardly do more than demonstrate that a division of social life into three spheres of interaction has a high degree of plausibility. It is evidently quite natural to distinguish forms of social integration according to whether they occur via emotional bonds, the granting of rights, or a shared orientation to values. Part of what is distinctive about the theories advocated by Hegel and Mead is that they trace these three spheres of interaction back to different patterns of mutual recognition, which are each supposed to correspond, furthermore, to a particular potential for moral development and to distinct types of individual relations-to-self. In order to be able to examine these ambitious claims, one needs to reconstruct the vividly familiar content of love, rights, and solidarity to the point at which it becomes possible to make fruitful connections to the results of research in individual sciences. In testing this conception against evidence from empirical studies, it will then have to be seen whether the three patterns of relationship can, in fact, be distinguished in such a way that they form independent types with regard to (a) the medium of recognition, (b) the form of the relation-to-self made possible, and (c) the potential for moral development.

I

In order to avoid having to speak of 'love' only in the restricted sense that the concept has acquired since Romanticism's revaluation of intimate sexual relationships, it is initially advisable to follow a usage that is as neutral as possible.[4] Love relationships are to be understood here as referring to primary relationships insofar as they – on the model of friendships, parent–child relationships, as well as erotic relationships between lovers – are constituted by strong emotional attachments among a small number of people. This proposed usage overlaps with Hegel's in that, for him too, 'love' denotes more than a sexually charged relationship between a man and a woman. Although his early writings in particular are still strongly influenced by early Romanticism's emphasis on emotional bonds between the sexes, it became clear in the course of our interpretation that he applies the concept also, for example, to the affectional relationship between parents and children within the family. Thus, for Hegel, love represents the first stage of reciprocal recognition, because in it subjects mutually confirm each other with regard to the concrete nature of their needs and thereby recognize each other as needy creatures. In the reciprocal experience of loving care, both subjects know themselves to be united in their neediness, in their dependence on each other. Since, moreover, needs and emotions can, to a certain extent, only gain 'confirmation' by being directly satisfied or reciprocated, recognition itself must possess the character of affective approval or encouragement. This recognition relationship is thus also necessarily tied to the physical existence of concrete others who show each other feelings of particular esteem. The key for translating this topic into a context of scientific research is represented by Hegel's formulation, according to which love has to be understood as 'being oneself in another'.[5] This way of speaking of primary affectional relationships as depending on a precarious balance between independence and attachment is much the same as the approach taken, as part of an attempt to determine the causes of pathological disorders, by psychoanalytic object-relations theory. With the turn in psychoanalysis to interactions in early childhood, affectional attachment to other persons is revealed to be a process whose success is dependent on the mutual maintenance of a tension between symbiotic self-sacrifice and individual self-assertion. For this reason, the research tradition of object-relations theory is especially well suited to rendering love intelligible as the interactive relationship that forms the basis for a particular pattern of reciprocal recognition.

In object-relations theory, conclusions are drawn, on the basis of the therapeutic analysis of relational pathologies, as to the conditions that can lead to a successful form of emotional attachment to other persons. Of course, before psychoanalysis could be brought to this sort of concentration on the interpersonal aspects of human action, a series of theoretical impulses were required, which were able to put into question the orthodox conception of how the child's instinctual life develops.[6] For Freud and his followers, the child's interaction partners were initially significant only to the degree to which they acted as the objects of libidinal charges stemming from the intrapsychic conflict between unconscious instinctual demands and gradually emerging ego-controls. Beyond this merely intermediate, secondary role, only the mother was granted the independent status of a significant other, because the threatened loss of the mother in the phase of psychological helplessness of the infant was considered to be the cause of all more mature varieties of anxiety.[7] Since this established a picture of the psychological development of children in which their relations to other persons were viewed merely as a function of the unfolding of libidinal instincts, the empirical studies of René Spitz were enough to raise the first doubts about this approach. For what his observations showed was that the withdrawal of maternal care also led to severe disturbances in the behaviour of the infant in cases in which otherwise all of its physical needs were taken care of.[8] As Morris Eagle has shown in his overview, *Recent Developments in Psychoanalysis*,[9] this first indication of the independent significance of emotional bonds for early childhood development was supported and strengthened by a series of further results from psychological research. Experimental investigations in ethology were able to demonstrate that the attachment of baby primates to their so-called substitute mothers cannot stem from an experience of the satisfaction of instincts but rather from the experience of 'comfort'.[10] The path-breaking studies by John Bowlby led to the conclusion that human infants develop an active willingness to produce interpersonal proximity, which provides the basis for all later forms of affectional bonds.[11] And Daniel Stern, inspired largely by the research of Spitz and Bowlby, has been able to provide convincing evidence for a conception of the interaction between 'mother' and child as a highly complex process, in which both participants acquire, through practice, the capacity for the shared experience of emotions and perceptions.[12]

All of this must have been extremely unsettling for psychoanalysis, or at least for those parts of the psychoanalytical world – as could be found in Britain and the USA after the war – that were still receptive to the results of research. For, contrary to the Freudian structural model of the ego and the id, the evidence seemed to point to the lasting significance of very early, prelinguistic interactive experiences. If the socialization process was predominantly dependent on experiences that children have in their first interpersonal relationships, then one could no longer maintain the orthodox idea that psychological development occurred as a sequence of organizational forms of 'monological' relations between libidinal drives and ego-capacity. Instead, the conceptual framework of psychoanalysis was in need of a fundamental extension along the separate dimension of the social interactions in which, through emotional relationships to other persons, children learn to see themselves as independent subjects. Finally, this theoretical conclusion was supported on the therapeutic side by the discovery that a growing number of patients suffered from mental illnesses that could not be traced back to intrapsychic conflicts between ego and id components but rather only to interpersonal disturbances in the process of the child's detachment. As they appeared in symptoms of borderline disorders or narcissism, these pathologies forced therapists to draw on explanatory approaches that accorded independent significance to the mutual bonds between children and significant others and that were thus incompatible with orthodox ideas.

Object-relations theory represents the first attempt at a conceptual response to the various challenges just outlined. It systematically takes into account the increased insight into the psychological status of interactive experiences in early childhood by supplementing the organization of libidinal drives with affective relationships to other persons as a second component of the maturational process. But what makes object-relations theory seem especially well suited to the purposes of a phenomenology of recognition relations is not the intersubjectivist extension of the psychoanalytic framework of explanation as such. Rather, it can convincingly portray love as a particular form of recognition only owing to the specific way in which it makes the success of affectional bonds dependent on the capacity, acquired in early childhood, to strike a balance between symbiosis and self-assertion. The path to this central insight, in which the intuitions of the young Hegel are confirmed to a surprising degree, was prepared by the English psychoanalyst Donald W. Winnicott. Since then, drawing on his writings, Jessica Benjamin has developed a first attempt at a psychoanalytic interpretation of the love relationship as a process of mutual recognition.

Winnicott wrote from the perspective of a psychoanalytically oriented paediatrician attempting, in the context of treating mental behavioural disorders, to gain an understanding of the 'good-enough' conditions for the socialization of young children.[13] What separates him from the approach found in the orthodox tradition of psychoanalysis is an insight that can easily be fitted into the theoretical framework constructed by Hegel and Mead. In the first months of life, infants are so dependent on the practical extension of their behaviour via the care they receive that it is a misleading abstraction on the part of psychoanalytic research to study the infant in isolation from all significant others, as an independent object of inquiry.[14] The care with which the 'mother' keeps the newborn baby alive is not added to the child's behaviour as something secondary but is rather merged with the child in such a way that one can plausibly assume that every human life begins with a phase of undifferentiated intersubjectivity, that is, of symbiosis. For Winnicott, this involves more than what Freudian theory describes under the heading of 'primary narcissism'. Not only does the infant hallucinate that all 'maternal' care flows from the infant's own omnipotence, but the 'mother' also comes to perceive, conversely, all of her child's reactions to be part and parcel of one single cycle of action. This initial, mutually experienced behavioural unit, for which the concept 'primary intersubjectivity' has established itself,[15] raises the central question that occupied Winnicott during his life: how are we to conceive of the interactional process by which 'mother' and child are able to detach themselves from a state of undifferentiated oneness in such a way that, in the end, they learn to accept and love each other as independent persons? Even just the formulation of the question indicates that Winnicott conceived the child's maturational process from the start as a task that can only be accomplished collectively, through the intersubjective interplay of 'mother' and child. Since both subjects are initially included in the state of symbiotic oneness in virtue of their active accomplishments, they must, as it were, learn from each other how to differentiate themselves as independent entities. Accordingly, the concepts that Winnicott uses to characterize the individual phases of this maturational process are always at the same time descriptions not merely of the psychological situation of one participant – the child – but rather of each of the states of the relationship between the 'mother' and the child. The progress that the child's development must make if it is to lead to a psychologically healthy personality is read off changes in the structure of a system of interactions and not off transformations in the organization of individual drive potential. To designate the first phase – that is, the relationship of symbiotic togetherness that begins immediately after birth – Winnicott generally introduces the category of 'absolute dependency'.[16] Here, both partners to interaction are entirely dependent on each other for the satisfaction of their needs and are incapable of individually demarcating themselves from each other. On the other hand, because the 'mother' identified herself projectively with the baby in the course of the pregnancy, she experiences the infant's helpless neediness as a lack of her own sensitivity. For this reason, her emotional attention is so completely devoted to the child that she learns to adapt her care and concern, as if out of an inner urge, to the infant's changing (and yet, as it were, empathically experienced) requirements. Corresponding to this precarious dependence of the 'mother' – whom Winnicott assumes to need the protective recognition of a third party[17] – there is, on the other hand, the utter helplessness of the infant, who is unable to articulate his or her physical and emotional needs communicatively. During the first months of life, the child is incapable of differentiating between self and environment, and moves within a horizon of experience, the continuity of which can only be assured by the supplemental assistance of a partner in interaction. To the extent that vitally necessary qualities of this undifferentiated experiential world include not only the release of instinctual tensions but also the provision of tender comfort, infants are helplessly dependent on the 'mother' to provide them with love by 'holding' them in the necessary ways. It is only in the protective space of 'being held' that infants can learn to coordinate their sensory and motor experiences around a single centre and thereby to develop a body-scheme. Because the activity of 'holding' is so extraordinarily significant for child development, Winnicott occasionally refers to the state of being merged as the 'holding phase'.[18]

Since, in this phase of symbiotic unity, 'mother' and child are mutually dependent on each other, they are also only able to end this phase once each of them has been able to acquire a bit of new-found independence. For the 'mother', this emancipatory shift begins at the moment in which she can once again expand her social field of attention, as her primary, bodily identification with the infant begins to disperse. The resumption of an everyday routine and the renewed openness to family and friends forces her to deny the child immediate gratification of the child's needs – which she still spontaneously intuits – in that she increasingly leaves the child alone for long periods of time. Corresponding to the 'mother's' 'graduated de-adaptation',[19] there is an intellectual development, on the part of the infant, in which the expansion of conditioned reflexes is accompanied by the capacity for cognitive differentiation between self and environment. At six months, on average, the child begins to interpret acoustic and optical signals as clues to the future satisfaction of needs, so that the child is slowly able to endure the temporary absence of the 'mother'. In thereby experiencing, for the first time, the 'mother' as something in the world that is outside of his or her omnipotent control, the child simultaneously begins to become aware of his or her dependence. The infant leaves the phase of 'absolute dependence', because the dependence on the 'mother' enters his or her field of view in such a way that the child now learns to orient personal impulses toward specific aspects of her care. This new stage of interaction, which Winnicott labels 'relative dependence',[20] encompasses all of the decisive steps in the development of the child's capacity to form attachments. For this reason, he devoted the largest and most instructive part of his analyses to these steps. These analyses depict the emergence, in the relation between mother and child, of the 'being oneself in another' that represents the model for all more mature forms of love.

For the child, once the 'mother' regains her autonomy and can no longer always be at the child's disposal, a process of disillusionment sets in, thereby generating a major and difficult challenge. The person who, until this point, had been imagined to be part of the child's subjective world has gradually slipped out of the child's omnipotent control, and the child must begin to come to a 'recognition of [the object] as an entity in its own right'.[21] The child is able to accomplish this task to the extent to which his or her social environment allows for the implementation of two psychological mechanisms, which together help the child work through this new experience emotionally. Winnicott addressed the first of these two mechanisms under the keyword 'destruction'. The second is presented within the context of his concept of 'transitional phenomena'.

In response to the gradually acquired awareness of a resistant reality, the infant soon begins to act aggressively, primarily towards the 'mother', who is now perceived by the child to be independent herself. As if to rebel against the loss of omnipotence, the infant attempts to destroy her body – which, until then, had been experienced as a source of pleasure – by hitting, biting, and kicking it. In earlier interpretive approaches, these outbursts of aggression were usually linked causally to the frustrations that inevitably set in with the experience of losing omnipotent control. For Winnicott, by contrast, they represent inherently purposive acts, by which the infant unconsciously tests out whether the affectively charged object does, in fact, belong to a reality that is beyond influence and, in that sense, 'objective'. If the 'mother' survives these destructive attacks without taking revenge, the child has thereby, in a manner of speaking, actively placed himself or herself into a world in which he or she exists alongside other subjects.[22] In this sense, the child's destructive, injurious acts do not represent the expression of an attempt to cope negatively with frustration, but rather comprise the constructive means by which the child can come to recognize the 'mother', unambivalently, as 'an entity in its own right'. If she survived the infant's destructive experiments as a person capable of resistance – indeed, if she, through her refusals, even provided the child with occasion for fits of temper – then the child will, by integrating its aggressive impulses, become able to love her. In the bond that has now been formed, the child is able to reconcile its (still symbiotically supported) devotion to the 'mother' with the experience of standing on its own:

> The mother is needed over this time and she is needed because of her survival value. She is an environment-mother and at the same time an object-mother, the object of excited loving. In this latter role she is repeatedly destroyed or damaged. The child gradually comes to integrate these two aspects of the mother and to be able to love and to be affectionate with the surviving mother at the same time.[23]

If we thus conceive the child's first process of detachment as the result of aggressive behavioural expressions, then there seems to be good reason to follow Jessica Benjamin's suggestion and introduce the Hegelian 'struggle for recognition' here as an instructive explanatory model.[24] For it is indeed only in the attempt to destroy his or her 'mother' – that is, in the form of a struggle – that the child realizes that he or she is dependent on the loving care of an independently existing person with claims of her own. But for the 'mother', in turn, this means that she too must first learn to accept the independence of the child if she wants to 'survive' these destructive attacks in the context of her re-established sphere of activity. What the aggressively charged situation demands of her, in fact, is that she understand the destructive wish-fantasies of her child as something that goes against her own interests and thus as something that can be ascribed to the child alone, as an already independent person. If, in the way just sketched, a first step of mutual demarcation is successfully taken, then mother and child can acknowledge their dependence on each other's love without having to merge symbiotically.

In a supplementary part of his analyses, Winnicott then claims that the child's capacity to strike a balance, in this early form, between independence and symbiosis varies with the degree of distortion in the development of a second coping mechanism. He presents this with the help of the concept of 'transitional objects'. The empirical phenomenon that Winnicott has in mind here consists in the strong tendency of children a few months in age to form highly affectively charged relationships to objects in their physical environment. Such objects – be it part of a toy, the corner of a pillow, or the child's own thumb – are treated as an exclusive possession, sometimes tenderly loved, sometimes passionately abused. For Winnicott, the key to explaining the function of these transitional objects is the fact that the child's partners to interaction also situate the objects in a domain of reality, with regard to which the question of fiction or reality becomes unimportant. As if by tacit agreement, they are transferred to an 'intermediate' realm, where it is up to the participants to decide whether to view it as belonging to an inner world of mere hallucinations or to the empirical world of objective facts:

> Of the transitional object it can be said that it is a matter of agreement between us and the baby that we will never ask the question: 'Did you conceive of this or was it presented to you from without?' The important point is that no decision on this point is expected. The question is not to be formulated.[25]

If one takes into consideration the developmental phase in which the discovery of these intermediate objects of significance occurs, then there are grounds for supposing that they represent surrogates for the 'mother', who has just been lost to external reality. Because they are ontologically ambiguous in nature, the child can actively use them to keep omnipotence fantasies alive, even after the experience of separation, and can simultaneously use them to creatively probe reality. In this playful yet reality-checking manner of utilization, it also becomes apparent that the function of transitional objects cannot be restricted to the symbiotic appropriation of the role of the 'mother' as experienced in the state of merging. The child relates to the objects he or she has selected not only with symbiotic tenderness but also with repeated attacks of rage and attempts to destroy it. Winnicott believes that one can conclude from this that, in the case of transitional objects, one is dealing with ontological links, as it were, that mediate between the primary experience of being merged and the awareness of separateness. In the playful interaction with these affectively charged objects, the child repeatedly attempts to bridge, symbolically, the painful gap between inner and outer reality. The fact that this coincides with the emergence of intersubjectively accepted illusions allows Winnicott to go even one step further and to arrive at a thesis with consequences both far-reaching and difficult to assess. Because this ontological, mediating sphere arises as the solution to a task that people continue to face throughout their lives, it is the psychological origin of all adult interests vis-à-vis cultural objectivations. Not without a sense for sharpening the speculative point of the matter, Winnicott writes:

> It is assumed here that the task of reality-acceptance is never completed, that no human being is free from the strain of relating inner and outer reality, and that relief from this strain is provided by an intermediate area of experience . . . which is not challenged (arts, religion, etc.). This intermediate area is in direct continuity with the play area of the small child who is 'lost' in play.[26]

This last phrase also offers a clue as to why the concept of 'transitional objects' is to be understood as a direct extension of Winnicott's interpretation of love in terms of a theory of recognition. According to him, the child is capable of being 'lost' in interaction with the chosen object only if, after the separation from the symbiotically experienced 'mother', the child can generate enough trust in the continuity of her care that he or she is able, under the protection of a felt intersubjectivity, to be alone in a carefree manner. The child's creativity – indeed, the human faculty of imagination in general – presupposes a 'capacity to be alone', which itself can arise only out of a basic confidence in the care of a loved one.[27] From this perspective, far-reaching insights emerge into the connection between creativity and recognition, which are of no further interest to us here. Of central importance, however, for the attempt to reconstruct love as a particular relationship of recognition is Winnicott's claim that the ability to be alone is dependent on the child's trust in the continuity of the 'mother's' care. The thesis thus outlined provides some insight into the type of relation-to-self that one can develop when one knows oneself to be loved by a person that one experiences as independent and for whom one, in turn, feels affection or love.

If the 'mother' managed to pass the child's unconscious test by enduring the aggressive attacks without withdrawing her love in revenge, she now belongs, from the perspective of the child, to a painfully accepted external world. As has been said, the child must now become aware, for the first time, of his or her dependence on the 'mother's' care. If the 'mother's' love is lasting and reliable, the child can simultaneously develop, under the umbrella of her intersubjective reliability, a sense of confidence in the social provision of the needs he or she has, and via the psychological path this opens up, a basic 'capacity to be alone' gradually unfolds in the child. Winnicott traces the young child's ability to be alone – in the sense of beginning to discover, without anxiety, his or her 'own personal life' – back to the experience of the 'continued existence of a reliable mother':[28] only to the extent to which there is 'a good object in the psychic reality of the individual'[29] can he or she become responsive to inner impulses and pursue them in an open, creative way, without fear of being abandoned.

The shift of focus to that part of one's own self that Mead called the 'I' thus presupposes that one trusts the loved person to maintain his or her affection, even when one's own attention is withdrawn. But this certainty is, for its part, just the outwardly oriented side of a mature confidence that one's own needs will lastingly be met by the other because one is of unique value to the other. To this extent, the 'capacity to be alone' is the practical expression of a form of individual relation-to-self, similar to what Erikson conceived of under the title of 'trust'. In becoming sure of the 'mother's' love, young children come to trust themselves, which makes it possible for them to be alone without anxiety.

In one of his typically cryptic asides, Winnicott claims that this communicatively protected ability to be alone is 'the stuff of which friendship is made'.[30] What he is evidently getting at here is the idea that every strong emotional bond between people opens up the possibility of both parties relating to themselves in a relaxed manner, oblivious to their particular situation, much like an infant who can rely on his or her 'mother's' emotional care. This suggestion can be understood as an invitation to identify, in the successful relationship between 'mother' and child, a pattern of interaction whose mature reappearance in adult life is an indication of successful affectional bonds to other people. In this way, we put ourselves methodologically in a position to draw conclusions from the maturational processes of early childhood about the communicative structure that makes love a special relationship of mutual recognition.

We can then proceed from the hypothesis that all love relationships are driven by the unconscious recollection of the original experience of merging that characterized the first months of life for 'mother' and child. The inner state of symbiotic oneness so radically shapes the experiential scheme of complete satisfaction that it keeps alive, behind the back of the subject and throughout the subject's life, the desire to be merged with another person. Of course, this desire for merging can only become a feeling of love once, in the unavoidable experience of separation, it has been disappointed in such a way that it henceforth includes the recognition of the other as an independent person. Only a refracted symbiosis enables the emergence of a productive inter-personal balance between the boundary-establishment and boundary-dissolution that, for Winnicott, belongs to the structure of a relationship that has matured through mutual disillusionment. There, the capacity to be alone constitutes the subject-based pole of an intersubjective tension, whose opposing pole is the capacity for boundary-dissolving merging with the other. The act of boundary-dissolution, in which subjects experience themselves to be reconciled with one another, can take a wide variety of forms, depending on the type of bond. In friendships, it may be the shared experience of an unselfconscious conversation or an utterly unforced moment together. In erotic rela-tionships, it is the sexual union in which one knows oneself to be reconciled with the other without difference. But in each case, the process of merging obtains its very condition of possibility solely from the opposite experience of encountering the other as someone who is continually re-establishing his or her boundary. It is only because the assurance of care gives the person who is loved the strength to open up to himself or herself in a relaxed relation-to-self that he or she can become an independent subject with whom oneness can be experi-enced as a mutual dissolution of boundaries. To this extent, the form of recognition found in love, which Hegel had described as 'being oneself in another', represents not an intersubjective state so much as a communicative arc suspended between the experience of being able to be alone and the experience of being merged; 'ego-relatedness' and symbiosis here represent mutually required counterweights that, taken together, make it possible for each to be at home in the other.

These conclusions lose some of their speculative character when we consider Jessica Benjamin's psychoanalytical research, in which she has studied pathological disorders of the love relationship. She too makes use of object-relations theory in order, on the basis of findings regarding the successful course of the separation of 'mother' and child, to draw conclusions about the structure of interaction essential to a successful bond between adults. But what primarily concerns her in this connection are the dynamics of the disorders of the love relationship that are clinically termed 'masochism' and 'sadism'.[31] It then turns out that one of the advantages of the concept of love found in the theory of recognition – as developed here, following Winnicott – is that it makes it possible to grasp failures of this sort in systematic terms, as one-sidedness in the direction of one of the two poles of the balance of recognition. In pathological cases, the reciprocity of the intersubjectively suspended arc is destroyed by the fact that one of the subjects involved is no longer able to detach himself or herself either from the state of egocentric independence or from that of symbiotic dependence. As Benjamin is able to show, these types of one-sidedness interrupt the continual exchange between ego-relatedness and boundary-dissolution, in that they replace it with a rigid scheme of mutual supplementation. The symbiotically sustained dependence of one partner is then ultimately just the complement to the aggressively tinged omnipotence fantasies upon which the other partner is fixated.[32] For Benjamin, there is of course no doubt but that these distortions of the balance of recognition are to be traced back to psychological disturbances, the cause of which lies in the abortive development of the child's detachment from the 'mother'. To support her position here, she can draw on therapeutic findings such as those presented by Otto F. Kernberg in his psychoanalytic study of the 'pathologies of love life'.[33]

What is of interest here, of course, are not the details of this type of genetic deduction but rather the fact that the basic objects of study here are relational disorders that can be assessed within the categories of mutual recognition. For if it is, in fact, possible to derive a criterion for what counts as a disorder, with regard to affectional bonds, from the idea of the unsuccessful reciprocity of certain tensely balanced states, then this also demonstrates, in turn, the empirical appropriateness of a concept of love conceived in terms of a theory of recognition.

From a therapeutic angle, the possibility of reinterpreting the clinical material on relational pathologies in terms of a structural one-sidedness in the balance of recognition supports the idea that, ideally speaking, the love relationship represents a symbiosis refracted by recognition. Accordingly, every prominent model of an instrumentally one-sided relational constellation – to which the love relationship in general is reduced in Sartre's phenomenological analysis[34] – can be seen as a psychoanalytically explicable deviation from a defensible ideal of interaction. Moreover, because this relationship of recognition prepares the ground for a type of relation-to-self in which subjects mutually acquire basic confidence in themselves, it is both conceptually and genetically prior to every other form of reciprocal recognition. This fundamental level of emotional confidence – not only in the experience of needs and feelings, but also in their expression – which the intersubjective experience of love helps to bring about, constitutes the psychological precondition for the development of all further attitudes of self-respect.[35]

II

If love can be said to represent a symbiosis refracted by mutual individuation, then, in loving, what one recognizes in the other is evidently only the other's individual independence. Thus, it might be thought that the love relationship is characterized solely by a type of recognition involving the cognitive acceptance of the other's independence. That this is not the case can already be seen in the fact that this release into independence has to be supported by an affective confidence in the continuity of shared concern. Without the felt assurance that the loved one will continue to care even after he or she has become independent, it would be impossible for the loving subject to recognize that independence. Because this experience must be mutual in love relationships, recognition is here characterized by a double process, in which the other is released and, at the same time, emotionally tied to the loving subject. Thus, in speaking of recognition as a constitutive element of love, what is meant is an affirmation of independence that is guided – indeed, supported – by care. Every love relationship, whether between friends, lovers, or parent and child, thus presupposes liking and attraction, which are out of individuals' control. And since positive feelings about other people are not matters of choice, the love relationship cannot be extended at will, beyond the social circle of primary relationships, to cover a larger number of partners to interaction. Although this means that love will always have an element of moral particularism to it, Hegel was nonetheless right to discern within it the structural core of all ethical life. For it is only this symbiotically nourished bond, which emerges through mutually desired demarcation, that produces the degree of basic individual self-confidence indispensable for autonomous participation in public life.

Compared to the form of recognition found in love – as it is presented here with the help of object-relations theory – legal relations differ in just about every essential respect. The only reason why both spheres of interaction are to be understood as two types of one and the same pattern of socialization is that the logic of each cannot be adequately explained without appeal to the same mechanism of recip-rocal recognition. In the case of law, Hegel and Mead drew this con-nection on the basis of the fact that we can only come to understand ourselves as the bearers of rights when we know, in turn, what vari-ous normative obligations we must keep vis-à-vis others: only once we have taken the perspective of the 'generalized other', which teaches us to recognize the other members of the community as the bearers of rights, can we also understand ourselves to be legal persons, in the sense that we can be sure that certain of our claims will be met.

In his later years, Hegel once again presented, with the desired clarity, this necessary interconnection, which allowed both him and Mead to conceive legal relations as a form of mutual recognition. In the summary of the *Encyclopedia*, he wrote:

> [I]n the state . . . man is recognized and treated as a *rational* being, as free, as a person; and the individual, on his side, makes himself worthy of this recognition by overcoming the natural state of his self-consciousness and obeying a universal, the will that is in essence and actuality will, the *law*; he behaves, therefore, toward others in a manner that is universally valid, recognizing them – as he wishes others to recognize him – as free, as persons.[36]

Admittedly, owing to the use of the predicate 'free', the formulation also makes clear that Hegel always intends the legal form of recogni-tion to refer to the specific constitution of modern legal relations, because it is only their claim that inherently applies to all people as free and equal beings. What mattered to him was demonstrating that the personal autonomy of the individual owes its existence to a par-ticular mode of reciprocal recognition that is incorporated in positive law. In his concept of the 'generalized other', by contrast, Mead was initially only interested in the logic of legal recognition as such. This difference, which we have thus far ignored in our historical recon-struction, must be clarified, at least in rough outline, before we can answer the question as to which specific type of recognition (along with the corresponding relation-to-self) is structurally inherent in legal relations. For in the distinction between tradition-bound and post-traditional law, it becomes clear that, unlike the case of love, the par-ticular form of reciprocity found in legal recognition can emerge only in the course of a historical development.

As we saw in the discussion of Mead's social psychology, the concept of 'legal recognition' refers, in the first place, only to the situation in which self and other respect each other as legal subjects for the sole reason that they are both aware of the social norms by which rights and duties are distributed in their community. A definition of this sort, however, lacks specifics as to both the type of rights accorded to individuals and the mode of legitimation by which they are generated within the society. Rather, what the definition refers to is just the fundamental fact that one can count as the bearer of rights of some kind only if one is socially recognized as a member of a community. For the individual, the socially accepted role of being the member of a social collective that is organized on the basis of the division of labour gives rise to certain rights, and the individual can normally ensure that these rights are adhered to by calling upon an authorized, sanctioning force.[37] This extremely weak concept of a legal order is well suited to revealing the general features of legal recognition in traditional societies. As long as an individual's legitimate claims are not yet infused with the universalistic principles of post-conventional morality, they amount to nothing more than the authority accorded to that individual as a member of a particular concrete community. Because his concept of the generalized other refers, in the first instance, to this sort of basic system of cooperative rights and duties, Mead had good reasons for attaching only limited normative significance to legal recognition. Here, the individual subject is recognized solely for its legitimate membership in a social collective organized on the basis of the division of labour. As we have already seen, even this traditional form of legal recognition grants one society's protection for one's human 'dignity'. But this is still completely fused with the social role accorded to one within the context of a generally unequal distribution of rights and burdens.

By contrast, the structure from which Hegel can derive his definitions of the legal person only takes on the legal form of recognition once it becomes dependent on the premises of a universalist conception of morality. With the transition to modernity, the post-conventional principles that had already been developed in philosophy and political theory made their way into established law and submitted it to the constraints of justification associated with the idea of rational agreement on disputed norms. From this point on, the legal system can be understood as the expression of the universalizable interests of all members of society, so that, according to the demand internal to it, exceptions and privileges are no longer admissible.[38] Since, in this connection, a willingness to adhere to legal norms can only be expected of partners to interaction if they have, in principle, been able to agree to the norms as free and equal beings, a new and highly demanding form of reciprocity enters the relationship of recognition based on rights. In obeying the law, legal subjects recognize each other as persons capable of autonomously making reasonable decisions about moral norms. For this reason, Hegel's characterizations, unlike those of Mead, apply to the legal order only to the degree to which it has been able to detach itself from the self-evident authority of ethical traditions and is reoriented towards a universalistic principle of justification.

This distinction gives rise to two questions concerning the structural characteristics that legal recognition has acquired under conditions of modern legal relations. First, we need to clarify the requisite structure of the form of recognition that brings to light the same quality of individual autonomy in all members of the community of citizens. One could already have learned from the young Hegel that this type of universal respect is not to be conceived of as an affective attitude but rather only as a purely cognitive accomplishment of comprehension, which sets almost internal limits on emotional promptings. To this extent, what will have to be explained is the constitution of a type of respect that, on the one hand, is supposed to be detached from feelings of liking and affection and yet, on the other hand, can actually influence individual behaviour.

Second, the question must be answered as to what it can mean to say that, under conditions set by modern legal relations, subjects reciprocally recognize each other with regard to their status as morally responsible. This trait, which is supposed to be shared by all subjects, cannot be taken to refer to human abilities whose scope or content is determined once and for all. It will rather turn out to be the case that the essential indeterminacy as to what constitutes the status of a responsible person leads to a structural openness on the part of modern law to a gradual increase in inclusivity and precision.

Although we were able to back up the explication of the form of recognition found in love with empirical research, this route is not available with respect to these two questions. I must instead be content here to sketch the answers with the help of an empirically supported conceptual analysis. The claim will be that, with the transition to modernity, individual rights have become detached from concrete role expectations because they must, from that point on, be ascribed in principle to every human individual as a free being. If this brief account turns out to be correct, then this already provides an indirect indication of the new character of legal recognition. We can take it for granted that, for tradition-bound legal relations, the recognition of someone as a legal person is, to a certain extent, still bound up with the social esteem accorded to individual members of society in light of their social status. The conventional ethical life of such a community constitutes a normative horizon in which the multiplicity of individual rights and duties remains tied to differently valued tasks within a system of social cooperation. Legal recognition is thus still situated hierarchically, in terms of the esteem that each individual enjoys as the bearer of a role, and this linkage breaks down only in the course of a historical process that submits legal relations to the requirements of post-conventional morality. From that point on, recognition of someone as a legal person – which, according to its inherent idea, must be directed toward every subject to the same degree – comes to be sufficiently separated from the level of social esteem for that person, so that two different forms of respect emerge, whose manner of functioning can also be analysed only separately. The subject-matter thus outlined reappears in the discussions that have been going on since the days of Kant and Schiller about the idea of respect or regard for other persons.[39] In the course of these discussions, a tendency emerged of drawing the same dividing-line between the two semantic aspects of 'respect' that first arose with the uncoupling of legal recognition from social esteem. In this connection, the context of 'law' will occupy us with the first usage of the concept, whereas it is the second semantic aspect that will be of interest for the explication of the form of recognition found in 'communities of value'.

Already towards the end of the last century, Rudolph von Ihering made a distinction with regard to the concept of 'respect' that broadly supports the historical decoupling of legal recognition and social esteem.[40] In the second volume of his book on the 'purpose within law' – which, largely for methodological reasons, was greatly to influence the development of legal studies in Germany – he worked out the categorial connection between the various forms of conduct that can contribute to the 'ethical' integration of a society. Because such patterns of action are composed, according to him, primarily of expressions of mutual recognition and respect, he had to attempt to distinguish, from a systematic point of view, different types of social respect. The fundamental division that Ihering arrived at in his conceptual analysis stems from the various possible ways of answering the question as to what it is about another human being that is respected: in the case of what Ihering himself calls 'legal recognition', the idea is expressed that every human subject must be considered to be an 'end in itself', whereas 'social regard' emphasizes the 'worth' of an individual, insofar as it can be measured according to criteria of social relevance.[41] As the use of the Kantian formulation indicates, we are dealing in the first case with universal respect for the 'freedom of the will of the person', and in the second case, by contrast, with the recognition of individual achievements, whose value is measured by the degree to which society deems them significant. Thus, the legal recognition of a human being as a person cannot admit of any further degrees, while the esteem for his or her traits and abilities appeals at least implicitly to a standard, in terms of which their 'more' or 'less' has to be determined.[42] For Ihering, these distinctions primarily have the function of allowing for a theoretically informed analysis of the customs and mores in which social esteem could historically take shape. But because his observations do not go beyond the bounds of the framework thus set out, the question remains unanswered of how to define accurately the detailed structure of legal recognition. Of some assistance here are the recent attempts by analytical philosophers to demarcate more clearly the various forms of interpersonal respect.

The theoretical argument that we can recognize human beings as persons without having to esteem their achievements or their character forms a bridge between Ihering's study and contemporary discussions. Stephen L. Darwall is also guided by the belief that we must distinguish two forms of respect by using the criterion of whether they presuppose evaluative gradations or precisely rule them out.[43] He begins by tracing the respect for a human being as a person back to a type of 'recognition respect', because it primarily involves cognitively recognizing the fact that, with regard to the other, one is dealing with a being possessed of personal qualities. To this extent, this form of universalized respect always retains something of the sense of being 'cognizant' of someone [*Zurkenntnisnahme*] that is semantically present in the word 'recognition' [*Anerkennung*].[44] But only when the interpretation of the situation is supplemented by practical knowledge of the constraints one must place on one's actions vis-à-vis human persons does one move from cognitive acknowledgement to what has been signified, since Kant, by the concept of moral respect: that to recognize every other human being as a person must then be to act, with regard to all of them, in the manner to which we are morally obligated by the features of a person. Although this does not take us all that far towards an answer to our question – since everything now turns on how the normatively obligating qualities of a person are to be defined – the structure of legal recognition has nonetheless become a bit less opaque. In legal recognition, two operations of consciousness flow together, so to speak, since, on the one hand, it presupposes moral knowledge of the legal obligations that we must keep vis-à-vis autonomous persons, while, on the other hand, it is only an empirical interpretation of the situation that can inform us whether, in the case of a given concrete other, we are dealing with an entity possessed of the quality that makes these obligations applicable. For this reason, the task of situation-specific application is an inviolable component of the structure of legal recognition, precisely because it is (under modern conditions) universalistically constituted. It must always be asked of a universally valid right – in light of empirical descriptions of the situation – what the circle of human subjects is, within which, because they belong to the class of morally responsible persons, the rights are supposed to be applicable. As we shall see, this zone of application and situation-interpretation represents one of the contexts of modern legal relations where a struggle for recognition can arise.[45]

What makes esteeming someone different from recognizing him or her as a person is primarily the fact that it involves not the empirical application of general, intuitively known norms but rather the graduated appraisal of concrete traits and abilities. It thus always presupposes – as Darwall, agreeing with Ihering, claims – an evaluative frame of reference that indicates the value of personality traits on a scale of more or less, better or worse.[46] Unlike Ihering, of course, Darwall is only interested in the narrow class of appraisals directed at the moral qualities of subjects. When we consider the form of recognition found in communities of value, we will have to address the question regarding the role of this particular form of moral respect in the whole context of social esteem. At the moment, all that matters are the conclusions that can be provisionally drawn from this comparison between legal recognition and social esteem. In both cases, human beings are respected because of certain traits. In the first case, however, this is a matter of the general feature that makes them persons at all, whereas in the second case, it is a matter of the particular characteristics that distinguish them from other persons. For this reason, the central question for legal recognition is how to define this constitutive quality of persons, while the question for social esteem is the constitution of the evaluative frame of reference within which the 'worth' of characteristic traits can be measured.

Thus formulated, this preliminary conclusion introduces a second problem, which had cropped up in connection with the structural qualities of legal recognition: there has to be a way of determining the capacity, with regard to which subjects mutually respect each other in recognizing each other as legal persons. An answer to the question thus posed is of all the greater importance because it provides the key to analysing the function of the granting of rights under post-traditional conditions. After becoming detached from ascriptions of status, its task must, by all appearances, be directed above all towards protecting and enabling not only the possession but also the exercise of this universal capacity, which characterizes a human being as a person in the first place. But the issue of which universal feature of legally capable subjects is supposed to be protected is decided by the new form of legitimation to which modern law is structurally bound. If a legal order can be considered to be valid and, moreover, can count on the willingness of individuals to follow laws only to the extent to which it can appeal, in principle, to the free approval of all the individuals it includes, then one must be able to suppose that these legal subjects have at least the capacity to make reasonable, autonomous decisions regarding moral questions. In the absence of such an ascription, it would be utterly inconceivable how subjects could ever have come to agree on a legal order. In this sense, because its legitimacy is dependent on a rational agreement between individuals with equal rights, every community based on modern law is founded on the assumption of the moral accountability of all its members.

But an ascription of this sort still does not indicate a feature that has sharp enough contours to be fixed once and for all. What is meant in saying that a subject is capable of acting autonomously on the basis of rational insight is something that is determined only relative to an account of what it means to speak of rational agreement. For depending on how the fundamental legitimating procedure is imagined, there will also be a change in the features that must be ascribed to a person, if he or she is to be able to participate as an equal in the process. The determination of the capacities that constitutively characterize a human being as a person is therefore dependent on background assumptions about the subjective prerequisites that enable participation in rational will-formation. The more demanding this procedure is seen to be, the more extensive the features will have to be that, taken together, constitute a subject's status as morally responsible. As the connection thus postulated already makes clear, these capacities – with regard to which members of a society mutually recognize each other, whenever they respect each other as legal persons – are open to change. But it is only with a glance at the actual development of the granting of individual rights under post-conventional conditions that the direction of these changes becomes transparent. The cumulative expansion of individual rights-claims, which is what we are dealing with in modern societies, can be understood as a process in which the scope of the general features of a morally responsible person has gradually increased, because, under pressure from struggles for recognition, ever-new prerequisites for participation in rational will-formation have to be taken into consideration. We came across a similar thesis earlier, in Hegel's speculative idea that the criminal forces the bourgeois legal order to extend its legal norms along the dimension of substantively equal opportunity.

Within legal studies, it has meanwhile become a matter of course to divide individual rights into civil rights guaranteeing liberty, political rights guaranteeing participation, and social rights guaranteeing basic welfare. The first category refers to negative rights that protect a person's life, liberty, and property from unauthorized state interference; the second category refers to the positive rights guaranteeing a person the opportunity to participate in processes of public will-formation; and the third category, finally, refers to the similarly positive rights that ensure a person's fair share in the distribution of basic goods. The approach to such a tripartite distinction can already be found in the work of Georg Jellinek, whose influential theory of status distinguished (alongside duties of obedience) the negative status, positive status, and active status of a legal person. Today, this approach is being pursued by Robert Alexy with the aim of systematically justifying basic individual rights.[47] For the context of our argumentation, however, it is of primary importance that the same distinction also underlies the now-famous attempt of T. H. Marshall to reconstruct the historical levelling of social class differences as a process moving in the direction of an expansion of basic individual rights.[48] Talcott Parsons took up this analysis in the context of his mature social theory, using it as the point of reference for his account of the development of modern law.[49]

Marshall starts out from the situation of upheaval depicted above, in terms of which the basic distinction between the traditional and the modern constitution of law is made. With the uncoupling of individual rights-claims from the ascription of social status, a general principle of equality emerges for the first time, which henceforth requires of every legal order that it allow no exceptions and privileges. Because this requirement makes reference to the role that the individual occupies as a citizen, the idea of equality simultaneously acquires here a sense of 'full-fledged' membership in a political community: independent of differences in the amount of economic power, every member of society is accorded all the rights that help to bring about the equal representation of his or her political interests. What interests Marshall here is the developmental pressure that basic individual rights had to come under, once they had been subjected to this demand for equality. The fact that, as the result of social struggles, one is forced to do justice to this demand has allowed the level of individual rights-claims to increase to a point at which, ultimately, even the pre-political, economic inequalities could no longer remain completely untouched.

Marshall's justification for this thesis, which implies much about how modern law has been gradually expanded in terms of recognition, takes the form of a historical reconstruction.[50] Within this framework, the classification in legal theory becomes applicable according to which the sum of all individual rights-claims can be divided systematically into three classes. Marshall gives this three-part division a historical formulation, which, in its roughest version, states that civil rights developed in the eighteenth century, political rights were established in the nineteenth century, and finally, social rights were created in the twentieth century. But for our purposes, what is significant about this suggestive periodization (which will be further refined in what follows) is the indication that, historically, the establishment of each new class of basic rights is consistently compelled by arguments that referred implicitly to the demand for full-fledged membership in the political community. Initially, political rights to participation thus arose merely as a secondary product of the civil rights that, to a large extent, had already been granted to at least the male portion of the growing population during the eighteenth century. In the beginning, only those who could demonstrate a certain measure of income or property had a positive claim to participation in the process of political will-formation. These previously status-bound rights to participation only became a distinct class of universal human rights once these rights were partially expanded and carved out and the legal-political climate had eventually changed to such a degree that there were no longer any convincing arguments with which to oppose the demands of excluded groups for equality. There came a moment during the first decades of the twentieth century in which the belief established itself, once and for all, that every member of a political community must be accorded equal rights to participation in the process of democratic will-formation.

As with rights to political participation, social welfare rights have also emerged in the course of an expansion – forced 'from below' – of the meaning attached to the idea of 'full-fledged' membership in a political community. Part of the prehistory of this category of human rights is to be found in battles fought in several countries during the nineteenth century for the introduction of universal mandatory education. The goal of this struggle was to provide not the child but the future adult with the measure of cultural education required for the equal exercise of citizens' rights. Once this point had been reached, the insight was not far away that political rights would have to remain a merely formal concession to the mass of the population as long as the possibility for actively taking advantage of them was not guaranteed by a certain social standard of living and degree of economic security. During the twentieth century, what then emerged from such demands for equality, at least in those Western countries that have followed a welfare state course, was a new class of social welfare rights, which are supposed to assure every citizen the possibility of asserting all his or her other rights-claims.

From this brief sketch of Marshall's analysis, it is not difficult to see the manner in which the successive expansion of basic individual rights remained linked to the normative principle that was there from the start as its guiding idea. For each enrichment of the legal claims of individuals can be understood as a further step in fleshing out the moral idea that all members of society must have been able to agree to the established legal order on the basis of rational insight, if they are to be expected to obey the law. The institutionalization of bourgeois liberties initiated, as it were, a permanent process of innovation that gave rise to at least two new classes of individual rights, because what was demonstrated again and again in subsequent history, under pressure from disadvantaged groups, was that not all of the appropriate preconditions were present for equal participation in a rational agreement: in order to be involved as morally responsible persons, individuals need not only legal protection from interference in their sphere of liberty, but also the legally assured opportunity for participation in the public process of will-formation, an opportunity that they can only actually take advantage of, however, if they also have a certain social standard of living. Thus, during the last few centuries, the enrichment of the legal status of the individual citizen was accompanied by the successive expansion of the core constellation of capacities that constitutively characterize a human being as a person. In particular, the characteristics that put a subject in a position to act autonomously on the basis of rational insight have since come to include a minimum of cultural education and economic security. In this sense, then, to recognize one another as legal persons means more today than it possibly could have at the start of the evolution of modern law. In being legally recognized, one is now respected with regard not only to the abstract capacity to orient oneself vis-à-vis moral norms, but also to the concrete human feature that one deserves the social standard of living necessary for this.

As Marshall's historical sketch also shows, this expansion – through social struggle – of basic individual rights is only one side of a process that took the form, on the whole, of an interlocking of two developmental paths that need to be distinguished. As a result of the introduction of the principle of equality into modern law, the status of a legal person was not only gradually broadened with regard to its content, in that it cumulatively incorporated new claims, but was also gradually expanded in the social sense that it was extended to an ever increasing number of members of society. Marshall can therefore summarize the results of his historical overview in the following concise thesis: 'the urge forward along the path thus plotted is an urge toward a fuller measure of equality, an enrichment of the stuff of which the status is made and an increase in the number of those on whom the status is bestowed'.[51] In the first case, as we have seen, the substantive content of law is augmented, generating an increased sensitivity to differences in individuals' opportunities for realizing socially guaranteed freedoms. In the second case, by contrast, legal relations are universalized, in the sense that a growing circle of previously excluded or disadvantaged groups are granted the same rights as all other members of society. Because both of these developmental possibilities are internal to the structure of modern legal relations, both Hegel and Mead are convinced of a continuation of the 'struggle for recognition' within the legal sphere. The practical confrontations that arise in reaction to being denied recognition or treated with disrespect thus represent conflicts over the expansion of both the substantive content and social scope of the status of a legal person.[52]

In preparing to characterize the experience of disrespect on which these social conflicts are based, there needs to be, in conclusion, a brief explication of the type of positive relation-to-self that legal recognition makes possible. The natural suggestion here, following Mead, is to consider the central psychological phenomenon associated with the granting of rights to be an increase in the ability to relate to oneself as a morally responsible person. Just as, in the case of love, children acquire, via the continuous experience of 'maternal' care, the basic self-confidence to assert their needs in an unforced manner, adult subjects acquire, via the experience of legal recognition, the possibility of seeing their actions as the universally respected expression of their own autonomy. The idea that self-respect is for legal relations what basic self-confidence was for the love relationship is already suggested by the conceptual appropriateness of viewing rights as depersonalized symbols of social respect in just the way that love can be conceived as the affectional expression of care retained over distance. Whereas the latter generates, in every human being, the psychological foundation for trusting one's own sense of one's needs and urges, the former gives rise to the form of consciousness in which one is able to respect oneself because one deserves the respect of everyone else. It is, of course, only with the establishment of universal human rights that this form of self-respect can assume the character associated with talk of moral responsibility as the respect-worthy core of a person. What is required are conditions in which individual rights are no longer granted disparately to members of social status groups but are granted equally to all people as free beings; only then will the individual legal person be able to see in them an objectivated point of reference for the idea that he or she is recognized for having the capacity for autonomously forming judgements. It is to these legal relations that a thought experiment of Joel Feinberg's is tailored, one that he developed in order to demonstrate the moral significance of the granting of rights. His discussion is well suited to revealing the conceptual, if not empirical, connection between legal recognition and the acquisition of self-respect.[53]

Feinberg presents the fictional state of a society in which there is an unusually high level of social goodwill and mutual considerateness, even though the institution of socially established rights has remained utterly unknown. In order not to make things too easy for himself, he supplements this model of a social collectivity he calls 'Nowheresville' in two further steps, by adding both an awareness of moral obligations and a system of positive law. Finally, having constructed the community in this way, Feinberg has good reasons for assuming that it would guarantee the well-being of its citizens at a level that is at least as high as that provided today in societies with basic individual rights. Everything that, in existing societies, stands people in good stead (in terms of assistance and respect), via legal claims, is guaranteed there by altruistic inclinations and a feeling of one-sided obligation. The sense that in a 'Nowheresville' type of society something is nevertheless missing, something that we generally reckon with, due to our moral intuitions, is precisely the point that interests Feinberg. Through an analysis of what this fictional community is lacking in spite of its wealth, he wants to ascertain the significance of individual rights for the individual. What gives him the key to solving this self-posed problem is the meaning that the expression 'rights' gains as soon as it is used in the sense of the possession of universal human rights. Once we realize that possessing rights under such circumstances means nothing else than being able to raise claims whose social redemption is considered justified, then it also becomes clear what is crucially lacking in 'Nowheresville'. For the individual member of society, to live without individual rights means to have no chance of developing self-respect:

Having rights enables us to 'stand up like men', to look others in the eye, and to feel in some fundamental way the equal of anyone. To think of oneself as the holder of rights is not to be unduly but properly proud, to have that minimal self-respect that is necessary to be worthy of the love and esteem of others. Indeed, respect for persons . . . may simply be respect for their rights, so that there cannot be the one without the other. And what is called 'human dignity' may simply be the recognizable capacity to assert claims.[54]

Although this line of thought is not free of unclarities or even contradictions,[55] one can derive an argument from it that provides a better basis for the account that Mead already suggested. Since possessing rights means being able to raise socially accepted claims, they provide one with a legitimate way of making clear to oneself that one is respected by everyone else. What gives rights the power to enable the development of self-respect is the public character that rights possess in virtue of their empowering the bearer to engage in action that can be perceived by interaction partners. For, with the optional activity of taking legal recourse to a right, the individual now has available a symbolic means of expression whose social effectiveness can demonstrate to him, each time anew, that he or she is universally recognized as a morally responsible person. If we introduce the points developed above into this context, we can conclude that in the experience of legal recognition, one is able to view oneself as a person who shares with all other members of one's community the qualities that make participation in discursive will-formation possible. And we can term the possibility of relating positively to oneself in this manner 'self-respect'.

For the moment, however, this conclusion is only a conceptual claim, for which empirical support is, as yet, completely lacking. The reason why it is so difficult, in the case of self-respect, to demonstrate the reality of the phenomenon is because, to a certain extent, it acquires a perceptible mass only in a negative form – specifically, only when subjects visibly suffer from a lack of it. The actual presence of self-respect can therefore be inferred only indirectly each time, by making empirical comparisons involving groups of people, from whose general behaviour one can draw conclusions about the forms in which the experience of disrespect is symbolically represented. One way out of this difficulty is provided by the occasional cases in which the groups involved have themselves publicly discussed the denial of basic rights from the perspective of how withheld recognition undermines the opportunity for individual self-respect. In these exceptional historical situations – such as the one represented by discussions in the civil rights movement of the fifties and sixties in the US – the psychological significance of legal recognition for the self-respect of excluded collectivities breaks to the linguistic surface: in the relevant publications one regularly finds talk of how the endurance of legal under-privileging necessarily leads to a crippling feeling of social shame, from which one can be liberated only through active protest and resistance.[56]

III

Both Hegel and Mead contrasted love and legal relations with a further form of mutual recognition and, although they chose to give different accounts of it, they were largely in agreement on its specific function: in order to be able to acquire an undistorted relation-to-self, human subjects always need – over and above the experience of affectionate care and legal recognition – a form of social esteem that allows them to relate positively to their concrete traits and abilities. In Hegel's Jena writings, the concept 'ethical life' was the term for this recognition relationship of mutual esteem. In Mead, by contrast, we found, instead of a purely formal conception of this form of recognition, the already institutionally concrete model of the cooperative division of labour. From the comparison between the two descriptive approaches, the conclusion could be drawn that this type of pattern of recognition could only be properly understood at all once one further supposed, as a prerequisite, the existence of an intersubjectively shared value-horizon. For self and other can mutually esteem each other as individualized persons only on the condition that they share an orientation to those values and goals that indicate to each other the significance or contribution of their qualities for the life of the other. An initial indication that our interpretation of Hegel and Mead did not lead to an empirically unsupportable conclusion ultimately arose from the analysis of modern legal relations. The fundamental, universalistic principle underlying these relations could only be reconstructed by conceiving of them as the outcome of an uncoupling of legal recognition from the forms of social regard in which subjects are recognized according to the socially defined worth of their concrete characteristics. In these historically shifting patterns of social esteem one can discern the early empirical forms of what Hegel and Mead each had in mind in introducing a third relation of mutual recognition. Its features can thus best be determined – in the sense of an empirically backed phenomenology – if we return to our line of analysis at the point where we left it, in the comparison between legal recognition and social esteem. In this connection, it turns out that with their concepts of 'ethical life' and a democratic division of labour, Hegel and Mead each sought to single out only one type – and, in normative terms, a particularly demanding type – of value-community, into which every form of esteem-granting recognition necessarily must be admitted.

Unlike modern legal recognition, social esteem is directed, as we have seen, at the particular qualities that characterize people in their personal difference. Thus, whereas modern law represents a medium of recognition that expresses the universal features of human subjects, this form of recognition demands a social medium that must be able to express the characteristic differences among human subjects in a universal and, more specifically, intersubjectively obligatory way. This task of mediation is performed, at the societal level, by a symbolically articulated – yet always open and porous – framework of orientation, in which those ethical values and goals are formulated that, taken together, comprise the cultural self-understanding of a society. Such a framework of orientation can serve as a system of reference for the appraisal of particular personality features, because their social 'worth' is measured by the degree to which they appear to be in a position to contribute to the realization of societal goals.[57] The cultural self-understanding of a society provides the criteria that orient the social esteem of persons, because their abilities and achievements are judged intersubjectively according to the degree to which they can help to realize culturally defined values. This form of mutual recognition is thus also tied to the presupposition of a context of social life, whose members, through their orientation towards shared conceptions of their goals, form a community of value. But if social esteem is determined by the dominant conceptions of ethical goals in a society, then the forms it can take are no less historically variable than those of legal recognition. Their societal scope and the measure of their symmetry then depend on both the degree of pluralization of the socially defined value-horizon and the character of the personality ideals singled out there. The more conceptions of ethical goals are open to different values and the more their hierarchical arrangement gives way to horizontal competition, the more clearly social esteem will be able to take on an individualizing character and generate symmetrical relationships. Thus, here too, it seems natural to analyse this specific form of recognition in terms of the historical, structural transformation that it went through in the transition from traditional to modern societies: as with legal relations, social esteem could only take on the shape familiar to us today after it had outgrown the framework of corporatively organized societies of the pre-modern period. The structural transformation that thereby got underway is marked, in terms of the history of concepts, by the transition from concepts of honour to categories of social 'standing' or 'prestige'.

As long as a society's conceptions of its ethical goals are still conceived of substantively and the corresponding value-ideas are hierarchically organized in such a way that a scale of more and less valuable forms of conduct can arise, a person's status is measured in terms of social honour. The conventional ethical life of such communities allows them to stratify areas of responsibility within society vertically, according to their purported contribution to the realization of central values and mapped further onto specific ways of leading one's life. And it is in adhering to these patterns that individuals can attain the 'honour' appropriate to their status. Thus, within corporatively organized societies, 'honour' designates the relative level of social standing that people can attain when they manage to conduct themselves habitually in line with the collective expectations that are 'ethically' linked to their social status: 'In content,' we read in Max Weber, 'status [*ständisch*] honor is normally expressed in the fact that above all else a specific *style of life* is expected from all those who want to belong to the circle'.[58] The personality traits towards which the social evaluation of a person is oriented, under these presuppositions, are thus not those of a biographically individuated subject but rather those of a culturally typified status group. It is according to the 'worth' of this group – which emerges, in turn, from the socially determined degree of their collective contribution to the realization of societal goals – that the social worth of each of its members is to be measured as well. 'Honourable' conduct is thus only what each individual must further accomplish in order to actually attain the level of social standing collectively accorded to his or her estate, on the basis of the culturally pre-given value order.[59]

When social esteem is organized according to the corporative pattern just sketched, the forms of recognition associated with it take on the character of internally symmetrical yet externally asymmetrical relationships between culturally typified members of an estate. Within the status group, subjects can esteem each other as persons who, because of their common social position, share traits and abilities that are accorded a certain level of social standing on the society's scale of values. Between status groups, one finds relations of hierarchically graded esteem, which allow members of society to esteem subjects outside their estate for traits and abilities that, to a culturally predetermined degree, contribute to the realization of collectively shared values. Of course, even this relatively stable system of recognition relations does not rule out the possibility that social groups would take the alternative route of a 'counterculture of compensatory respect',[60] in order to rectify, through demonstrative stylizations, what they feel to be an unjust appraisal of the worth of their collective characteristics. And one can view it as equally typical for corporative societies that, as Max Weber observed, social groups tend to try to deny non-members access to the distinguishing features of their group, in order to monopolize long-term chances for high social prestige.[61] But all of these dimensions of an everyday struggle for honour remain bound to the framework of a corporative system of recognition relations, as long as it does not directly put into question the substantive value-hierarchy that marks the cultural self-understanding of traditional societies in general.

This gradual devaluation of traditional ethical life began at the moment at which the post-conventional ideas of philosophy and political theory had gained so much cultural influence that they could not leave the status of socially integrative value-convictions untouched. In the transition to modernity, it is not simply the case that relations of legal recognition became detached, as we have seen, from the hierarchical order of social esteem. In addition, this order itself was submitted to a tough, conflict-ridden process of structural transformation, because in the wake of cultural innovations, the conditions for the validity of a society's ethical goals changed as well. Even though the societal value-system had been able to serve as an evaluative system of reference with which to determine – objectively, as it were – the patterns of honourable conduct specific to an estate, this was primarily due to the particular cognitive givenness of the value-system. In fact, it still owed its social currency to the undiminished convincing force of a religious or metaphysical heritage and was thus anchored in cultural self-understanding as a meta-social point of reference. But as soon as this epistemic threshold was crossed on a broad scale – that is, as soon as ethical obligations were recognized to be the result of inner-worldly decisions – the everyday understanding of the character of society's value-system had to change, as the preconditions for the validity of law had done before. Stripped of the transcendental basis for its self-evidence, this value-system could no longer be viewed as an objective system of reference in which class-specific expectations as to one's conduct could provide unambiguous information about the relative measure of social honour. Along with the metaphysical foundation for validity, the value-cosmos lost both its objective character and its ability to fix, once and for all, a scale of social prestige in a way that could govern conduct. For this reason, the struggle against the nobility's notions of honour that the bourgeoisie took up at the threshold of modernity represents not only the collective attempt to establish new value-principles but also the initiation of a confrontation over the status, in general, of such value-principles. For the first time, it came to be open to dispute whether a person's social standing is to be measured in terms of the predetermined worth of traits that are attributed, as types, to entire groups. It is only from this point on that the subject entered the contested field of social esteem as an entity individuated in terms of a particular life-history.

In the course of the upheaval described above, a significant part of the social esteem guaranteed to individuals via corporatively stratified principles of honour made its way into the newly formed legal relations, where it attained universal currency in the concept of 'human dignity'.[62] In modern catalogues of human rights, all human beings are guaranteed equal legal protection for their standing in society, even though it remains unclear even today what practical legal consequences this should actually have. But legal relations cannot integrate all dimensions of social esteem as is already clear simply from the fact that, in accordance with its overall function, social esteem can only apply to those traits and abilities with regard to which members of society differ from one another. Persons can feel themselves to be 'valuable' only when they know themselves to be recognized for accomplishments that they precisely do not share in an undifferentiated manner with others. Although such differences among characteristics had previously been defined collectivistically, in order to tie one's level of social honour to one's membership in status group, this possibility disappears here with the gradual dissolution of the traditional hierarchy of values. The bourgeoisie's struggle against the compulsion to conduct oneself in a manner suitable to one's 'estate', to which they had been yoked by the old system of recognition relations, led to an individualization of the notion of who contributed to the realization of societal goals. Because it is no longer to be determined in advance which ways of leading one's life are considered ethically admissible, social esteem begins to be oriented not towards collective traits but towards the capacities developed by the individual in the course of his or her life. The individualization of achievement is inevitably accompanied by the opening of societal value-ideas for differing forms of personal self-realization. From this point on, it is a form of value pluralism – albeit one defined in class-specific and gender-specific terms – that constitutes the cultural framework of orientation within which individuals' level of accomplishment and thus their social worth are defined. It is in this context that the concept of social honour gradually becomes watered down into a concept of social prestige.[63]

One side of this historical process of conceptual transformation involves the decline of the category of 'honour' – up to this point linked to ways of leading one's life specific to a status group or 'estate' – into a different context of application, that of the private sphere. From here on, 'honour' designates only the subjectively definable standard for those aspects of one's self-understanding that unconditionally deserve to be defended. The place that the concept of honour had previously held in the public arena gradually comes to be occupied by the categories of 'standing' or 'prestige', which are supposed to capture the measure of esteem that individuals are socially accorded for their individual accomplishments and abilities. Now the new organizational pattern that this form of recognition thus acquires can, of course, only refer to the narrow stratum of a person's worth which is left over from the two processes of, on the one hand, the universalization of 'honour' into 'dignity' and, on the other hand, the privatization of 'honour' into subjectively defined 'integrity'. Thus, social esteem is henceforth no longer linked to legal privileges of any sort, and does not constitutively include the designation of moral qualities of one's personality.[64] Rather, 'prestige' or 'standing' signifies only the degree of social recognition the individual earns for his or her form of self-realization by thus contributing, to a certain extent, to the practical realization of society's abstractly defined goals. With regard to this new, individualized system of recognition relations, everything now depends, therefore, on the definition of this general value-horizon, which is supposed to be open to various forms of self-realization and yet, at the same time, must also be able to serve as an overarching system of esteem.

With these conflicting tasks a tension is introduced into the modern organization of social esteem, a tension that renders it permanently subject to cultural conflict. For, however the societal goals are defined – whether in terms of a seemingly neutral idea of 'achievement' or in terms of an open horizon of plural values – there is always a need for a secondary interpretive practice, before they can operate within the social lifeworld as criteria of esteem. The abstract guiding ideas of modern societies provide so little in the way of a universally valid system of reference with which to measure the social worth of particular traits and abilities that they must always be made concrete through supplemental cultural interpretations before they can be applied in the sphere of recognition. For this reason, the worth accorded to various forms of self-realization and even the manner in which the relevant traits and abilities are defined fundamentally depend on the dominant interpretations of societal goals in each historical case. But since the content of such interpretations depends in turn on which social groups succeed in publicly interpreting their own accomplishments and forms of life in a way that shows them to be especially valuable, this secondary interpretive practice cannot be understood to be anything other than an ongoing cultural conflict. In modern societies, relations of social esteem are subject to a permanent struggle, in which different groups attempt, by means of symbolic force and with reference to general goals, to raise the value of the abilities associated with their way of life.[65] To be sure, it is not only the power of specific groups to control these means of symbolic force but also the climate of public attention (never easily influenced) that partly decides, in each case, the temporarily stable outcome of such struggles. The more successful social movements are at drawing the public sphere's attention to the neglected significance of the traits and abilities they collectively represent, the better their chances of raising the social worth or, indeed, the standing of their members. Since, beyond this, relations of social esteem are, as Georg Simmel already saw, indirectly coupled with patterns of income distribution, economic confrontations are also constitutive for this form of struggle for recognition.

With this development, social esteem develops a pattern that lends the associated form of recognition the character of an asymmetrical relationship between biographically individuated subjects. Of course, the cultural interpretations that must, in each case, render abstract societal goals concrete within the lifeworld are still determined by social groups' interests in the revaluation of their abilities and traits, but within value-systems (which have emerged via conflict) the social standing of subjects is indeed measured in terms of what they can accomplish for society within the context of their particular forms of self-realization. It is this type of organizational pattern of social esteem that Hegel and Mead are each aiming at in their proposals, found respectively in the concept of 'ethical life' and the idea of a democratic division of labour. For in their proposed solutions, both envisioned a social value-system in which societal goals had gone through such a complex and detailed explication that every individual would basically have the chance to attain some degree of social standing. I have already attempted to describe the theoretical dead-ends in which both Hegel and Mead admittedly ended up in working out their shared core idea. It remains to be asked why the category of 'solidarity' recommends itself as the overarching concept for these suggested solutions. A clarification of this question is only possible, however, after the type of individual relation-to-self accompanying the experience of social esteem has been revealed.

As long as the form of recognition found in esteem is organized in terms of status groups, the corresponding experience of social distinction can generally refer only to the collective identity of one's own group. The accomplishments in terms of whose societal worth individuals are recognized are then still so little abstracted from the typified collective traits of the status group that only the group as a whole can feel itself to be the addressee of esteem. The practical relation-to-self that such an experience of recognition allows individuals to attain is thus a feeling of group-pride or collective honour. Here, the individual knows himself or herself to be a member of a social group that can collectively accomplish things whose worth for society is recognized by all other members of society. In the internal relations of such groups, forms of interaction normally take on the character of relationships of solidarity, since each member knows himself or herself to be esteemed by all others to the same degree. This is because, to a first approximation, 'solidarity' can be understood as an interactive relationship in which subjects mutually sympathize with their various different ways of life because, among themselves, they esteem each other symmetrically.[66] This suggestion also explains the fact that up to now the concept of 'solidarity' has been applied primarily to group relations that arise in the experience of collective resistance to political oppression. Here, it is the all-dominating agreement on a practical goal that instantly generates an intersubjective value-horizon, in which each participant learns to recognize the significance of the abilities and traits of the others to the same degree.[67] The mechanism of symmetrical esteem can also be used to explain the fact that war often represents a collective event that is able to create spontaneous relationships of solidarity and sympathy across social boundaries. Here again, in the shared experience of great strain and sacrifice a new constellation of values suddenly emerges, which allows subjects to esteem one another for accomplishments and abilities that had previously been without societal significance.

Up to now, however, we have only clarified the type of practical relation-to-self that allows individuals to gain social esteem as long as it is still organized along corporative lines. But with the individualization (depicted above) of this form of recognition, the practical relationship with themselves that this enables subjects to enter into changes as well. Now the individual no longer has to attribute to an entire collective the respect that he or she receives for accomplishments that fit social standards but can refer them positively back to himself or herself instead. Under these altered conditions, the experience of being socially esteemed is accompanied by a felt confidence that one's achievements or abilities will be recognized as 'valuable' by other members of society. We can meaningfully term this type of practical relation-to-self (for which, in everyday speech, the expression 'feeling of self-worth' predominates) 'self-esteem', as the parallel category to the concepts of 'basic self-confidence' and 'self-respect'.[68] To the extent to which every member of a society is in a position to esteem himself or herself, one can speak of a state of societal solidarity (see figure 2).

In modern societies, therefore, social relations of symmetrical esteem between individualized (and autonomous) subjects represent a prerequisite for solidarity. In this sense, to esteem one another symmetrically means to view one another in light of values that allow the abilities and traits of the other to appear significant for shared praxis. Relationships of this sort can be said to be cases of 'solidarity', because they inspire not just passive tolerance but felt concern for what is individual and particular about the other person. For only to the degree to which I actively care about the development of the other's characteristics (which seem foreign to me) can our shared goals be realized. The fact that 'symmetrical' cannot mean here that we esteem each other to the same degree is already clear from the essential openness to interpretation of every societal value-horizon. It is simply impossible

Mode of recognition	emotional support	cognitive respect	social esteem
Dimension of personality	needs and emotions	moral responsibility	traits and abilities
Forms of recognition	primary relationships (love, friendship)	legal relations (rights)	community of value (solidarity)
Developmental potential	—	generalization, de-formalization	individualization, equalization
Practical relation-to-self	basic self-confidence	self-respect	self-esteem
Forms of disrespect	abuse and rape	denial of rights, exclusion	denigration, insult
Threatened component of personality	physical integrity	social integrity	'honour', dignity

Figure 2 The structure of relations of recognition

to imagine a set of collective goals that could be fixed quantitatively in such a way that it would allow for an exact comparison of the value of individual contributions; 'symmetrical' must mean instead that every subject is free from being collectively denigrated, so that one is given the chance to experience oneself to be recognized, in light of one's own accomplishments and abilities, as valuable for society. For this reason too, the social relations that we have conceived of here in terms of the concept of 'solidarity' open up, for the first time, the horizon within which individual competition for social esteem can then acquire a form free from pain, that is, a form not marred by experiences of disrespect.

6

Personal Identity and Disrespect: The Violation of the Body, the Denial of Rights, and the Denigration of Ways of Life

Inherent in our everyday use of language is a sense that human integrity owes its existence, at a deep level, to the patterns of approval and recognition that we have been attempting to distinguish. For up to the present day, in the self-descriptions of those who see themselves as having been wrongly treated by others, the moral categories that play a dominant role are those – such as 'insult' or 'humiliation' – that refer to forms of disrespect, that is, to the denial of recognition. Negative concepts of this kind are used to designate behaviour that represents an injustice not simply because it harms subjects or restricts their freedom to act, but because it injures them with regard to the positive understanding of themselves that they have acquired intersubjectively. Without the implicit reference to the claims to recognition that one makes to one's fellow human beings, there is no way of using these concepts of 'disrespect' and 'insult' meaningfully. In this sense, our ordinary language contains empirical indications of an indissoluble connection between, on the one hand, the unassailability and integrity of human beings and, on the other hand, the approval of others. What the term 'disrespect' [*Mißachtung*] refers to is the specific vulnerability of humans resulting from the internal interdependence of individualization and recognition, which both Hegel and Mead helped to illuminate. Because the normative self-image of each and every individual human being – his or her 'me', as Mead put it – is dependent on the possibility of being continually backed up by others, the experience of being disrespected carries with it the danger of an injury that can bring the identity of the person as a whole to the point of collapse.[1]

Admittedly, all of what is referred to colloquially as 'disrespect' or 'insult' obviously can involve varying degrees of depth in the psychological injury to a subject. There is a categorial difference between, say, the blatant degradation involved in the denial of basic human rights, on the one hand, and the subtle humiliation that accompanies a public allusion to a person's failings, on the other. And the use of a single term threatens to efface this difference. But even just the fact that we have been able to identify systematic gradations for the complementary concept of 'recognition' points to the existence of internal differences between individual forms of disrespect. If it is the case that the experience of disrespect signals the withholding or withdrawing of recognition, then the same distinctions would have to be found within the field of negative phenomena as was met with in the field of positive phenomena. In this sense, the distinctions between three patterns of recognition gives us a theoretical key with which to separate out just as many kinds of disrespect. Their differences would have to be measured by the various degrees to which they are able to disrupt a person's practical relation-to-self by denying him or her recognition for particular claims to identity. Only by proceeding from this set of divisions can one take on the question that neither Hegel nor Mead were able to answer: how is it that the experience of disrespect is anchored in the affective life of human subjects in such a way that it can provide the motivational impetus for social resistance and conflict, indeed, for a struggle for recognition?

In light of the distinctions worked out thus far it would appear sensible to start from a type of disrespect that affects a person at the level of physical integrity. The forms of practical maltreatment in which a person is forcibly deprived of any opportunity freely to dispose over his or her own body represent the most fundamental sort of personal degradation. This is because every attempt to gain control of a person's body against his or her will – irrespective of the intention behind it – causes a degree of humiliation that impacts more destructively than other forms of respect on a person's practical relation-to-self. For what is specific to these kinds of physical injury, as exemplified by torture and rape, is not the purely physical pain but rather the combination of this pain with the feeling of being defencelessly at the mercy of another subject, to the point of feeling that one has been deprived of reality.[2] Physical abuse represents a type of disrespect that does lasting damage to one's basic confidence (learned through love) that one can autonomously coordinate one's own body. Hence the further consequence, coupled with a type of social shame, is the loss of trust in oneself and the world, and this affects all practical dealings with other subjects, even at a physical level. Thus, the kind of recognition that this type of disrespect deprives one of is the taken-for-granted respect for the autonomous control of one's own body, which itself could only be acquired at all through experiencing emotional support as part of the socialization process. The successful integration of physical and emotional qualities of behaviour is, as it were, subsequently broken up from the outside, thus lastingly destroying the most fundamental form of practical relation-to-self, namely, one's underlying trust in oneself.

Since such forms of basic psychological self-confidence carry emotional preconditions that follow a largely invariant logic associated with the intersubjective balance between fusion and demarcation, this experience of disrespect also cannot simply vary with the historical period or the cultural frame of reference. Whatever the construction of the system of legitimation that tries to justify it, the suffering of torture or rape is always accompanied by a dramatic breakdown in one's trust in the reliability of the social world and hence by a collapse in one's own basic self-confidence. By contrast, the other two types of disrespect in our tripartite division are embedded in a process of historical change. Here, what it is that is perceived, in each case, to be a moral injury is subject to the same historical transformations as the corresponding patterns of mutual recognition.

Whereas the first form of disrespect is inherent in those experiences of physical abuse that destroy a person's basic self-confidence, we have to look for the second form in those experiences of denigration that can affect a person's moral self-respect. This refers to those forms of personal disrespect to which an individual is subjected by being structurally excluded from the possession of certain rights within a society. We have initially construed the term 'rights', only roughly, as referring to those individual claims that a person can legitimately expect to have socially met because he or she participates, with equal rights, in the institutional order as a full-fledged member of a community. Should that person now be systematically denied certain rights of this kind, this would imply that he or she is not being accorded the same degree of moral responsibility as other members of society. What is specific to such forms of disrespect, as exemplified by the denial of rights or by social ostracism, thus lies not just in the forcible restriction of personal autonomy but also in the combination with the feeling of not enjoying the status of a full-fledged partner to interaction, equally endowed with moral rights. For the individual, having socially valid rights-claims denied signifies a violation of the intersubjective expectation to be recognized as a subject capable of forming moral judgements. To this extent, the experience of this type of disrespect typically brings with it a loss of self-respect, of the ability to relate to oneself as a legally equal interaction partner with all fellow humans.[3] Thus, the kind of recognition that this type of disrespect deprives one of is the cognitive regard for the status of moral responsibility that had to be so painstakingly acquired in the interactive processes of socialization. This form of disrespect represents a historically variable quantity because the semantic content of what counts as a morally responsible agent changes with the development of legal relations. Therefore, the experience of the denial of rights is always to be measured not only in terms of the degree of universalization but also in terms of the substantive scope of the institutionally established rights.

Finally, this second type of disrespect, which injures subjects with regard to their self-respect, is to be set off from a third type of degradation, one that entails negative consequences for the social value of individuals or groups. Not until we consider these, as it were, evaluative forms of disrespect – the denigration of individual or collective ways of life – do we arrive at the form of behaviour ordinarily labelled 'insulting' or 'degrading' today. As we saw, a person's 'honour', 'dignity', or, to use the modern term, 'status' refers to the degree of social esteem accorded to his or her manner of self-realization within a society's inherited cultural horizon. If this hierarchy of values is so constituted as to downgrade individual forms of life and manners of belief as inferior or deficient, then it robs the subjects in question of every opportunity to attribute social value to their own abilities. For those engaged in them, the result of the evaluative degradation of certain patterns of self-realization is that they cannot relate to their mode of life as something of positive significance within their community. For individuals, therefore, the experience of this social devaluation typically brings with it a loss of personal self-esteem, of the opportunity to regard themselves as beings whose traits and abilities are esteemed. Thus, the kind of recognition that this type of disrespect deprives a person of is the social approval of a form of self-realization that he or she had to discover, despite all hindrances, with the encouragement of group solidarity. Of course, one can only relate these kinds of cultural degradation to oneself as an individual person once the institutionally anchored patterns of social esteem have been historically individuated, that is, once these patterns refer evaluatively to individual abilities instead of collective traits. Hence, this experience of disrespect, like that of the denial of rights, is bound up with a process of historical change.

It is typical of the three groups of experiences of disrespect analytically distinguished in this way that their individual consequences are always described in terms of metaphors that refer to states of deterioration of the human body. Psychological studies of the personal after-effects of torture or rape frequently speak of 'psychological death'. In research concerned with how victims of slavery collectively cope with the denial of rights and exclusion from society, the concept of 'social death' is now well established. And with regard to the type of disrespect associated with the cultural denigration of forms of life, one regularly speaks of 'scars' and 'injuries'.[4] These metaphorical allusions to physical suffering and death articulate the idea that the various forms of disregard for the psychological integrity of humans play the same negative role that organic infections take on in the context of the reproduction of the body. The experience of being socially denigrated or humiliated endangers the identity of human beings, just as infection with a disease endangers their physical life. If this interpretation, suggested by our linguistic practice, turns out to be not entirely implausible, then it contains two implicit suggestions that are relevant for our purposes. First, the comparison with physical illness prompts the idea of identifying, for the case of suffering social disrespect as well, a stratum of symptoms that, to a certain extent, make the subjects aware of the state they are in. The hypothesis here is that what corresponds to physical indications here are the sort of negative emotional reactions expressed in feelings of social shame. Second, however, the comparison also provides the opportunity to draw conclusions, on the basis of an overview of the various forms of disrespect, as to what fosters the 'psychological health' or integrity of human beings. Seen this way, the parallel to the preventive treatment of illnesses would be the social guarantees associated with those relations of recognition that are able to protect subjects most extensively from suffering disrespect. Although this second comparison will only be of interest to us when we examine the normative implications of this connection between personal integrity and disrespect (in chapter 9), the first comparison is already significant for the argument to be developed here. For the negative emotional reactions accompanying the experience of disrespect could represent precisely the affective motivational basis in which the struggled-for recognition is anchored.

Neither in Hegel nor in Mead did we find any indication as to how experiencing social disrespect can motivate a subject to enter a practical struggle or conflict. There was, as it were, a missing psychological link that would lead from mere suffering to action by cognitively informing the person in question of his or her social situation. I would

like to defend the thesis that this function can be performed by negative emotional reactions, such as being ashamed or enraged, feeling
hurt or indignant. These comprise the psychological symptoms on the
basis of which one can come to realize that one is being illegitimately
denied social recognition. The reason for this can again be seen in the
constitutional dependence of humans on the experience of recognition.
In order to acquire a successful relation-to-self, one is dependent on
the intersubjective recognition of one's abilities and accomplishments.
Were one never to experience this type of social approval at some
stage of one's development, this would open up a psychological gap
within one's personality, into which negative emotional reactions
such as shame or rage could step. Hence, the experience of disrespect
is always accompanied by affective sensations that are, in principle,
capable of revealing to individuals the fact that certain forms of recognition are being withheld from them. In order to give this complex
thesis some plausibility, at least in outline, it would be advisable to
connect it to a conception of human emotions of the sort developed by
John Dewey in his pragmatist psychology.

In several early essays, Dewey turned against the widespread view
that human states of emotional excitation had to be conceived of as
expressions of inner feelings. He wanted to show that such a conception, which could still be found in William James, necessarily overlooks the function of emotions for action by assuming the psychological
event to be something 'inner' and prior to actions, which it views as
something directed 'outwards'.[5] Against this, Dewey's argument proceeds from the observation that, within the human horizon of experience, insofar as feelings appear at all, they appear in either positive or
negative dependence on actions: either they accompany the experience of particularly successful 'communications' (with people or things)
as bodily states of excitement, or they emerge as the experience of
being repelled by a failed, interrupted attempt to execute an action.
The analysis of such experiences of being repelled provides Dewey
with the key to devising an action-theoretical conception of human
emotions. According to this conception, negative feelings such as
anger, indignation, and sorrow constitute the affective side of the shift
of attention towards one's own expectations that inevitably occurs as
soon as one has difficulty making the step one planned to make upon
completing an action. Positive feelings such as joy or pride, by contrast, arise when one is suddenly freed from a burdensome state of
excitement, because one has been able to find a suitable, successful
solution to a pressing action problem. In general, then, Dewey views

feelings as the affective reactions generated upon succeeding or failing to realize our intentions.

Starting from this general point, we can differentiate emotions still further once we distinguish more precisely the types of 'disruptions' on which habitual human action can founder. Since these disruptions or failures are to be assessed against the background of the orienting expectations that precede the act in each case, we can make an initial, rough division on the basis of two different types of expectations. Routine human actions can come up against obstacles either in the context of expectations of instrumental success or in the context of normative behavioural expectations. Should actions oriented towards success fail as a result of unanticipated obstructions, this leads to 'technical' disruptions in the broadest sense. By contrast, should actions guided by norms be repelled by situations because the norms taken to be valid are violated, this leads to 'moral' conflicts in the social lifeworld. This second class of disrupted actions constitutes the experiential horizon in which moral emotional reactions are situated practically. They can be understood, in Dewey's sense, as the emotional excitations with which human beings react to having their actions unexpectedly repelled owing to a violation of normative expectations. The differences between the individual feelings can be measured quite elementarily in terms of whether the violation of the norm hindering the action is caused by the subject or by the interaction partner. In the first case, the subject experiences the hindrance to the action in feelings of guilt and, in the second case, in emotions of moral indignation. What is true of both cases, however, is something that Dewey considered to be typical of situations of emotionally experiencing one's action thrown back upon itself, namely, that with the shift of attention to one's own expectations, one also becomes aware of the cognitive components – in this case, moral knowledge – that had informed the planned and (now) hindered action.

The most open of our moral feelings is shame – to the extent that it does not refer simply to the evidently deep-seated shyness about having one's body exposed. In the case of shame, it is not fixed from the outset which party to the interaction is responsible for violating the norm, a norm that the subject now lacks, as it were, for the routine continuation of an action. As both psychoanalytical and phenomenological approaches have shown, the emotional content of shame consists, to begin with, in a kind of lowering of one's own feeling of self-worth. Ashamed of oneself as a result of having one's action rejected, one experiences oneself as being of lower social value than one

had previously assumed. In psychoanalytic terms, this means that what
is negatively affected by the action-inhibiting violation of a moral norm
is not the super-ego but the subject's ego-ideals.[6] This type of shame
– which is only experienced in the presence of a real or imaginary
interaction partner, playing as it were the role of witness to the injured
ego-ideals – can be caused by oneself or by others. In the first case, one
experiences oneself as inferior because one has violated a moral norm,
adherence to which had constituted a principle of one's ego-ideals. In
the second case, however, one is oppressed by a feeling of low self-
esteem because one's interaction partners violate moral norms that,
when they were adhered to, allowed one to count as the person that,
in terms of one's ego-ideals, one wants to be. Hence, the moral crisis
in communication is triggered here by the agent being disappointed
with regard to the normative expectations that he or she believed
could be placed on another's willingness to respect him or her. In this
sense, the second type of moral shame represents the emotion that
overwhelms subjects who, as a result of having their ego-claims disregarded, are incapable of simply going ahead with an action. In these
emotional experiences, what one comes to realize about oneself is that
one's own person is constitutively dependent on the recognition of
others.[7]

In the context of the emotional responses associated with shame, the
experience of being disrespected can become the motivational impetus
for a struggle for recognition. For it is only by regaining the possibility
of active conduct that individuals can dispel the state of emotional
tension into which they are forced as a result of humiliation. But what
makes it possible for the praxis thus opened up to take the form of
political resistance is the opportunity for moral insight inherent in
these negative emotions, as their cognitive content. It is only because
human subjects are incapable of reacting in emotionally neutral ways
to social injuries – as exemplified by physical abuse, the denial of
rights, and denigration – that the normative patterns of mutual recognition found in the social lifeworld have any chance of being realized.
For each of the negative emotional reactions that accompany the experience of having one's claims to recognition disregarded holds out
the possibility that the injustice done to one will cognitively disclose
itself and become a motive for political resistance.

Of course, the weakness of this foothold of morality within social
reality is shown by the fact that, in these affective reactions, the injustice
of disrespect does not inevitably *have to* reveal itself but merely *can*.
Empirically, whether the cognitive potential inherent in feeling hurt or
ashamed becomes a moral-political conviction depends above all on

how the affected subject's cultural-political environment is constructed: only if the means of articulation of a social movement are available can the experience of disrespect become a source of motivation for acts of political resistance. The developmental logic of such collective movements can, however, only be discovered via an analysis that attempts to explain social struggles on the basis of the dynamics of moral experiences.

Part III

Social-philosophical Perspectives:

Morality and Societal Development

Using the resources of an empirically grounded phenomenology, we have been able to show that Hegel's and Mead's tripartite distinction among forms of recognition did not entirely miss its mark in social reality. Indeed, it turned out to be thoroughly capable of fruitfully disclosing the moral infrastructure of interactions. As a result, it was also possible (as both authors had supposed) to map these various patterns of recognition onto different types of practical relations-to-self, that is, onto ways of relating positively to oneself. It was then no longer difficult to distinguish, in a second step, forms of social disrespect in terms of the specific level of persons' practical relations-to-self they can damage or even destroy. The very provisional distinction between the violation of the body, the denial of rights, and the denigration of ways of life provides us with the conceptual means for making fairly plausible what renders Hegel's and Mead's common approach so provocative: the thesis that the moral force within lived social reality that is responsible for development and progress is a struggle for recognition. This is a strong claim, one that sometimes seems to suggest a philosophy of history, and in order to give it a theoretically defensible form, evidence would have to be presented to the effect that the experience of disrespect represents the affective source of knowledge for social resistance and collective uprisings. But that, too, is not something that I can directly prove here. Instead, I must settle for an indirect historical and illustrative approach.

To this end, I shall first return to the effort to bring up to date the tradition of social philosophy found in the work of Hegel and Mead. When we examine the history of post-Hegelian thought in search of theories with comparable theoretical intentions, we encounter a number of approaches in which historical development is viewed – drawing, in part, on Hegel, but never with reference to Mead – as the agonistic process found in the struggle for recognition. The systematic differentiation of the three forms of recognition can now help to make transparent the confusions upon which post-Hegelian conceptions have previously always run aground. The social philosophies of Marx, Sorel, and Sartre represent the most significant examples of an intellectual current that theorizes social conflicts as charged with demands for recognition (in opposition to Hobbes and Machiavelli) but without ever really being able to see through to their moral infrastructure (chapter 7).

The further critical development of this tradition requires an account of the historical, empirical indicators that allow it to seem at all plausible to speak of a 'struggle for recognition' setting the pace of historical transformations. For this reason, I shall attempt, second, to explicate briefly the moral logic of social struggles in such a way that it no longer appears to be completely misguided to suppose that these struggles represent the actual source of motivation for social progress (chapter 8).

If, in this sense, Hegel's conception of the 'struggle for recognition' – as corrected by Mead's social psychology – is to be made the guiding thread of a critical social theory, then this requires, finally, a philosophical justification for its underlying normative principle. This is to be attempted, in the final chapter, by way of a formal conception of ethical life, in which intersubjective conditions for personal integrity will be interpreted, taken together, as presuppositions for individual self-realization (chapter 9).

7

Traces of a Tradition in Social Philosophy: Marx, Sorel, Sartre

The differentiated, recognition-based model of conflict that Hegel worked out in his Jena years was never able to exercise any significant influence upon the history of social philosophy. It remained forever in the shadow of the methodologically sophisticated and, from a literary standpoint, certainly more impressive *Phenomenology of Spirit*, in which the topic of a 'struggle for recognition' was restricted to the issue of the conditions for the emergence of 'self-consciousness'. The chapter on 'lordship and bondage' was nevertheless sufficiently suggestive to bring about a change in political theory, as a consequence of which the central themes of the earlier writings could still, in essence, remain present. By suggesting that the conflict between the lord and the bondsman be interpreted as a struggle over the recognition of identity-claims, Hegel was able to initiate an intellectual movement in which social diremption [*Entzweiung*] could be traced back – *pace* Machiavelli and Hobbes – to the experience of moral claims being violated. The author in whose work this epoch-making redefinition of social struggle left its first and, up to the present day, most influential traces is Karl Marx. In his theory of class struggle, the intuitive moral theory guiding the young Hegel enters into a tension-ridden, highly ambivalent synthesis with currents of utilitarianism. After decades of economistic reductionism within Marxism, Georges Sorel then attempted to reintroduce the process of social transformation into the perspective of a struggle for recognition. Influenced more by Vico and Bergson than by Hegel, his contributions to overcoming social-scientific utilitarianism represent an almost dangerously failed attempt to interpret history in terms of a theory of recognition. In the most recent past, finally, it was above all Jean-Paul Sartre who contributed to the idea of making a 'struggle for recognition' fruitful for the purposes of a critically oriented social theory. From the beginning, however, his existentialist version of the Hegelian conception was in tension with themes – suggestive of a theory of recognition – found in his political commentaries. In each of these cases, the decisive reason for the failure of the theoretical approach represented by Marx, Sorel, and Sartre is clearly the same. The process of social development is always considered only in terms of one of the three moral aspects of the movement of recognition that we have systematically distinguished, drawing on the early Hegel. Despite this, these various theories represent the fragments of a tradition of thought that, in its subsequent development, indicates what an interpretation of moral progress in terms of a theory of recognition must accomplish.

Already in the case of Marx, who had access to the *Phenomenology of Spirit* but not the *Realphilosophie*, the idea of a struggle for recognition is discussed (in the Paris manuscripts) in the narrowed version found in the dialectic of lordship and bondage. As a result, at the start of his creative work, Marx succumbed to the problematic tendency to reduce the spectrum of demands for recognition to the dimension of self-realization through labour.[1] But Marx bases his initial philosophical anthropology on a concept of labour which is so normatively charged that he can construe the act of production itself as a process of intersubjective recognition. In the course of fully integrated labour – which is conceived of on the model of artistic or craft activities[2] – the experience of having an ability objectified is so intertwined with the mental [*geistige*] anticipation of a possible consumer that this experience gives the individual an intersubjectively mediated feeling of self-worth. Thus, in his excerpt from James Mill's political economy (written at the same time as the Paris manuscripts),[3] Marx speaks of the 'double affirmation' – vis-à-vis both oneself and the other – that one experiences through labour: in the mirror of the object produced, one can not only experience oneself as an individual possessed of particular abilities but also understand oneself to be a person capable of providing for the needs of a concrete partner in interaction.[4] From this perspective, Marx views capitalism – that is, a single class's control of the means of production – as a social order that inevitably destroys the interpersonal relations of recognition mediated by labour. For, in being cut off from the means of production, workers also have the possibility for independently controlling their activity torn away from them, control that represents a social precondition for their being able to recognize each other as cooperative partners within a context of community life. But if the capitalist organization of society results in the destruction of labour-mediated relationships of recognition, then the historical conflict this generates has to be understood as a struggle for recognition. Thus, in line with the lordship and bondage dialectic of the *Phenomenology*, the early Marx can interpret the social confrontations of his time as a moral struggle waged by oppressed workers for the restitution of social opportunities for full recognition. Initially, he conceives of class struggle not as a strategic battle over the acquisition of material goods or instruments of power but rather as a moral conflict in which what is at issue is the 'emancipation' of labour as the crucial condition for both symmetrical esteem and basic self-confidence. Admittedly, this interpretation involved a series of speculative assumptions about the philosophy of history, as Marx soon acknowledged, at least to the extent that he retained only a weakened form of them in the further course of his scientific analysis of capitalism.

The young Marx was able to connect up with the recognition-based model of conflict found in Hegel's *Phenomenology* only because, in his anthropological concept of labour, he directly identified the element of personal self-realization with that of intersubjective recognition. His model has to be read as claiming that, in producing, one not only realizes oneself (in gradually objectifying one's individual abilities) but also, at the same time, affectively recognizes all of one's interaction partners, since one anticipates them to be needy co-subjects. But once this unified activity is fragmented by capitalist relations of production, every struggle for self-realization has to be understood as being a contribution to the reinstatement of reciprocal relationships of recognition as well. This is because the recovery of the possibility of autonomous labour would re-establish, in a single stroke, the social conditions under which subjects mutually affirm each other as needy species-beings. The fact that a model of this sort represents a highly problematic confluence of elements from Romanticism's expressionist conception of human nature, Feuerbach's concept of love, and British political economy is something that Marx, for lack of distance, was never really able to recognize. Nonetheless, the untenable premises behind his speculations on the philosophy of history must soon have become sufficiently evident to him that he abandoned them by moving in a new theoretical direction. Even when labour is thought of in terms of an aesthetics of production – as an artistic or craft activity – it is impossible to conceptualize labour simply as a process of the objectification of essential 'inner' energies;[5] nor is it plausible to conceive of labour, in and of itself, as the complete realization of relationships of intersubjective recognition. The objectification model creates the mistaken impression of individual traits and abilities being something always already fully present in the mind, which can then be subsequently expressed only in the act of production. And although the idea that, in working with objects, other subjects must remain present as possible consumers – indeed, that they are recognized as needy beings – does bring to light an intersubjective level of all creative work, it reduces the possible relationships of recognition between people to the satisfaction of material needs. In his early writings, then, Marx narrows Hegel's model of the 'struggle for recognition' in the direction of an aesthetics of production. As a result, however, all aspects of intersubjective recognition that do not stem directly from the process of cooperative, self-managed labour get excluded from the moral spectrum of the social struggles occurring in Marx's day. And, in this way, Marx secretly tied them to the goal of self-realization through production. Of course, with its intentional overstatement, his concept of 'alienated labour' (laden, as it was, with presuppositions taken from the philosophy of history) did focus attention on the phenomena of degradation resulting from the capitalist organization of labour.[6] Indeed, in so doing, he opened up, for the first time, the very possibility of conceptualizing social labour itself as a medium of recognition and, accordingly, as an arena of possible disrespect. At the same time, because his model of conflict is so one-sidedly committed to an aesthetics of production, Marx was prevented from locating the alienation of labour within the fabric of relationships of intersubjective recognition in a way that could reveal its moral importance for the social struggles of his time.

Marx was able to free himself from this one-sided model of conflict only after he had rid the 'anthropological' concept of labour found in his early work of its excessive claims regarding the philosophy of history to such an extent that he could make it the categorial foundation for his critique of political economy.[7] At this point, however, the restriction of the moral theory in terms of which he had always perceived the social struggles of his time became the gateway for utilitarian themes.[8] For the purposes of the analysis of capital, Marx retained his earlier idea that labour represents not only the societal creation of value but also the externalization of essential human energies. For, by itself, the conception of human labour activity as both a factor of production and an act of expression made it possible for him to view capitalist society as both a socio-economic formation and a particular relationship of human self-reification. In the meantime, however, what Marx gave up along the path to the analysis of capitalism is the Feuerbachian idea that every act of unalienated labour had to be interpreted as a kind of loving affirmation of the neediness of all other members of the species. In so doing, however, Marx gave up the resource that had previously allowed him to connect up, in terms of the philosophy of history, with Hegel's model of the struggle for recognition: if individual self-realization through labour no longer automatically entails a recognizing reference to other subjects, then interpreting the struggle of workers as a struggle over the social conditions for recognition is no longer a matter of course. This put him in an awkward situation, since, in giving up this assumption, he also lost the key for interpreting class struggle in terms of the philosophy of history. To extricate himself from this situation, he appropriated a utilitarian model of social conflict: in his analysis of capitalism, he let the laws of motion of the conflict between different classes be fixed – in accordance with his new set of basic concepts – by the antagonism between economic interests. For Marx, class struggle now no longer represents a struggle for recognition (as Hegel interpreted it) but is conceptualized along the lines of the traditional model of a struggle for (economic) self-assertion. The theoretical position occupied by a moral conflict resulting from the destruction of conditions for mutual recognition is suddenly taken by structurally conditioned competition over interests.

Marx could clearly adopt this new model of conflict all the more easily because he had already indirectly prepared the way by narrowing the moral theory of the initial interpretive approach. For, in retrospect, by reducing the goals of class struggle to only those demands that are directly connected to the organization of social labour, he made it easy to abstract from all the political concerns stemming from the violation of moral claims as such. Marx's early works already contain, in germ, the possibility of a transition to a utilitarian model of struggle, since they restrict the spectrum of demands for recognition down to one dimension, which – following the discontinuation of the additional interpretation in terms of philosophical anthropology – could easily be made into a merely economic interest. For this reason, in his critique of political economy – to the extent that Marx discusses the social struggle of workers at all as part of his immanent analysis of the growing autonomy of capital – he generally attributes only those aspirations to it that stem from the 'objective' interests of the proletariat. By contrast, the idea that there is a connection between one's position in the production process and one's moral experiences resulting from disappointed identity-claims is nowhere to be found. This is not significantly altered even by those passages in *Capital* in which Marx refers to social confrontations that seem to follow the pattern of a collective struggle for the extension of legal claims.[9] For his highly ambivalent relation to the achievements of modern legal universalism prevented Marx from seeing in such conflicts the entirely benign evidence of a battle that workers must wage against the legal neglect of their class-specific concerns. Marx was much too convinced of the idea that the bourgeois ideas of freedom and equality serve the capitalist economy's need for legitimation to be able to treat the legal aspects of the struggle for recognition as something unambiguously positive.[10]

One does, however, find a genuine alternative to these utilitarian tendencies in those parts of Marx's mature work devoted not to the development of economic theory but to historical and political analysis. Here, he is guided by a model of social conflict that contrasts with the model found in the writings on the theory of capital to the extent that it takes into account, in an almost Herderian sense, the culturally inherited forms of life of various social groups.[11] Initially, this broadening of Marx's perspective is simply a result of his methodological intention to provide, in his historical studies, a narrative depiction of the actual course of the processes that he had studied in his economic analyses under the sole and, to a certain extent, functionalist standpoint of the establishment of capitalist relations. Hence, Marx's account now has to take into consideration all the aspects of social reality that influence how, in actual conflicts, the estranged groups experience their situation and, accordingly, act politically. But, for Marx, this incorporation of class-specific everyday culture necessarily alters the model in terms of which behaviour in political conflict is itself to be explained: if it is the case that culturally inherited lifestyles are what shape the way in which social circumstances and privations are experienced, then the question of which objectives the various groups in a political confrontation are pursuing can no longer be decided on the basis of a pure weighing of interests. Thus Marx had to take his explanatory approach in a different direction, so that conflict would come to be seen as depending on the values reflected in each of the culturally inherited forms of life: in these social struggles, groups or classes confront each other in an attempt to defend and establish the values that guarantee their identities. This is why the model of conflict underlying Marx's 'Eighteenth Brumaire' and 'Civil War in France' is best termed 'expressivist'.[12]

This concept is not meant to refer only to the fact that the behaviour of participants in conflict is to be understood as an expressive phenomenon, that is, on the model of an expressive action in which feelings and attitudes are made known. That, of course, is the primary reason why Marx incorporates within his investigations empirical information about the religious traditions and everyday lifestyles of the different groups, since these facts provide the best resource for identifying collective values. In addition, however, 'expressivist' is also meant to characterize the tendency in these writings to present the course of social confrontations themselves in terms of the literary genre of a drama, by portraying the clashing class fractions as actors in a fight in which their very existence is at stake.[13] In his political-historical studies, Marx explicates class struggle – in clear contrast to his writings on the theory of capitalism – according to the model of an ethical diremption [*ethische Entzweiung*]. In the social events that he so dramatically recounts, the collective actors opposing each other are oriented towards divergent values, owing to their positions within society. In taking this approach, Marx again – against his utilitarian inclinations – moved closer to Hegel's model of a 'struggle for recognition'. At the same time, he committed himself no further on the issue of whether the struggles he portrayed actually entail moral demands that are linked to the structure of relationships of recognition. In this context, the term 'expressivist' has, instead, yet a third meaning: it emphasizes the tendency in Marx's historical works to conceive of class struggle merely as a confrontation over collective forms of self-realization. But, on this view, the conflicts depicted would not actually represent moral phenomena that admit of the possibility of a social resolution but rather historical excerpts from an eternal struggle between inherently incompatible values.

Marx himself was nowhere able to connect systematically the utilitarian approach of the economic writings and the expressivist approach of the historical studies, so as to keep these two models of conflict from clashing in his mature work. The principle of economically determined, interest-based conflict stands, unmediated, alongside the relativistic explanation of all conflicts in terms of incompatible aspirations for self-realization. But Marx was never able to comprehend in systematic terms the struggle of social classes – which does, after all, constitute a core component of his own theory – as a form of morally motivated conflict over the expansion of (analytically distinct) recognition relations. For this reason, it was never really possible for him to anchor the normative aspirations of his own project within the same social process that consistently held his attention under the heading of 'class struggle'.

It is against these utilitarian tendencies – which, owing to Marx's privileging of the model of interest-oriented agents, quickly spread through the tradition of historical materialism – that George Sorel battled in all his writings. His theoretical oeuvre represents one of the most original and yet, politically, most ambivalent products of the history of Marxism. By temperament easily enthused, Sorel does not shy away either from switching political fronts frequently or from appropriating the most diverse currents of thought in a manner that clearly transcends the bounds of eclecticism. In the course of his practical engagement, he sympathized with the monarchist Right no less than with Russian Bolsheviks, and his work on a new version of Marxism was inspired by Vico as well as Bergson, by Durkheim as much as by the American pragmatists.[14] But, from the start, the basic theoretical conviction that runs like a thread through his life-work and explains, in retrospect, the abrupt transitions is the intention of overcoming utilitarianism as the system of thought that allows Marxism to misidentify, with enormous consequences, its own ethical goals:[15] for Sorel, the notion that human action would reduce to the purposive-rational pursuit of interests is a fundamental barrier to discovering the moral drives that actually guide people in their creative accomplishments. Along the path set out for his theoretical work by this starting position, Sorel was destined to arrive at a moral conception of social struggle that would overlap with the young Hegel's model of conflict at not a few points.

The foundation of Sorel's theory is found in a concept of social action that is oriented towards the creative generation of the new, instead of the purposive-rational pursuit of interests. But already in his discussion of Vico's work, from which he gained his first insights into the social role of human creativity, this starting-point in utilitarianism is further modified in terms of moral theory. The creatively generated idea-complexes that constitute the cultural horizon of a historical epoch are primarily composed of the ideas that establish what is to count as ethically good and humane. The next step, in which Sorel attempts to make this conceptual framework more precise, also owes a great deal to an interpretation of Vico's views: because there is no agreement on the criteria according to which notions of the ethically good are measured, the historical process in which new ideas are creatively produced takes the form of a struggle between classes. Social classes are constantly trying to formulate their own norms and their notions of honour in more universal terms, so as to demonstrate the appropriateness of these ideas for the organization of society as a whole. But since a socially encompassing means of expression for particularistic conceptions of morality is to be found only in the medium of rights, class struggle inevitably takes the form of legal confrontations:

> History is made in the struggles of groups. But Vico realized that these
> struggles are not all of the same sort, something that contemporary

Marxists often forget. There are conflicts that serve to seize political power ... and there are others over the acquisition of rights. The latter struggles may be considered only when one is speaking of class struggle in Marx's sense. In order to avoid misunderstandings, it would perhaps be good to label this 'class struggle over rights', in order to indicate that they have, as their principle, the existence of conflict between juridical conceptions.[16]

Of course, this principle also does not yet reveal, in any detail, how to view the social opposition between legal norms and class-specific morality, which is supposed to give rise to the 'ethical nature of the class struggle'.[17] Essentially, up to now, all that has been shown is that social groups must always translate their ideas about what is ethically good into legal concepts before they are able to introduce them into the field of societal confrontations. What impelled Sorel to illuminate the relationship between law and morality further was his encounter with 'ethical socialism', as a current of thought that is primarily concerned with the foundations of Marxism in moral theory. Sorel did not, admittedly, appropriate this new approach – which attempts to ground the claims of Marxian theory rigorously in Kantian ethics – as such but rather gave it an original and, as it were, Hegelianized reinterpretation, which ultimately led to an empirical hypothesis about the character of our everyday moral conceptions. At this point, Sorel traced the ethical norms repeatedly introduced into legal confrontations by oppressed classes back to affective experiences within the specific sphere of social life that the young Hegel had summarized under the category of 'natural ethical life': in the family, every human individual acquires, via the practice of 'reciprocal devotion and respect',[18] a moral sensorium that constitutes the core of all his or her later ideas about what is ethically good. These mature moral conceptions represent, therefore, nothing but the socially generalized version of values that the individual was able, as a child, to acquire through experience, values regarding what constitutes the conditions for an 'honourable life'.[19] But these affectively anchored standards and norms do not provide 'any means of constructing a new juridical system', even if they have become an established component of collective notions about morality, since, as Sorel concisely puts it, they can contain only 'negations'.[20] What is meant here is that only negative emotional reactions reveal to individuals or social groups their conception of the ethical good. For Sorel, morality represents the sum total of all the feelings of hurt and violation with which we react every time we confront something that we consider to be morally indefensible. In this sense, the distinction between morality and law is to be measured in terms of the fundamental difference between negative emotional reactions and positively established norms.

In light of this, the picture of inter-class conflicts over rights that Sorel has been developing undergoes a significant extension. He now sees the motivational force perpetuating the moral struggle of oppressed classes to be the collective feelings of having been treated with injustice or disdain. The ethical demands acquired by that social group through familial devotion take the form of social feelings of having been unjustly treated and flow into the social life-process in such a way that they necessarily lead to a confrontation with the dominant, legally established system of norms. To express this idea, Sorel makes use of a conceptual distinction between 'historical' (established) and 'human' (moral) mandates:

> Then the historical mandate, the basis of all social organization, enters into conflict with the human claim, which morality teaches us to consider. This opposition can long rest without effect, but there are always cases when the pleas of the oppressed individual seem more sacred to us than traditions, the necessities of order, the principles on which society rests.[21]

What this line of thought also reveals, however, is that Sorel bases his normative model of class struggle on a relativistically foreshortened concept of law. For him, the legal order of a society is just the expression of the positive norms into which the class that has attained political power has been able to transform its own previous feelings of having been socially disrespected. Hence, conversely, every oppressed class that tries to fight the selective legal system of the ruling social order also must creatively transform its (initially only negative) conceptions of morality into positive legal norms before it can compete for political power. Hence, the legal order of every state represents merely the embodiment of the particularistic feelings of having been unjustly treated possessed by every social class that, for morally contingent reasons, is in power at any given moment. By thus conceiving of 'law' exclusively in terms of techniques of power, Sorel makes himself hopelessly blind to the universalistic potential of legal recognition, and his final modification of the basic theoretical model does nothing to change this. Having come under the strong influence of Bergson,[22] he developed a concept of social myth, on the basis of Bergson's vitalism [*Lebensphilosophie*], that is supposed to reveal the cognitive constitution of the process by which new legal ideas are collectively produced: because, as primarily affective beings, humans have intuitive access to vivid images more easily than to rational argumentation, what best enables oppressed classes' 'ardent sentiment of indignation'[23] to be transformed into positive legal principles are social myths in which an indeterminate future is given a vivid depiction.

The doctrine of social myth merely put the seal on the tendency that eventually came to dominate Sorel's attempt to transform Marxism in terms of moral theory. Although he, like no other, equipped the interpretive framework provided by the idea of a struggle for recognition with the empirical material of moral feelings, he steered this approach back onto the tracks of the Machiavellian tradition. Since, in principle, every group-specific claim to an 'honourable life' is backed by the same interest in legal recognition, any legal system can lay claim to the same validity, as long as it is based on political power. This relativistic consequence is due to a tacit elision of the distinction between two forms of recognition, which Hegel and Mead had each held neatly apart: for if the need for collective self-respect, on which Sorel largely focused, is suddenly conceived as a demand that can be completely met within the legal form of recognition, then its pressure towards formal universalization necessarily has to be forced out of the picture. With regard to group-specific feelings of having been unjustly treated, which his entire theory is tailored to analysing, Sorel does not distinguish sufficiently between disrespect for values and the violation of expectations associated with autonomy. This is why he does not view law as a medium in which subjects' universalizable claims to autonomy are recognized, but rather as a means for expressing conceptions of a virtuous life, conceptions that serve particularistic needs. As a result, he lacks a normative criterion for distinguishing between morally justified and unjustified legal systems, so that, in the end, the inner constitution of a legal system is simply left to political power-struggles. The theoretical decisiveness with which Sorel reduced the struggle for recognition down to that one dimension of self-realization could not but have fatal consequences for his political orientations. Because he never managed to separate the moral achievements of the bourgeois state from its class-specific implementation, he was always on the side that – independent of any other political or normative differences – had set about radically destroying it.[24] This is even true of those indirect students of Sorel's who, like Hendrik de Man, were inspired by his writings, at least to the extent of analysing the social resistance of the working class along lines of injured feelings of honour instead of economic interests. In de Man as well, the peculiar inability to perceive the universalistic content of the sphere of modern law eventually led him to sympathize with populist currents of the political right.[25]

Sorel's work is something that Sartre – the third representative of the intellectual movement that interests us here – referred to with only the greatest disdain.[26] Nevertheless, in his later writings, he shared with Sorel the theoretical view that social conflicts are to be understood, above all, as disruptions in relationships of recognition between collective actors. First, of course, Sartre had to wrest this interpretive model – which is primarily a component of his analyses of politics and events of the day – away from his existentialist beginnings through continual revision. For, in his main early work (that is, in *Being and Nothingness*), he was so strongly convinced of the intrinsic impossibility of successful interaction between people that he could not take into account the vantage-point of social communication that was only partially distorted.

Sartre's initial theory of intersubjectivity, in which the 'struggle for recognition' finds itself eternalized as an existential fact of human *Dasein*, resulted from applying the ontological dualism of 'being-for-itself' and 'being-in-itself' to the transcendental philosophical problem of the existence of the other. Because, as a being-for-itself, every human subject lives in a state of permanent transcendence of current plans for action, one must experience the gaze of the other – the only way by which one can reach self-consciousness at all – as objectivating, in that it defines one in terms of only one of the ways in which one could possibly exist. Hence, the only way to avoid the danger of an objectivation of this sort (which is signalled by negative emotions) is to invert the direction of the gaze-relationship and to define the other in terms of one single life-project. These dynamics of reciprocal reification introduce an element of conflict into all forms of social interaction, so that the prospect of a state of interpersonal reconciliation is, as it were, ontologically excluded.[27]

Soon, however, in his writings in political philosophy, Sartre allowed this negativistic theory of intersubjectivity, the conceptual weaknesses of which have since been illuminated from a number of sides,[28] to recede quietly behind a more strongly historicizing approach. In the short study *Anti-Semite and Jew*, which marks a clear point of theoretical reorientation, Sartre views anti-Semitism as a form of social disrespect whose causes are to be found in the historical dimension of class-specific experiences of the petty bourgeoisie. And, accordingly, he examines Jews' social norms of conduct as expressions of a desperate attempt to maintain a kind of collective self-respect under conditions of denied recognition.[29] This change in the subject-matter of Sartre's phenomenological analysis also clandestinely altered the logic that was supposed to determine interactive relationships between people. Because the position previously occupied by existential experiences of individual subjects came to be taken by historical experiences of social collectives, the possibility of modification came into view. The conceptual model thus outlined indicates the path that Sartre then took in a series of further studies on the political situation of his time. The struggle for recognition no longer represented an inescapable and unfathomable structural feature of human existence. Rather, it came to be interpreted as a phenomenon that is caused by an asymmetrical relationship between social groups and is, in principle, open to being overcome. This historically relativized model of conflict came to dominate the essays Sartre composed on the anti-colonialist movement of *négritude* in particular.[30] There, colonialism is understood as a social situation that distorts intersubjective relationships of reciprocal recognition in such a way that the participant groups are pressed into a quasi-neurotic scheme of behaviour. The only way that the colonizers can work through the self-contempt that they feel for themselves as a result of systematically denigrating the native people is through cynicism or heightened aggression, and the only way the colonized are able to endure the 'common degradation' is by splitting their conduct into the two parts of ritual transgression and habitual over-accommodation.[31]

Although Sartre's points may seem overdone or even crude, compared with studies in social psychology, they are based on a communications-theoretic interpretation that is quite interesting for empirical purposes: for Sartre, the asymmetrical patterns of communication between the settler and the native that are found in the colonial system represent interactive relations that demand from both sides the simultaneous denial and maintenance of relationships of mutual recognition. For, in order for interaction to be possible at all, the colonial master has to both recognize and disrespect the native as a human person in just the way that the latter is forced into 'laying claims to and denying the human condition at the same time'.[32] As a label for the type of social relationship that must result from this reciprocal denial of claims to recognition (that are nevertheless raised), Sartre introduced the concept of 'neurosis' at this point, even though he will provide the systematic foundation for this concept only later, in the ambitious study of Flaubert: here, as there, 'neurotic' is meant to designate not an individual behavioural disorder with a psychological aetiology but rather a pathological distortion of relations of interaction stemming from the reciprocal denial of relationships of recognition that are still effective below the surface.[33]

Admittedly, it is precisely the essays on colonialism that make

especially clear the extent to which Sartre was still in the dark as to
what is actually supposed to make human beings worthy of recognition. On the one hand, he selected, as the criterion for the disrespect
done to native peoples within the colonial system, the intentional denial
of 'human rights'. But, normatively speaking, such a definition presupposes a form of universalism with regard to human rights, something that he asserted, at another point, to be 'nothing but an ideology
of lies, a perfect justification for pillage'.[34] Hence, in the same context,
one finds the view that the native peoples within the colonial system
remain without social recognition for their 'status as a human being'
because, structurally, their specific ways of life and forms of self-
realization are not tolerated. On their own, both accounts are meaningful, as long as they are neatly separated. In Sartre's hands, however,
they come to be confounded – within one and the same text – to such
an extent that each of them loses its normative significance.

This conceptual imprecision betrays the fact that the development
of Sartre's philosophical theory was never quite able to keep up with
the development of his political analyses. For, despite several attempts,
he was never able to provide a systematic justification for the normative presuppositions that had to be employed in viewing conflicts
from the moral standpoint that is based on the reciprocity of relationships of recognition.[35] In the philosophical writings of the late Sartre,
one finds a normative conception of mutual recognition frequently
hinted at but never developed to the level of explication that would
have been required for its precise use in analysing events of the day.
Hence, in his political writings, Sartre ultimately succumbed to the same
conceptual confusion which so shaped Sorel's political theory. Because
Sartre, too, failed to draw an analytically clear line between law-based
and law-transcending forms of mutual recognition, he could not avoid
confounding the pursuit of self-realization and the pursuit of an expansion of rights, just as Sorel had done. Like Sorel, Sartre was thus
unable to give the formalism of bourgeois law the moral significance
that it is revealed to have once one distinguishes, following Hegel and
Mead, the three different levels of the 'struggle for recognition'.

The current of thought represented by the examples of Marx, Sorel,
and Sartre was certainly able to extend and enrich the model of a
struggle for recognition with which Hegel, in the Jena writings, had
boldly opposed modern social philosophy. Marx succeeded, thanks to
the overall outline of his basic concepts, in showing labour to be a
central medium of mutual recognition, even though he did so in the
exaggerated terms of a philosophy of history. Sorel was able to reveal,
as the affective side of struggle on which Hegel had focused, many of

the collective feelings of being disrespected that are rarely considered by academic theories; and Sartre, finally, used the concept of 'objective neurosis' to lay the groundwork for a perspective from which it appears possible to understand social structures of domination in general as a pathology of recognition relations. But none of the three authors was able to contribute to the further systematic development of the conception founded by Hegel and deepened by Mead. Although, in empirical contexts, they often made virtuoso use of the model of recognition, its normative implication remained too opaque, too alien even, for them to be able to move it to a new level of explication.

Disrespect and *Resistance:* The *Moral Logic of* *Social Conflicts*

At a pretheoretical level, Marx, Sorel, and Sartre – the three repre-
sentatives of the tradition brought to light above – could always count
on the fact that the self-understanding of the social movements of
their day was shot through with the semantic potential of a vocabu-
lary of recognition. For Marx, who followed the working class's attempts at organizing from the closest distance, it was beyond doubt
that the overarching aspirations of the emerging movement could be
brought together under the concept of 'dignity'. Sorel, a theoretical fore-
runner of French syndicalism, employed the conservative-sounding
category of 'honour' to express the moral content of the political demands of the workers' movement. And the Sartre of the fifties encoun-
tered in Frantz Fanon's famous book an anti-colonialist manifesto that
attempted to explicate the experience of oppressed Black Africa by
drawing directly on Hegel's doctrine of recognition.[1] However much
the idea of tracing social conflicts to the violation of implicit rules of
mutual recognition may have been an essential element of the everyday political observations of these three theorists, this experience was
hardly reflected in the conceptual framework of the emerging social
sciences: in the contexts in which the category of social struggle plays
any constitutive role at all in revealing social reality, it quickly came
to be defined, under the influence of Darwinian or utilitarian models,
in terms of competition over material opportunities.

   Although Emile Durkheim and Ferdinand Tönnies both approached
the development of empirical sociology with the intention of critically
diagnosing the moral crises of modern societies, neither of them give
the phenomenon of social confrontation a systematic role in their basic
concepts. However many insights they may have had into the moral

preconditions for social integration, they drew few theoretical conclusions from this for the category of social conflict. Max Weber, on the other hand, who sees the process of socialization as virtually geared towards a conflict of social groups, excludes every aspect of moral motivation from his conceptual definition of 'struggle'. According to the famous formulations of his 'Basic Sociological Concepts', an action context involves a social relationship of struggle 'insofar as the action is oriented intentionally to carrying out the actor's own will against the resistance of the other party or parties' in order to increase the actor's power or chance of survival.[2] And Georg Simmel, finally, who devotes a famous chapter of his *Sociology* to the socializing function of conflict, systematically considers a form of social 'sensitivity to difference' (along with 'hostility') as a source of conflict, but he does so little to trace this dimension of personal or collective identity back to intersubjective preconditions associated with recognition that it is impossible for moral experiences of disrespect to come into view as the occasions for social conflicts.[3] Once again, as in so many respects, the sociological work of the pragmatist 'Chicago School' constitutes a notable exception.[4] In the textbook edited by Robert Park and Ernest Burgess under the title *Introduction to the Science of Sociology*, the discussion of 'conflict' refers to a 'struggle for recognition'[5] with regard to the particular case of confrontations between nationalities or ethnic groups. Nevertheless, aside from the mere mention of 'honor, glory, and prestige', this discussion also does not have much to say about how the moral logic of social struggles is to be appropriately defined.

Thus, within academic sociology, the internal connection that often holds between the emergence of social movements and the moral experience of disrespect has, to a large extent, been theoretically severed at the start. The motives for rebellion, protest, and resistance have generally been transformed into categories of 'interest', and these interests are supposed to emerge from the objective inequalities in the distribution of material opportunities without ever being linked, in any way, to the everyday web of moral feelings. Relative to the predominance that the Hobbesian conceptual model acquired within modern social theory, the incomplete, even misguided, proposals of Marx, Sorel, and Sartre have remained mere fragments of an invisible, undeveloped theoretical tradition. Today, anyone who tries to reconnect with this disrupted effective history of Hegel's counter-model, in order to acquire the foundations for a normatively substantive social theory, will have to rely primarily on a concept of social struggle that takes as its starting-point moral feelings of indignation, rather than pre-given interests. In what follows, I want to reconstruct the essential features of an alternative – Hegelian and Meadian – paradigm of this sort, up to the point at which it begins to become apparent that recent trends within historiography can support the asserted connection between moral disrespect and social struggle.

Even just our effort to develop an empirically grounded phenomenology of forms of recognition made clear that none of the three fields of experience can be adequately described without reference to an inherent conflict: the experience of a particular form of recognition was shown to be bound up with the disclosing of new possibilities with regard to identity, which necessarily result in a struggle for the social recognition of those new forms of identity. Of course, the three spheres of recognition do not all contain the type of moral tension that can set social conflicts in motion, for a struggle can only be characterized as 'social' to the extent that its goals can be generalized beyond the horizon of individuals' intentions, to the point where they can become the basis for a collective movement. With regard to the distinctions made above, the initial implication of this is that love, as the most basic form of recognition, does not entail moral experiences that could lead, of their own accord, to the formation of social conflicts. Every love relationship does, to be sure, involve an existential dimension of struggle, insofar as the intersubjective balance between fusion and ego-demarcation can only be maintained through the overcoming of resistance on both sides. But the goals and desires connected with this cannot be generalized beyond the circle of primary relationships, at least not in a way that would make them matters of public concern. The forms of recognition associated with rights and social esteem, by contrast, do represent a moral context for societal conflict, if only because they rely on socially generalized criteria in order to function. In light of norms of the sort constituted by the principle of moral responsibility or the values of society, personal experiences of disrespect can be interpreted and represented as something that can potentially affect other subjects. Whereas here, in the case of legal relations and communities of value, individual goals are, in principle, open to social universalization, in love relationships they are necessarily enclosed within the narrow boundaries of a primary relationship. This categorial restriction already gives us an initial, rough idea of how a social struggle must be understood within the context of our discussion. We are dealing here with a practical process in which individual experiences of disrespect are read as typical for an entire group, and in such a way that they can motivate collective demands for expanded relations of recognition.

What is striking about this provisional definition, to begin with, is the purely negative fact that it is neutral with regard to the usual distinctions within the sociology of conflict.[6] If one interprets social struggle from the perspective of moral experiences in the manner mentioned, there is no theoretical pre-commitment in favour of either non-violent or violent resistance. Instead, at the level of description, it is left entirely open whether social groups employ material, symbolic, or passive force to publicly articulate and demand restitution for the disrespect and violation that they experience as being typical. The suggested conception is also neutral with respect to the traditional distinction between intentional and unintentional forms of social conflict, since it asserts nothing about the degree to which actors have to be aware of the driving moral motivation of their action. Here, one can easily imagine cases in which social movements intersubjectively misidentify, as it were, the moral core of their resistance by explicating it in the inappropriate terms of mere interest-categories. Finally, the idea that personal and impersonal goals represent exclusive alternatives does not entirely apply to a struggle understood in this way, since the struggle can, in principle, only be determined by those *universal* ideas and appeals in which individual actors see their particular experiences of disrespect eliminated in a positive manner. There must be a semantic bridge between the impersonal aspirations of a social movement and their participants' private experiences of injury, a bridge that is sturdy enough to enable the development of collective identity.

The descriptive openness that thus characterizes the suggested concept of social struggle stands in contrast to the fixed core of its explanatory content. Unlike all utilitarian models of explanation, it suggests the view that motives for social resistance and rebellion are formed in the context of moral experiences stemming from the violation of deeply rooted expectations regarding recognition. These expectations are internally linked to conditions for the formation of personal identity in that they indicate the social patterns of recognition that allow subjects to know themselves to be both autonomous and individuated beings within their socio-cultural environment. If these normative expectations are disappointed by society, this generates precisely the type of moral experience expressed in cases where subjects feel disrespected. Hurt feelings of this sort can, however, become the motivational basis for collective resistance only if subjects are able to articulate them within an intersubjective framework of interpretation that they can show to be typical for an entire group. In this sense, the emergence of social movements hinges on the existence of a shared semantics that enables personal experiences of disappointment to be interpreted as something affecting not just the individual himself or herself but also a circle of many other subjects. As Mead saw, the need for such semantics is met by the moral doctrines or ideas that are able normatively to enrich our notions of social community. Along with the prospect of broadened recognition relations, these languages open up an interpretive perspective for identifying the social causes of individual injuries. Thus, as soon as ideas of this sort have gained influence within a society, they generate a subcultural horizon of interpretation within which experiences of disrespect that, previously, had been fragmented and had been coped with privately can then become the moral motives for a collective 'struggle for recognition'.

When we try to grasp, in this way, the process by which social struggles emerge, they turn out to involve the experience of recognition in more than just the regard mentioned. The collective resistance stemming from the socially critical interpretation of commonly shared feelings of being disrespected is not solely a practical instrument with which to assert a claim to the future expansion of patterns of recognition. For the victims of disrespect – as has been shown in philosophical discussions, in literature, and in social history[7] – engaging in political action also has the direct function of tearing them out of the crippling situation of passively endured humiliation and helping them, in turn, on their way to a new, positive relation-to-self. The basis for this secondary motivation for struggle is connected to the structure of the experience of disrespect itself. As we have seen, social shame is a moral emotion that expresses the diminished self-respect typically accompanying the passive endurance of humiliation and degradation. If such inhibitions on action are overcome through involvement in collective resistance, individuals uncover a form of expression with which they can indirectly convince themselves of their moral or social worth. For, given the anticipation that a future communication-community will recognize them for their present abilities, they find themselves socially respected as the persons that they cannot, under present circumstances, be recognized for being. In this sense, because engaging in political struggle publicly demonstrates the ability that was hurtfully disrespected, this participation restores a bit of the individual's lost self-respect. This may, of course, be further strengthened by the recognition that the solidarity within the political groups offers by enabling participants to esteem each other.

The foregoing may seem to suggest that all social confrontations and forms of conflict follow the same pattern of a struggle for recognition. On this view, the emergence of every collective act of resistance and rebellion would be traceable to an invariant framework of moral experiences, within which social reality would be interpreted in terms of a historically changing grammar of recognition and disrespect. A thesis of this sort would lead, however, to the fatal consequence of requiring one to dispute, from the outset, the possibility of social struggles that obey a logic of the more-or-less conscious pursuit of collective interests. That this is not the case – that is, that not all forms of resistance have their roots in injury to moral claims – is clearly shown by the many historical cases in which it was purely the securing of economic survival that motivated massive protest and revolt. Interests are basic goal-directed orientations that accompany the economic and social circumstances of individuals, if only because individuals must try to obtain the conditions for their own reproduction. Such interests become collective attitudes to the extent to which various subjects become aware of the commonality of their social situation and, because of this, come to see themselves as confronting similar tasks of reproduction. Feelings of having been disrespected, on the other hand, form the core of moral experiences that are part of the structure of social interaction because human subjects encounter one another with expectations for recognition, expectations on which their psychological integrity turns. Feelings of having been unjustly treated can lead to collective actions to the extent to which they come to be experienced by an entire circle of subjects as typical for their social situation. The models of conflict that start from collective interests are those that trace the development and course of social struggles back to attempts on the part of social groups to obtain or enlarge control over certain opportunities for their reproduction. This same line is also taken by all those approaches that want to broaden the spectrum of these interest-guided struggles by including cultural and symbolic goods within the definition of group-specific opportunities for reproduction.[8] By contrast, the models of conflict that start from collective feelings of having been unjustly treated are those that trace the emergence and the course of social struggles back to moral experiences of social groups who face having legal or social recognition withheld from them. In the first case, we are dealing with the analysis of competition for scarce goods, whereas in the second case, we are dealing with the analysis of a struggle over the intersubjective conditions for personal integrity.

It is important to stress, however, that this second model of conflict, based on a theory of recognition, should not try to replace the first, utilitarian model but only extend it. It will always be an empirical question as to the extent to which a social conflict follows the logic of the pursuit of interests or the logic of the formation of moral reactions.

That notwithstanding, social theory's fixation on the dimension of interests has so thoroughly obscured our view of the societal significance of moral feelings that today recognition-theoretic models of conflict have the duty not only to extend but possibly to correct. The collective interest behind a conflict does not have to be seen as something ultimate or original but may rather have been constituted within a horizon of moral experience that admits of normative claims to recognition and respect. This is the case, for example, wherever the social esteem for a person or group is so obviously correlated to the level of control over certain goods that only the acquisition of those goods can lead to the corresponding recognition. A number of historical studies point in the direction of just such a corrective interpretation of social conflicts by focusing on the everyday moral culture of the lower social classes. The results of these studies can help to lend empirical support to the model of conflict developed here and to defend it against obvious criticisms.

Not least under the influence of utilitarian currents of thought, historical research on political movements was, for a long time, so wedded to the standard model of the collective pursuit of interests that the moral grammar of social struggles had to remain hidden from it. This only changed in a lasting fashion after the methodological intersection of social anthropology and cultural sociology gave rise, two decades ago, to a form of historiography that was able to perceive more broadly and more accurately the normative presuppositions of the way lower social classes engaged in conflict. The advantage of this approach over conventional historiography lies in its heightened attention to the horizon of moral norms of action that are subtly involved in everyday life. Aided by the tools of anthropological field research, it became possible for historical studies to reveal the implicit rules of the normative consensus on which the political reactions of various subcultures depend. The impetus for this sort of reorientation, by which the utilitarian presuppositions of the earlier tradition could be replaced by normative premises, undoubtedly came from the English historian E. P. Thompson. His investigations of the everyday moral conceptions that motivated the English lower classes to resist the introduction of capitalist industrialization prepared the way for an entire line of research.[9] Thompson took his lead from the idea that social rebellion can never be merely a direct expression of experiences of economic hardship and deprivation. Rather, what counts as an unbearable level of economic provision is to be measured in terms of the moral expectations that people consensually bring to the organization of the community. Hence, practical protest and resistance typically arise when a change in the economic situation is experienced as a violation of this tacit but effective consensus. In this sense, the investigation of social struggles presupposes an analysis of the moral consensus that un-officially governs, within a context of social cooperation, the distribu-tion of rights and responsibilities between the dominators and the dominated.

To be sure, this shift of perspective was not yet enough to generate the results that, at a historical level, would support the thesis that social confrontations can in principle be understood in terms of the moral pattern of a struggle for recognition. For that, the further point needed to be demonstrated that every violation of an implicit consen-sus among those affected is experienced as something that denies them social recognition and, as a result, injures their feelings of self-worth. The first approach to explicating a motivational nexus of this sort has been developed in historical studies that have taken Thompson's approach and extended it along the dimension of individual or collec-tive identity. Once the component of subjects' practical relation-to-self was taken into account, it quickly became apparent that, for partici-pants, the existing consensus in each historical case amounts to a normative order that organizes relationships of mutual recognition. In this field, pioneering work has been done by Barrington Moore, and it is no coincidence that his concept of an 'implicit social contract' connects up with Thompson's idea of a 'moral economy'. His com-parative studies of revolutionary uprisings in Germany between 1848 and 1920 concluded that the active and militant subgroups within the working class were primarily those that felt their previously recog-nized self-understanding to be massively threatened by socio-political changes.[10] Moore treats the implicit social contract – that is, the nor-mative consensus among the cooperating groups within a community – as a loosely organized system of rules that determine the conditions for mutual recognition. Hence, as soon as an implicit consensus of this sort is disrupted by politically imposed innovations, this leads almost inevitably to social disrespect for the inherited identity of individual subgroups. And, in Moore's view, it is only this jeopardizing of the possibility for collective self-respect that generates broad-based polit-ical resistance and social revolts.

Today, Moore's position is strengthened by historical studies that locate the motivational impetus for political uprisings in the injury inflicted upon group-specific notions of honour. This research – well exemplified by Andreas Griessinger's study of eighteenth-century journeyman artisans[11] – adds the further component of identity to Thompson's approach by systematically connecting the political disappointment of moral expectations with the overthrow of traditionally conceived relations of recognition.

Studies of this sort provide sufficient experiential detail to serve as initial empirical support for the thesis that social confrontations follow the pattern of a struggle for recognition. A serious disadvantage arises, however, from the fact that the role these works ascribe to the internal logic of recognition relations is too limited to admit of anything but a historical account of particular lifeworlds. Whether they are spontaneous revolts, organized strikes, or passive forms of resistance, the events depicted always retain something of the character of mere episodes, because their position within the moral development of society does not, as such, become clear. But this gap between individual processes and an overarching developmental process can only be bridged once the logic according to which recognition relationships are expanded itself becomes the referential system for historical accounts.

Posing the task in this way makes it necessary to conceive of the model of conflict discussed so far no longer solely as an explanatory framework for the emergence of social struggles, but also as an interpretive framework for a process of moral formation. Even just the reference back to the logic of the expansion of recognition relationships allows for the systematic classification of what would otherwise remain an uncomprehended occurrence. Every unique, historical struggle or conflict only reveals its position within the development of society once its role in the establishment of moral progress, in terms of recognition, has been grasped. In addition, of course, the radical broadening of the perspective from which historical processes are to be observed demands a change in our view of the primary research material. The feeling of being unjustly treated and the experience of being disrespected, both of which are relevant for the explanation of social struggles, no longer appear only as motives for action but also come to be examined with regard to the moral role that must be attributed to each of them in the development [*Entfaltung*] of relations of recognition. As a consequence, moral feelings – until now, the emotional raw materials of social conflicts – lose their apparent innocence and turn out to be retarding or accelerating moments within an overarching developmental process. Of course, this last formulation also makes unmistakably clear the challenges facing a theoretical approach that is supposed to be able to model the struggle for recognition as a historical process of moral progress: in order to be able to distinguish between the progressive and the reactionary, there has to be a normative standard that, in light of a hypothetical anticipation of an approximate end-state, would make it possible to mark out a developmental direction.

Hence, the general framework of interpretation on which we must rely describes the process of moral development through which, in the course of an idealized sequence of struggles, the normative potential of mutual recognition has unfolded. A model of this sort finds its point of departure in the theoretical distinctions learned from Hegel and Mead. Taken together, the three forms of recognition – love, rights, and esteem – constitute the social conditions under which human subjects can develop a positive attitude towards themselves. For it is only due to the cumulative acquisition of basic self-confidence, of self-respect, and of self-esteem – provided, one after another, by the experience of those three forms of recognition – that a person can come to see himself or herself, unconditionally, as both an autonomous and an individuated being and to identify with his or her goals and desires. But even this tripartite division owes its existence to a theoretical projection of differentiations that are found only in modern societies back into a hypothetically supposed original situation. For, as we have seen in our analysis, legal relations are unable to dislodge themselves from a customarily ethical framework of social esteem until they have been subjected to the claims of post-conventional morality. Insofar as this is the case, it is natural to assume, as the original situation of the formative process to be described, a form of social interaction in which these three patterns of recognition are still intertwined in an undifferentiated manner. One thing that may speak in favour of this is the existence of an archaic group morality, in which aspects of care are not fully separated from either the rights of tribal members or their social esteem.[12] Thus, the moral learning process that the envisioned interpretive framework is supposed to model has to accomplish two completely different tasks: it must both differentiate the various patterns of recognition and then, within the spheres of interaction thus established, unleash the inherent potential of each. If we distinguish, in this sense, between the establishment of new levels of recognition and the development of their own internal structures, then it is not difficult to see that only the second process directly provides the occasion for social struggles.

Although the differentiation of patterns of recognition stems from social struggles that involve demands for recognition only in the very broad sense of releasing potentials for subjectivity, the result of this process marks the attainment of a socio-cultural level at which each of these structures, with its own internal logic, can become effective. Once love for persons is separated, at least in principle, from legal recognition and social esteem, three forms of mutual recognition have emerged that are geared towards specific developmental potentials as well as distinct types of struggle. At this point, for the first time, we find normative structures built into legal relations (with the possibilities for universalization and de-formalization [*Materialisierung*]) and into communities of value (with the possibilities for individualization and equalization) – normative structures that can become accessible via emotionally laden experiences of disrespect and that can be appealed to in the struggles resulting from these experiences. The breeding-ground for these collective forms of resistance is prepared by sub-cultural semantics in which a shared language is found for feelings of having been unjustly treated, a language that points – however indirectly – to possibilities for expanding relationships of recognition. It is the task of the envisioned interpretive framework to describe the idealized path along which these struggles have been able to unleash the normative potential of modern law and of esteem. This framework lets an objective-intentional context emerge, in which historical processes no longer appear as mere events but rather as stages in a conflictual process of formation, leading to a gradual expansion of relationships of recognition. Accordingly, the significance of each particular struggle is measured in terms of the positive or negative contribution that each has been able to make to the realization of undistorted forms of recognition. To be sure, such a standard cannot be obtained independently of a hypothetical anticipation of a communicative situation in which the intersubjective conditions for personal integrity appear to be fulfilled. Thus, ultimately, Hegel's account of a struggle for recognition can only be brought up to date again (albeit with less ambitious claims) if his conception of ethical life can also – in a modified, desubstantialized form – regain its plausibility.

9

Intersubjective Conditions for Personal Integrity: A Formal Conception of Ethical Life

If the idea of a 'struggle for recognition' is to be viewed as a critical framework for interpreting the processes by which societies develop, there needs to be, by way of completing the model, a theoretical justification for the normative point of view from which these processes can be guided. In order to describe the history of social struggles as moving in a certain direction, one must appeal hypothetically to a provisional end-state, from the perspective of which it would be possible to classify and evaluate particular events. In the case of Hegel as well as of Mead, we found at this point the proposed model of a post-traditional relationship of recognition, a relationship that integrates legal and ethical (if not familial) patterns of mutual recognition into a single framework. For, as it turns out, both thinkers shared the conviction that it is in modern society that subjects are to be recognized as both autonomous and individualized beings. Even just this brief reminder of the earlier discussion is enough to suggest that the end-state to be sketched is not to be grasped in terms of concepts drawn from a narrow understanding of morality. In general, 'morality' is conceived today, within the Kantian tradition, as the point of view that allows all subjects to be accorded the same respect or to have their interests taken into consideration in the same, fair way. But a formulation of this sort is too narrow to include all the aspects that constitute the goal of undistorted and unrestricted recognition. Prior to any substantive explication, therefore, one must first clarify the methodological status of a normative theory that is capable of depicting the hypothetical end-point of an expansion of relations of recognition. One can, it seems to me, speak here of a formal concept of the good life or, indeed, of ethical life [*Sittlichkeit*]. Only once this methodological justification has been completed can one then take the second step and reappropriate the intentions of Hegel and Mead, in order to outline the idea of a post-traditional relationship of recognition. The concept of such a relationship has to contain everything that is intersubjectively presupposed today in order for subjects to know that the conditions for their self-realization are safeguarded.

I

In the tradition going back to Kant, 'morality' is understood, to repeat, as the universalist attitude in which one respects all subjects equally as 'ends in themselves' or as autonomous persons; 'ethical life', on the other hand, refers to the settled *ethos* of a particular lifeworld, and normative judgements are to be made about this *ethos* only to the extent to which it is more or less able to approach the demands of universal moral principles.[1] Today, this devaluation of ethical life is opposed by its revaluation in movements within moral philosophy that return to Hegel or to Classical ethics. Here, the Kantian tradition is criticized for leaving a crucial question unanswered, in that it is unable to locate the purpose of morality as a whole within the concrete goals of human subjects. And it is to this end that critics of Kant advocate again reversing the relation of morality to ethical life, as it were, by making the validity of moral principles dependent on historically variant conceptions of the good life.[2] The line of argument that we have been following in the reconstruction of the model of recognition, however, points to a position that does not seem to fit clearly into either of these two alternatives. Our approach departs from the Kantian tradition in that it is concerned not solely with the moral autonomy of human beings but also with the conditions for their self-realization in general. Hence, morality, understood as the point of view of universal respect, becomes one of several protective measures that serve the general purpose of enabling a good life. But in contrast to those movements that distance themselves from Kant, this concept of the good should not be conceived as the expression of substantive values that constitute the *ethos* of a concrete tradition-based community. Rather, it has to do with the structural elements of ethical life, which, from the general point of view of the communicative enabling of self-realization, can be normatively extracted from the plurality of all particular forms of life. To this extent, insofar as we have developed it as a normative concept, our recognition-theoretic approach stands in the middle between a moral theory going back to Kant, on the one hand, and communitarian ethics, on the other. It shares with the former the interest in the most general norms possible, norms which are understood as conditions for specific possibilities; it shares with the latter, however, the orientation towards human self-realization as an end.[3]

Admittedly, this basic characterization of the position does not yet get us very far, since it remains completely unclear how, in methodological terms, this kind of a formal conception of ethical life is supposed to be possible. The concept of 'ethical life' is now meant to include the entirety of intersubjective conditions that can be shown to serve as necessary preconditions for individual self-realization. But how can one make general assertions about such enabling conditions if every explication of the structure of self-realization runs the risk of becoming an interpretation of particular, historically unique visions of the good life? The desired characterizations must, then, be formal or abstract enough not to raise the suspicion of representing merely the deposits of concrete interpretations of the good life; on the other hand, they must also have sufficient substantive content to be of more help than Kantian references to individual autonomy in discovering the conditions for self-realization. In this connection, a review of the results of our reconstruction of the various forms of recognition provides the key to a further clarification.

Our empirically oriented investigation was able to show in detail what had already begun to emerge in Mead's naturalistic transformation of Hegel's theory of recognition, namely, that the various patterns of recognition distinguished by Hegel could be conceptualized as the intersubjective conditions under which human subjects reach various new ways of relating positively to themselves. The connection between the experience of recognition and one's relation-to-self stems from the intersubjective structure of personal identity. The only way in which individuals are constituted as persons is by learning to refer to themselves, from the perspective of an approving or encouraging other, as beings with certain positive traits and abilities. The scope of such traits – and hence the extent of one's positive relation-to-self – increases with each new form of recognition that individuals are able to apply to themselves as subjects. In this way, the prospect of basic self-confidence is inherent in the experience of love; the prospect of self-respect, in the experience of legal recognition; and finally the prospect of self-esteem, in the experience of solidarity.

This brief review has greater implications for our present purposes than may at first appear. For the fact that the possibility of a positive relation-to-self emerges only with the experience of recognition can be interpreted as pointing to necessary conditions for individual self-realization. As in other contexts, a negative approach provides a preliminary justification: unless one presupposes a certain degree of self-confidence, legally guaranteed autonomy, and sureness as to the value of one's own abilities, it is impossible to imagine successful self-realization, if that is to be understood as a process of realizing, without coercion, one's self-chosen life-goals. With regard to such a process, 'lack of coercion' and 'freedom' cannot be understood simply as the absence of external force or influence, but must rather signify the lack of inner barriers as well as psychological inhibitions and fears.[4] But this second form of freedom is to be understood, to put it positively, as a form of trust directed inward, which gives individuals basic confidence in both the articulation of their needs and the exercise of their abilities. What we have already seen, however, is that this sort of confidence, these unanxious ways of dealing with oneself, constitute aspects of a positive relation-to-self that can only be gained through the experience of recognition. To this extent, the freedom associated with self-realization is dependent on prerequisites that human subjects do not have at their disposal, since they can only acquire this freedom with the help of their interaction partners. The three distinct patterns of recognition then represent intersubjective conditions that we must further presuppose, if we are to describe the general structures of a successful life.

It is not hard to see that the conditions thus outlined satisfy the methodological criteria for a formal conception of ethical life established earlier. On the one hand, the three patterns of recognition – which now can count as just as many preconditions for successful self-realization – are defined in a sufficiently abstract, formal manner to avoid raising the suspicion that they embody particular visions of the good life. On the other hand, from the perspective of their content, the explication of these three conditions is detailed enough to say more about the general structures of a successful life than is entailed by general references to individual self-determination. The forms of recognition associated with love, rights, and solidarity provide the intersubjective protection that safeguards the conditions for external and internal freedom, upon which the process of articulating and realizing individual life-goals without coercion depends. Moreover, since they do not represent established institutional structures but only general patterns of behaviour, they can be distilled, as structural elements, from the concrete totality of all particular forms of life.

A further difficulty for the conception under discussion here stems from the fact that two of the three patterns of recognition have the potential for further normative progress. As we have seen, legal relations as well as communities of value are open to transformative processes that move in the direction of increased universality and equality. This internal potential for development is accompanied by the introduction, as part of the normative conditions for self-realization, of a historical index, and this places limits on what our formal conception of ethical life can claim to accomplish. What can count as an intersubjective prerequisite for a successful life becomes historically variable and is determined by the actual level of development of the patterns of recognition. The formal conception loses its ahistorical character in that, hermeneutically speaking, it winds up dependent on what constitutes, in each case, the inescapable present.

II

A formal conception of ethical life encompasses the qualitative conditions for self-realization that, insofar as they form general prerequisites for the personal integrity of subjects, can be abstracted from the plurality of all particular forms of life. But since, for their part, such conditions are open to possibilities for normative progress, a formal conception of this sort does not escape all historical change but rather, quite the opposite, is tied to the unique initial situation presented by its period of origin. For our purposes, this restriction generates the obligation to introduce the three patterns of recognition historically and to do so in such a way that they can be viewed as elements of ethical life only at the highest level of development of each. The character of intersubjective prerequisites for self-realization becomes visible only under the historical conditions of the present, which in every case has already opened the prospect of further normative development regarding relations of recognition. The idea of post-traditional, democratic ethical life – as it begins to emerge as a consequence of this sort of argument – was first proposed by the young Hegel and further developed, on postmetaphysical premises, by Mead. Despite their many differences, what both had in mind was the same ideal of a society in which the universalistic achievements of equality and individualism would be so embedded in patterns of interaction that all subjects would be recognized as both autonomous and individuated, equal and particular persons. Furthermore, both thinkers conceived these specifically modern patterns of social interaction as forming a network of different relations of recognition, in each of which individuals can know that they are affirmed in a dimension of their self-realization. In this, Hegel and Mead came as close as one can imagine anyone coming to the normative idea that we have tried to outline here with the help of a historically grounded yet formal conception of ethical life. At the same time, an unmediated recourse to one of their models is already ruled out by the fact that, in both cases, the historical prejudices of their times slipped into the models in a problematic way.

In the case of Hegel, this is can already be seen in his treatment of the relationship of recognition that, as a fundamental condition for self-realization, is to represent the intersubjective core of a post-traditional form of ethical life as well. In the discussion of 'love' in his *Philosophy of Right*, Hegel lets himself be influenced so strongly by the institutional arrangements of his day that, ultimately, he has to end up with the patriarchal model of bourgeois family relations.[5] Once this misdirected concretization is removed, an idea remains, which has been developed here using the example of psychoanalytic object-relations theory: in the tense balance between fusion and ego-demarcation, the resolution of which is part of every successful form of primary relationship, subjects mutually experience themselves to be loved in their individuality only insofar as they are not afraid of being alone. This mode of basic self-confidence represents the basic prerequisite for every type of self-realization in the sense that it allows individuals to attain, for the first time, the inner freedom that enables them to articulate their own needs. Accordingly, the experience of love, whatever historical form it takes, represents the innermost core of all forms of life that qualify as 'ethical' [*sittlich*]. Because it does not admit of the potential for normative development, the integration of love into the intersubjective network of a post-traditional form of ethical life does not change its fundamental character. On the other hand, however, it is possible that the development of its invariant basic structures will be all the freer from distortion and coercion, the more rights come to be shared by partners in a friendship or love relationship. In this sense, a formal conception of post-traditional ethical life must be constructed in such a way that it can defend the radical egalitarianism of love against external forces and influences. It is at this point that the explication of the pattern of recognition involved in love touches on that of legal relations, which must be considered the second condition for personal integrity.

It turned out to be impossible to reconstruct the patterns of recognition corresponding to legal relations without referring to the normative development which has governed them since the formation of modern society. It became clear from this that, on its own, legal recognition holds a moral potential, one which can be developed via social struggles in the direction of an increase in both generality and context-sensitivity. This is, however, something that both Hegel and Mead failed to consider adequately, in including modern legal relations as a central condition for post-traditional ethical life. What remains convincing, however, are the reasons that both thinkers introduced in order to substantiate the significance of individual civil rights for the purpose of human self-realization. Subjects are equally in a position to determine their life-goals without external influence only to the extent to which the establishment of civil law gives them all, in principle, individual freedom to make decisions. In short, self-realization is dependent on the social prerequisite of legally guaranteed autonomy, because only with its help can subjects come to conceive of themselves as persons who can deliberate about their own desires. On the other hand, however, Hegel and Mead restricted modern legal relations to the mere existence of liberal civil rights, and they did so to such an extent that neither was able to realize how heavily the individual enjoyment of these liberties can also depend on the legal improvement of the conditions for their application. The legal prerequisites of self-realization represent something that can develop, since they can be improved in the direction of increased consideration for the particular circumstances of the individual without losing their universal content. For this reason, it is only once modern legal relations are expanded to include substantive components of this sort that they can find their place as a second element in the intersubjective network of post-traditional ethical life.

Admittedly, within this ethical framework, rights (thus conceived) have a restricting effect on love relationships as well as on conditions of solidarity, still to be explained. Patterns of recognition based on law extend into the inner sphere of primary relations, because individuals must be protected against the danger of physical violence that is structurally inherent in the precarious balance of every emotional bond. Today, the intersubjective conditions that enable personal integrity include not only the experience of love but also legal protection against the injuries that can be causally connected with love. Modern legal relations have a different influence, however, on conditions of solidarity. Here, they establish normative limitations to which the formation of community-generating value-horizons must generally be subject. The question, therefore, as to whether solidarity is to be included as a further element among the conditions for post-traditional ethical life cannot be settled without some reference to legal principles.

It is once again Hegel and Mead who have provided the crucial arguments as to why, even under conditions of modernity, subjects continue to be dependent on an encompassing value-horizon. Since individuals must know that they are recognized for their particular abilities and traits in order to be capable of self-realization, they need a form of social esteem that they can only acquire on the basis of collectively shared goals. Both thinkers, however, failed to address this third pattern of recognition in a form that they could have discovered empirically. Instead, they gave it a crucial reformulation in normative terms. For them, it was to be understood as referring only to those ethical value-horizons that are sufficiently open and pluralistic to give every member of society, in principle, the chance to know that he or she is socially esteemed with regard to his or her abilities. In thus sharpening the normative point of the category of a community of value, this move yields two theoretical advantages, the extent of which was clear to neither Hegel nor Mead: on the one hand, because it contains the possibility of further equalization and individualization, the course of development that is already laid out in the recognition relationship associated with social esteem only needs to be extended beyond the present into the future for it to reach the idea they outlined; on the other hand, however, this idea is itself so constituted as to admit only community-generating values that are structurally compatible with the moral conditions of modern law, that is, with the individual autonomy of every individual. Both Mead and the young Hegel wanted to imagine a future of modern society in such a way that it brought forth a new, open value-system, within the horizon of which subjects learn to esteem each other mutually with regard to their freely chosen life-goals. In so doing, both got to the threshold of a concept of social solidarity that is geared towards the possibility of symmetrical esteem among legally autonomous citizens. But with regard to answering the question of how to fill in the details of a modern idea of solidarity, not only do the two thinkers part ways in their attempts at a solution; they both, in their own ways, also fail.

As is clear from the foregoing, our formal conception of post-traditional ethical life would be incomplete if it were unable to indicate the position occupied by substantive values. For the attempt to start out from the intersubjective conditions for personal integrity in order to reach the normative universals of a successful life must, in the end, also include the pattern of recognition associated with social solidarity, which can only grow out of collectively shared goals. The fact that these, for their part, are subject to the normative restrictions set by the legally sanctioned autonomy of all subjects stems from the fact that these aspirations are situated within a relational network and need to coexist with the two other patterns of recognition, that is, love and rights. In his Jena writings, the young Hegel tried to fill in this position with a concept of the 'solidarity' of all citizens, which he still understood as a form of communication. But the advantage of greatest possible formality, which his proposal doubtless had brought him, had been paid for with the disadvantage of no longer having any reference to the experiences in terms of which the emergence of such feelings of solidarity could be explained. Mead, on the other hand – like Durkheim, at about the same time – had conceived the social division of labour as the framework of collective goals that is supposed to give rise to solidarity-generating forces [*solidierende Kräfte*], through which all subjects could know themselves to be esteemed. His suggestion was destined to founder, however, on the fact that, if not the organization of the social division of labour, then most certainly the evaluation of the diverse occupational achievements depends, itself, on ethical values. That, however, is precisely what was supposed to be neutralized by the reference to technical requirements.

Both Hegel and Mead fell equally short of their goal of defining an abstract horizon of ethical values that would be open to the widest variety of life-goals without losing the solidarity-generating force of collective identity-formation. The two hundred years separating us from Hegel's early writings and the nearly one hundred years separating us from Mead's speculations have only heightened the need for an integration of this sort. Indeed, in the meantime, social-structural upheavals in developed societies have so greatly expanded the possibilities for self-realization that the experience of individual or collective difference has become the impetus for a whole series of political movements. In the long run, their demands can only be satisfied once culture has been transformed so as to radically expand relations of solidarity. In this new situation, the only lesson that the conception sketched here has to learn from the failure of Hegel's and Mead's proposals is to be content with an ineluctable tension: we cannot refrain from allowing substantive values – which are supposed to be in a position to generate post-traditional solidarity – to take their place alongside the forms of recognition found in love and developed legal relations; nor, however, can the present proposal, on its own, fill the position that is thereby circumscribed as the locus of the particular in the fabric of relationships belonging to a modern form of ethical life. For, whether these substantive values point in the direction of a political republicanism, an ecologically based asceticism, or a collective existentialism, whether they presuppose changes in socio-economic circumstances or are compatible with the conditions of a capitalist society – this is no longer a matter for theory but rather for the future of social struggles.

Notes

Translator's Introduction

1 Charles Taylor, 'The politics of Recognition', in Amy Gutmann (ed.), *Multiculturalism and 'The Politics of Recognition'* (Princeton, NJ: Princeton University Press, 1992), pp. 25–73; here, p. 26.

2 This distinguishes Honneth's critique of the Hobbesian tradition from that of Durkheim or Parsons, in that Honneth is focused here on the conditions for self-realization rather than the problem of social order. For his perspective on issues of social integration, however, see the essays in his *Desintegration: Soziologische Exkurse* (Frankfurt: Fischer, 1994).

3 See *Critique of Power: Reflective Stages in a Critical Social Theory*, tr. Kenneth Baynes (Cambridge, Mass.: MIT Press, 1991), ch. 1 and the Introduction to *The Fragmented World of the Social: Essays in Social and Political Theory*, ed. Charles Wright (Albany, NY: SUNY Press, 1995). In a pivotal early essay, Honneth has formulated this point as a critique of Habermas: 'Moral consciousness and class domination: some problems in the analysis of hidden morality', *Praxis International*, 2 (Apr. 1982). [Reprinted in *The Fragmented World of the Social*.]

4 For similar views, see Jürgen Habermas, 'Individualization through socialization: on George Herbert Mead's theory of subjectivity', in *Postmetaphysical Thinking*, tr. William Mark Hohengarten (Cambridge, Mass.: MIT Press, 1992), pp. 149–204; and Ernst Tugendhat, *Self-consciousness and Self-determination*, tr. Paul Stern (Cambridge, Mass.: MIT Press, 1986).

5 Here, Honneth's account owes much to Elaine Scarry's phenomenology of torture: *The Body in Pain: The Making and Unmaking of the World* (Oxford: Oxford University Press, 1985).

6 Erik H. Erikson, 'Growth and crises of the healthy personality', in *Identity and the Life Cycle* (New York: Norton, 1980), pp. 57–67.

7 See also Axel Honneth and Hans Joas, *Human Nature and Social Action* (Cambridge, Mass.: MIT Press, 1988).

8 For a parallel analysis of this distinction, see David Sachs, 'How to distinguish self-respect from self-esteem', *Philosophy and Public Affairs*, 10: 4 (1981), pp. 346–60.

9   This is the central idea behind Jürgen Habermas's recent work on democratic and legal theory: *Faktizität und Geltung: Beiträge zur Diskurstheorie des Rechts und des demokratischen Rechtsstaat* (Frankfurt: Suhrkamp, 1992).

10 Joel Feinberg, 'The nature and value of rights', in his *Rights, Justice, and the Bounds of Liberty: Essays in Social Philosophy* (Princeton, NJ: Princeton University Press, 1980), p. 151.

11 It is interesting to note the parallel here with Peter Strawson's account of the ascription of responsible agency in everyday situations: insofar as one reacts to others with ordinary feelings (such as resentment) – rather than taking an 'objective', non-participatory attitude – one implicitly *recognizes* them as morally responsible for their actions. Furthermore, the mutual ascription of this status constitutes the intersubjective domain within which we can respond to each other morally. (See Strawson, 'Freedom and resentment', *Proceedings of the British Academy*, 48 (1962), pp. 1–25.) From Honneth's perspective, of course, this recognition of responsibility represents a necessary but hardly sufficient dimension of 'respect'.

12 This volume, p. 114.

13 Honneth has argued this point explicitly in connection with the discourse ethics of Habermas and Karl-Otto Apel: 'Equal opportunity for participation in practical discourse requires . . . the degree of social recognition and corresponding individual self-respect that is necessary in order for one to voice and defend one's moral intuitions publicly; this is because expressing moral beliefs presupposes, on the part of the subject involved, the feeling of being recognized by all others as a forthright and competent judge.' (Honneth, 'Diskursethik und implizites Gerechtigkeitskonzept', in W. Kuhlmann (ed.), *Moralität und Sittlichkeit: Das Problem Hegels und die Diskursethik* (Frankfurt: Suhrkamp, 1985), pp. 183–93; here, p. 192.)

14 See Charles Taylor, *The Ethics of Authenticity* (Cambridge, Mass.: Harvard University Press, 1992), pp. 35f.: 'Defining myself means finding what is significant in my difference from others. I may be the only person with exactly 3,732 hairs on my head . . . but so what?'

15 George Herbert Mead, *Mind, Self, and Society from the Standpoint of a Social Behaviorist*, ed. Charles W. Morris (Chicago: University of Chicago Press, 1934), p. 205.

16 Here Honneth is quite close to Taylor's idea that self-evaluation takes place in a horizon of values that individuals find themselves 'always already' in. See 'The limits of liberalism' in *The Fragmented World of the Social* and Honneth's afterword to the German edition of Taylor's collected papers: *Negative Freiheit? Zur Kritik des neuzeitlichen Individualismus* (Frankfurt: Suhrkamp, 1988), pp. 295–314.

17 This volume, p. 129.

18 E. P. Thompson, *The Making of the English Working Class* (London: Gollancz, 1963) and, more recently, *Customs in Common* (New York: New Press, 1991); and Barrington Moore, *Injustice: The Social Bases of Obedience and Revolt* (White Plains, NY: M. E. Sharpe, 1978).

19 This controversial critique of Hegel as a 'philosopher of consciousness' is also a common theme in Habermas's writings on Hegel; see, in particular, 'Labor and Interaction: Remarks on Hegel's Jena *Philosophy of Mind*', in *Theory and Practice*, tr. John Viertel (Boston: Beacon Press, 1973), pp. 142–69; and *The Philosophical Discourse of Modernity*, tr. Frederick G. Lawrence (Cambridge, Mass.: MIT Press, 1987), ch. 2. For a rather different recent

perspective on these issues, see Robert R. Williams, *Recognition: Fichte and Hegel on the Other* (Albany, NY: SUNY Press, 1992).

20 In addition to the works cited in n. 4 above, see Hans Joas, *G. H. Mead: A Contemporary Re-examination of his Thought*, tr. Raymond Meyer (Cambridge, Mass.: MIT Press, 1985).

21 Honneth has developed this point further, in more explicitly psychoanalytic terms, in his paper 'Decentered autonomy: lessons from the critique of the subject', read at the 1992 meeting of the Society for Phenomenology and Existentialist Philosophy.

22 This is a central theme in Honneth's criticisms of Habermas, particularly with regard to the latter's distinction between 'system' and 'lifeworld'; see *Critique of Power*, 'Afterword to the second German edition' and ch. 9.

23 For helpful comments on this introduction and on the translation as a whole, I am indebted to James Bohman, Larry May, and William Rehg. I would also like to thank Rainer Forst, Joe Heath, Elliot Jurist, Pauline Kleingeld, Thomas McCarthy, and Chris Zurn for further assistance. I am especially grateful to Axel Honneth for his unfailing support and cooperation throughout the translation process. Needless to say, the responsibility for remaining errors is entirely my own.

Introduction

1 See the 'Afterword to the second German edition', in my *Critique of Power: Reflective Stages in a Critical Social Theory*, tr. Kenneth Baynes (Cambridge, Mass.: MIT Press, 1991), pp. xii–xxxii. The first two chapters contain portions of a reconstruction of Hegel's views that I have published elsewhere: Axel Honneth, 'Moral development and social struggle: Hegel's early social-philosophical doctrines', in A. Honneth et al. (eds), *Cultural-political Interventions in the Unfinished Project of Enlightenment*, tr. Barbara Fultner (Cambridge, Mass.: MIT Press, 1992), pp. 197–217.

2 See my inaugural lecture in Frankfurt am Main: 'Integrity and disrespect: principles of a conception of morality based on the theory of recognition', *Political Theory*, 20: 2 (May 1992), pp. 187–201. [Reprinted in *The Fragmented World of the Social: Essays in Social and Political Philosophy*, ed. Charles Wright (Albany, NY: SUNY Press, 1994).]

3 See e.g. Seyla Benhabib, *Situating the Self: Gender, Community, and Postmodernism in Contemporary Ethics* (New York: Routledge, 1992); Iris Marion Young, *Justice and the Politics of Difference* (Princeton, NJ: Princeton University Press, 1990); Andrea Bambey, *Das Geschlechtervehältnis als Anerkennungsstruktur. Zum Problem der Geschlechterdifferenz in feministischen Theorien*, Studientexte zur Sozialwissenschaften, Sonderband 5 (Frankfurt, 1991).

4 Here I am thinking of, among others, Klaus Roth, *Die Institutionalisierung der Freiheit in den Jenaer Schriften Hegels* (Rheinfelden/Berlin: Schäuble, 1991).

Part I

1 See Joachim Ritter, 'Morality and ethical life: Hegel's controversy with Kantian ethics', in *Hegel and the French Revolution: Essays on the 'Philosophy*

of Right', tr. Richard Dien Winfield (Cambridge, Mass.: MIT Press, 1982), pp. 151–82; and Odo Marquard, 'Hegel und das Sollen', in *Schwierigkeiten mit der Geschichtsphilosophie* (Frankfurt: Suhrkamp, 1973), pp. 37ff.

2 I shall be refering primarily to the following:

  1 *System of Ethical Life* (1802/03):
    English: *'System of Ethical Life' (1802/03) and 'First Philosophy of Spirit' (Part III of the System of Speculative Philosophy 1803/04)*, ed. and tr. H. S. Harris and T. M. Knox (Albany, NY: SUNY Press, 1979), pp. 97–186.
    German: *System der Sittlichkeit*, ed. Georg Lasson (Hamburg: Meiner, 1967).

  2 'First Philosophy of Spirit' (1803/04), previously referred to as '*Realphilosophie, I*':
    English: *'System of Ethical Life' (1802/03) and 'First Philosophy of Spirit' (Part III of the System of Speculative Philosophy 1803/04)*, ed. and tr. H. S. Harris (Albany, NY: SUNY Press, 1979), pp. 187–265.
    German: *System der spekulativen Philosophie* (Hamburg: Meiner, 1986), part III.

  3 '*Realphilosophie*' (1805/06), previously referred to as '*Realphilosophie, II*':
    English: 'Jena Lectures on the Philosophy of Spirit', in *Hegel and the Human Spirit: A Translation of the Jena Lectures on the Philosophy of Spirit (1805–6) with Commentary*, ed. and tr. Leo Rauch (Detroit: Wayne State University Press, 1983).
    German: *Jenaer Realphilosophie* (Hamburg: Meiner, 1969).

  Beyond this, I refer to Hegel's natural law essay: *Natural Law: The Scientific Ways of Treating Natural Law, its Place in Moral Philosophy, and its Relation to the Positive Sciences of Law*, tr. T. M. Knox (Philadelphia: University of Pennsylvania Press, 1975). [German: 'Über die wissenschaftlichen Behandlungsarten des Naturrechts', in *Werke in 20 Bänden*, vol. II: *Jenaer Schriften 1801–07*, ed. Eva Moldenhauer and Karl Markus Michel (Frankfurt: Suhrkamp, 1971), pp. 434–530.] An overview of the development of these works can be found in Heinz Kimmerle, 'Zur Entwicklung des Hegelschen Denkens in Jena', *Hegel-Studien*, Suppl. 4 (1968).

Chapter 1   The Struggle for Self-preservation

1 See Jürgen Habermas, 'The classical doctrine of politics in relation to social philosophy', in *Theory and Practice*, tr. John Viertel (Boston: Beacon Press, 1973), pp. 41–81, esp. pp. 50ff.

2 See the outstanding study by Herfried Münkler: *Machiavelli: Die Begründung des politischen Denkens der Neuzeit aus der Krise der Republik Florenz* (Frankfurt: Europäische Verlagsanstalt, 1984), esp. part III, chs 1 and 2.

3 See e.g. Niccolò Machiavelli, *The Prince*, ed. Quentin Skinner and Russell Price (Cambridge: Cambridge University Press, 1988), ch. 17, pp. 58–61; as well as *The Discourses*, tr. Leslie J. Walker (London: Routledge & Kegan Paul, 1950), Book 1, ch. 29, pp. 277–80.

4 Hans Freyer has developed this thesis in his *Machiavelli* (Weinheim: Verlagsgesellschaft, 1986), esp. pp. 65ff.; for a similar recent approach, see Wolfgang Kersting, 'Handlungsmächtigkeit: Machiavellis Lehre vom politischen Handeln', *Philosophisches Jahrbuch*, 3: 4 (1988), pp. 234ff.

5 See again Habermas, 'The classical doctrine of politics', pp. 62ff. Still well worth reading in this connection is Franz Borkenau, *Der Übergang vom feudalen zum bürgerlichen Weltbild* (Darmstadt: Wissenschaftliche Buchgesellschaft, 1971), pp. 439ff.

6 See e.g. the famous formulation in Thomas Hobbes, *Leviathan*, ed. Richard Tuck (Cambridge: Cambridge University Press, 1991), p. 70. On Hobbes's political anthropology as a whole, see the informative study by Günther Buck, 'Selbsterhaltung und Historizität', in Hans Ebeling (ed.), *Subjektivität und Selbsterhaltung. Beiträge zur Diagnose der Moderne* (Frankfurt: Suhrkamp, 1976), pp. 144ff.

7 Buck, 'Selbsterhaltung', esp. pp. 144ff.

8 See the famous ch. 13 of *Leviathan*, pp. 86–90.

9 Münkler, *Machiavelli*.

10 See Habermas, 'Classical doctrine of politics'; see also Ernst Bloch, *Natural Law and Human Dignity*, tr. Dennis J. Schmidt (Cambridge, Mass.: MIT Press, 1986), ch. 9.

Chapter 2   Crime and Ethical Life

1 See Dieter Henrich, 'Hegel und Hölderlin', in *Hegel im Kontext* (Frankfurt: Suhrkamp, 1971), pp. 9ff.; see also his 'Historische Voraussetzungen von Hegels System', ibid., pp. 41ff., esp. pp. 61ff.

2 See Karl-Heinz Ilting, 'Hegels Auseinandersetzung mit der aristotelischen Politik', *Philosophisches Jahrbuch* 71 (1963/4), pp. 38ff. On Hegel's polis-enthusiasm, see also Jacques Taminaux, *La Nostalgie de la Grèce à l'aube de l'idealisme allemand: Kant et les Grecs dans l'itineraire de Schiller, de Hölderlin et de Hegel* (The Hague, 1967), esp. chs 1 and 5.

3 On this complex of problems as a whole, see Rolf-Peter Horstmann, 'Über die Rolle der bürgerlichen Gesellschaft in Hegels politischer Philosophie', in M. Riedel (ed.), *Materialen zu Hegels Rechtsphilosophie*, vol. 2 (Frankfurt: Suhrkamp, 1975), pp. 276ff. [Reprinted from *Hegel-Studien*, 9 (1974), pp. 209–40.] On the reception of British political economy, see also Georg Lukács, *The Young Hegel*, tr. Rodney Livingstone (London: Merlin Press, 1975), esp. ch. 2, v, and ch. 3, v.

4 Hegel, *Natural Law*, p. 70. [*Werke*, 2: 475.] (See above, ch. 1 n. 2.)

5 Ibid., esp. pp. 64f. [446f.]

6 Ibid., esp. pp. 74ff. [458ff. Translation modified.] Here, Hegel can build on the critical results of his 1801 treatise on *The Difference between the Fichtean and Schellingian Systems of Philosophy*, tr. H. S. Harris and Walter Cerf (Albany, NY: SUNY Press, 1977). On this topic as a whole, see Manfred Riedel, 'Hegel's criticism of natural law theory', in *Between Tradition and Revolution: The Hegelian Transformation of Political Philosophy*, tr. Walter Wright (Cambridge: Cambridge University Press, 1984), pp. 76–104.

7 Hegel, *Natural Law*, esp. pp. 64ff. [*Werke*, 2: 445ff.]

8 Ibid., p. 68. [448.]

9 See 'Das Älteste Systemprogramm des deutschen Idealismus', *Werke in 20 Bänden*, vol. I, pp. 234–6 [English: 'The oldest systematic programme of German Idealism', in Henry S. Harris, *Hegel's Development: Toward the Sunlight* (Oxford: Clarendon Press, 1972) pp. 510–12.] On the status of

this discussion, see Christoph Jamme and Helmut Schneider (eds), *Mythologie der Vernunft. Hegels 'älteste Systemprogramm' des deutschen Idealismus* (Frankfurt: Suhrkamp, 1984).

10 Hegel, *Natural Law*, p. 67. [*Werke*, 2: 471.]

11 On the systematic significance of the concept of *Sitte* in this context, see the good presentation in Miguel Giusti, *Hegels Kritik der modernen Welt* (Würzburg: Könighausen & Neumann, 1987), pp. 35ff.

12 Hegel, *Natural Law*, p. 116. [*Werke*, 2: 508.]

13 See again Horstmann, 'Über die Rolle der bürgerlichen Gesellschaft in Hegels politischer Philosophie', esp. (with regard to Hegel's *Natural Law*) pp. 279–87.

14 Hegel, *Natural Law*, p. 113. [*Werke*, 2: 505. The quote is from *Politics* 1253a, 25–9, where Aristotle speaks of the *'polis'* rather than the 'nation'.]

15 Besides Ilting's essay, 'Hegels Auseinandersetzung mit der aristotelischen Politik', Giusti is very clear on this: *Hegels Kritik der modernen Welt*, pp. 49ff.

16 Hegel, *Natural Law*, p. 113. [*Werke*, 2: 505.]

17 Ibid., p. 470. [507.]

18 Ibid.

19 The importance of Fichte for the young Hegel's account of recognition has been worked out recently in two excellent studies, which have significantly stimulated my own thinking: Ludwig Siep, 'Der Kampf um Anerkennung. Zu Hegels Auseinandersetzung mit Hobbes in den Jenaer Schriften', *Hegel-Studien*, 9 (1974), pp. 155ff.; Andreas Wildt, *Autonomie und Anerkennung. Hegels Moralitätskritik im Lichte seiner Fichte-Rezeption* (Stuttgart: Klett-Cotta, 1982). These studies were preceded by Manfred Riedel's important essay 'Hegel's criticism of natural law theory'. Another strand of Hegel's theory of recognition leads back to Rousseau. In his *Discourse on Inequality*, he introduced mutual recognition [*s'apprécier mutuellement*] as a central dimension of human socialization through which, he claimed, every sort of crime transforms itself into a form of insult: see Jean-Jacques Rousseau, *A Discourse on Inequality*, tr. Maurice Cranston (Harmondsworth: Penguin, 1984), pp. 114ff. (I am grateful to Hinrich Fink-Eitel for pointing this out to me.)

20 As Hegel puts it in his 'Differenzschrift': Hegel, *The Difference between the Fichtean and Schellingian Systems of Philosophy*, p. 62. [*Werke*, 2: 83.]

21 J. G. Fichte, 'Grundlage des Naturrechts nach Prinzipien der Wissenschaftslehre', in Immanuel Hermann Fichte (ed.), *Fichtes Werke*, vol. III (Berlin: de Gruyter, 1971), pp. 1ff., esp. 17ff.; on Fichte's doctrine of 'challenge' as a whole, see Ludwig Siep, *Anerkennung als Prinzip der praktischen Philosophie. Untersuchungen zu Hegels Jenaer Philosophie des Geistes* (Freiburg/Munich: Alber, 1979).

22 On Hegel's confrontation with the Hobbesian model of the state of nature, see Siep's excellent essay, 'Den Kampf um Anerkennung'. On Hegel's confrontation with Hobbes in the Jena writings, see Siep, *Anerkennung als Prinzip der praktischen Philosophie*.

23 Thus, Ilting, 'Hegels Auseinandersetzung mit der aristotelischen Politik', section 3.

24 In the *System of Ethical Life*, Hegel's account uses the method of alternately subsuming intuition and concept. Formally speaking, this procedure

generates three main parts of the text: the chapter on 'natural ethical life' as the subsumption of intuition under the concept; the chapter on 'crime' as the subsumption of the concept under intuition; and, finally, the chapter on 'absolute ethical life' as the 'indifference' of intuition and the concept. If I am not mistaken, however, this methodological procedure is generally unconnected to the social-philosophical content of the text.

25   Hegel, *System of Ethical Life*, p. 111. [*System der Sittlichkeit*, 18.]
26   Ibid., p. 124. [33.]
27   Ibid. [Translation modified.]
28   See Solange Mercier-Josa, 'Combat pour la reconnaissance et criminalité', in Dieter Henrich and Rolf-Peter Horstmann (eds) *Hegels Philosophie des Rechts* (Stuttgart: Klett-Cotta, 1982), pp. 75ff.
29   See Wildt's observations in *Autonomie und Anerkennung*, pp. 100ff.
30   Hegel, *System of Ethical Life*, p. 130. [*System der Sittlichkeit*, 39. Translation modified.]
31   Ibid., p. 135. [44. Translation modified.]
32   Ibid., p. 135. [45. Translation modified.]
33   Here I am following the interpretations of Wildt, *Autonomie und Anerkennung* p. 324, and Siep, *Anerkennung als Prinzip der praktischen Philosophie*, p. 39.
34   Hegel, *System of Ethical Life*, p. 136. [*System der Sittlichkeit*, 46.]
35   Ibid., p. 137. [47.]
36   Ibid., p. 138. [47. Interpolation Honneth's: the Knox translation has 'personality of both' in place of 'of a person'.]
37   Here I am of course contradicting the interpretation developed by Manfred Riedel of the chapter on crime: 'Hegel's criticism of natural law theory', p. 89. Riedel does not believe that the conflictual phenomena discussed by Hegel represent, in any way, a transition to the stage of 'absolute ethical life'.
38   Hegel, *System of Ethical Life*, p. 140. [*System der Sittlichkeit*, 50.]
39   Ibid., p. 144. [54.]
40   I owe the idea of using the concept of 'solidarity' to interpret certain aspects of the young Hegel's theory of ethical life to a suggestion that Andreas Wildt develops in an essay on 'Hegels Kritik des Jakobinismus', in Oskar Negt (ed.), *Aktualität und Folgen der Philosophie Hegels* (Frankfurt: Suhrkamp, 1970), pp. 277ff. In contrast to him, I link the concept more directly to the form of social relationship that Hegel wanted to specify by means of his recognition-based conception of ethical life. Gillian Rose has suggested a comparable, very strong interpretation of the concept of 'mutual recognition', according to which it designates a relationship 'which does not dominate or suppress but recognizes the difference and sameness of the other'. See Gillian Rose, *Hegel contra Sociology* (London: Athlone, 1981), p. 69
41   On the status of this text as a whole, see the informative commentary by Klaus Düsing and Heinz Kimmerle in their Introduction to G. W. F. Hegel, *System der spekulativen Philosophie* (Hamburg: Meiner, 1986), pp. vii ff.
42   Excellent on this topic generally: Rolf-Peter Horstmann, 'Probleme der Wandlung in Hegels Jenaer Systemkonzeption', *Philosophische Rundschau*, 19 (1972), pp. 87ff.
43   Ibid., pp. 114ff.; on this see also Siep, *Anerkennung als Prinzip der praktischen Philosophie*, pp. 182ff.

44 Hegel, 'First Philosophy of Spirit', p. 212. [*System der spekulativen Philosophie*, 189.] (See above, ch. 1 n. 2.)
45 Ibid., p. 236. [217.]
46 Ibid., p. 237 n. 46. [218 n. 2; interpolation in the Harris–Knox translation.]
47 Wildt provides a more extensive interpretation of the implications of this thesis for a theory of consciousness: *Autonomie und Anerkennung*, pp. 336ff.
48 Hegel, 'First Philosophy of Spirit', p. 242. [*System der spekulativen Philosophie*, 223.]

Chapter 3   The Struggle for Recognition

1 Hegel, 'Jena Lectures on the Philosophy of Spirit', p. 173 [*Realphilosophie*, p. 263. Translation modified.] (See above, pt. I intro., n. 2.)
2 On these difficulties, see Jürgen Habermas, 'Labor and interaction: remarks on Hegel's Jena *Philosophy of Mind*', *Theory and Practice*, pp. 142–69. [Translator's note: The text Habermas discusses is the same as the text being discussed here.]
3 The clearest and most detailed interpretation that I have found of part I of the 'Jena Lectures on the Philosophy of Spirit' – also with regard to the methodological problems – is in Wildt, *Autonomie und Anerkennung*, pp. 344f.
4 Hegel, 'Jena Lectures on the Philosophy of Spirit', p. 99. [*Realphilosophie*, 194.]
5 On the Jena-Hegel's theory of the will, see Wildt, *Autonomie und Anerkennung*, pp. 344ff.
6 Hegel, 'Jena Lectures on the Philosophy of Spirit', p. 99. [*Realphilosophie*, 194. Translation modified.]
7 Ibid., p. 103. [197.]
8 Ibid., p. 102. [196. Translation modified.]
9 Ibid., p. 103. [197. Translation modified.] On the issue of Hegel's externalization-model of labour, see Ernst Michael Lange, *Das Prinzip Arbeit* (Frankfurt/Berlin/Vienna, 1980), esp. ch. 1.3 and 1.4.
10 Hegel, 'Jena Lectures on the Philosophy of Spirit', p. 105. [*Realphilosophie*, 199f.]
11 Ibid., p. 106. [201: Translation modified.] I shall not here go into the further complications of this thesis that are generated by Hegel's initial ascription of different types of desire to the two genders; on this, however, see Wildt, *Autonomie und Anerkennung*, pp. 354f.
12 Hegel, 'Jena Lectures on the Philosophy of Spirit', p. 107. [*Realphilosophie*, 202 n. 1.]
13 Ibid., p. 107. [202. Translation modified.]
14 Wildt interprets this thesis in a similar way; see Wildt, *Autonomie und Anerkennung*, p. 356.
15 Hegel, 'Jena Lectures on the Philosophy of Spirit', p. 108. [*Realphilosophie*, 203.]
16 Hegel, 'Jena Lectures on the Philosophy of Spirit', p. 109. [203.]
17 On this entire complex of problems, see the enlightening study by Siegfried Blasche, 'Natürliche Sittlichkeit und bürgerliche Gesellschaft. Hegels Konstruktion der Familie als sittliche Intimität im entsittlichten Leben', in Riedel, *Materialen zur Hegels Rechtsphilosophie*, vol. 2, pp. 312ff.

18 Hegel, 'Jena Lectures on the Philosophy of Spirit', p. 109 [*Realphilosophie*, 204; Honneth's interpolations. Translation modified.]

19 Ibid., p. 110. [205.]

20 Ibid. The reason why, in what follows, I have treated so extensively the passage in which Hegel develops his critique of the natural law doctrine is because it is there that the theoretical premises of his model of a 'struggle for recognition' emerge in their most pregnant form. With regard to the more restricted context, see Siep, 'Kampf um Anerkennung'. The reconstruction that Steven B. Smith has offered for Hegel's description of the state of nature is also impressive: *Hegel's Critique of Liberalism: Rights in Context* (Chicago: University of Chicago Press, 1989), pp. 155ff.; with regard to the broader context, see also Norberto Bobbio, 'Hegel und die Naturrechtslehre', in Riedel , *Materialen zu Hegels Rechtsphilosophie*, vol. 2, pp. 81ff.

21 Hegel, 'Jena Lectures on the Philosophy of Spirit', p. 110. [*Realphilosophie*, 205. Translation modified.]

22 Ibid., p. 111. [206.]

23 Ibid. [Translation modified.]

24 Ibid.

25 Ibid., p. 115. [209.]

26 Ibid. [209f.]

27 Ibid. [210.]

28 Ibid.

29 Ibid. [Translation corrected.]

30 Ibid., p. 116. [210. Translation modified.]

31 Ibid., p. 117. [211.]

32 Ibid., p. 116. [211. Translation modified.]

33 Ibid., p. 117. [211. Translation modified.]

34 Ibid., p. 118. [212.]

35 Wildt, *Autonomie und Anerkennung*, p. 361.

36 Alexandre Kojève, *Introduction to the Reading of Hegel*, tr. James Nichols (New York: Basic Books, 1969), ch. 5; see also Thomas H. Macho, *Todesmetaphern. Zur Logik der Grenzerfahrung* (Frankfurt: Suhrkamp, 1987), ch. 2.

37 For an approach of this sort see e.g. Emmanuel Lévinas, *La Mort et le temps* (Paris, 1991).

38 For a similar account, see Wildt, *Autonomie und Anerkennung*, pp. 364f.

39 Hegel, 'Jena Lectures on the Philosophy of Spirit', p. 120. [*Realphilosophie*, 213.]

40 Ibid.

41 Ibid., p. 121. [215.]

42 Ibid., p. 123. [216.]

43 Ibid., p. 125. [218.]

44 Ibid., p. 128. [222.]

45 Ibid., p. 126. [219.]

46 Ibid., p. 125. [219.]

47 Ibid., p. 126. [220. Translation modified.]

48 Ibid., pp. 130f. [224. Translation corrected.]

49 Ibid., p. 131. [224f.]

50 Wildt suggests this interpretation in *Autonomie und Anerkennung*, pp. 364f.

51 Immanuel Kant, 'Elements of Right: Part Two', *The Metaphysics of Morals*, tr. Mary Gregor (Cambridge: Cambridge University Press, 1991), pp. 123ff. [German: *Metaphysik der Sitten*, Prussian Akademie edn, vol. 6 (Berlin: de Gruyter, 1968), pp. 309ff.]

52 Hegel, 'Jena Lectures on the Philosophy of Spirit', p. 131. [*Realphilosophie*, 224.]

53 Ibid., p. 153. [245.]

54 I owe this formulation to Vittorio Hösle's concise characterization of Hegel's later model of ethical life: Vittorio Hösle, *Hegels System*, vol. 2: *Philosophie der Natur und des Geistes* (Hamburg: Meiner, 1987), pp. 471f. Hösle is drawing here on the conclusions of Michael Theunissen's brilliant study, 'Die verdrängte Intersubjektivität in Hegels Philosophie des Rechts', in Dieter Henrich and Rolf-Peter Horstmann (eds), *Hegels Philosophie des Rechts*, pp. 317ff.

55 Hegel, 'Jena Lectures on the Philosophy of Spirit', p. 155. [*Realphilosophie*, 246.]

56 Ibid., pp. 155f. [246. Translation modified.]

57 Ibid., p. 159. [250. Translation modified.]

58 Ibid., p. 158. [249.]

59 Ibid., p. 157. [248.]

60 Hegel, *Phenomenology of Spirit*, trans. A. V. Miller (Oxford: Oxford University Press, 1977).

Part II

1 On this topic as a whole, see Jürgen Habermas, *The Philosophical Discourse of Modernity*, trans. Frederick G. Lawrence (Cambridge, Mass.: MIT Press, 1987), ch. 3.

2 This is what I understand Ludwig Siep's intention to be in his excellent reconstruction of the theory of recognition found in Hegel's Jena writings (Siep, *Anerkennung als Prinzip der praktischen Philosophie*). Siep believes that, by making use of the standard of complete recognition, a kind of 'normative genesis' of the formation of societal institutions can be worked out: on the basis of the 'evaluative framework' provided by the principle of recognition that Hegel explicates teleologically, one can reconstructively judge whether historically developed institutions serve a necessary and, in that sense, legitimate function in the formative process of the human species (ibid., pp. 259ff.). I share with Siep the view that, once it has undergone a transformation within a postmetaphysical context, Hegel's theory of recognition can be conceived of as an account of the necessary conditions for human socialization. But I consider the idea of deducing a normative standard with which to evaluate institutions to be mistaken, because we cannot, in principle, ever know what institutional form the lending of specific, necessary recognition is to take. In attempting to develop a normative theory of institutions, Siep relies too heavily on the social-scientific content of Hegel's practical philosophy. The decisive difference between Siep's project and the present work, however, results from the fact that I would like to use the normative presuppositions of the relationship of recognition, additionally, as a point of reference with which to explain historical,

empirical processes of societal change. As a result, I am under greater pressure to 'sociologize' Hegel's conceptual model than Siep is.

3   This sort of extension of morality, in terms of a theory of subjectivity, is apparently the goal that Andreas Wildt is pursuing in his reconstruction of the young Hegel's theory of recognition (Wildt, *Autonomie und Anerkennung*). Wildt is interested in 'normative conditions for qualitative ego-identity' (ibid., p. 9). To this end and clearly in the sense of philosophical psychology, he analyses Hegel's theory from the standpoint of the question as to which stages of mutual recognition need to be taken into account in order to arrive at a conception of a successful development of practical subjectivity. The point of his reconstruction is that stable elements of 'non-legal morality' [*nichtrechtsförmiger Moralität*] – that is, attitudes of beneficence, concern, and friendship that cannot be demanded on legal grounds – represent necessary conditions for the development of a qualitative identity. In keeping with this guiding thesis, Wildt's interpretation tends towards a psychologization of Hegel's account of recognition. He has to read the assertion of a repeated 'struggle for recognition' as a hypothesis about necessary conflicts in the socialization process of the individual. Thus, in contrast to Siep, but also in contrast to my own suggested interpretation, Wildt is not at all interested in the social-theoretical implications of Hegel's theory. Whereas I read the Jena writings as a theoretical proposal regarding the moral development of societies (in the sense of Mead or Durkheim), Andreas Wildt apparently wants to have it be understood as the embryonic form of a theory of the moral development of the self. Accordingly, the meaning of 'struggle' is utterly different in the two interpretive approaches: for Wildt, it points to an intrapsychic conflict; for me, it indicates the logic of social conflicts. A similar goal is pursued by Edith Düsing – though in a less suggestive and, hence, meta-ethically more modest manner – in her *Intersubjektivität und Selbstbewußtsein* (Cologne: Verlag für Philosophie J. Dinter, 1986).

Chapter 4   Recognition and Socialization

1   See in general Hans Joas, *G. H. Mead: A Contemporary Re-examination of his Thought*, tr. Raymond Meyer (Cambridge, Mass.: MIT Press, 1985); see further Jürgen Habermas, 'Individuation through socialization: On George Herbert Mead's theory of subjectivity', in *Postmetaphysical Thinking: Philosophical Essays*, tr. William Mark Hohengarten (Cambridge, Mass.: MIT Press, 1992), pp. 149–204.

2   In this chapter, I am relying primarily on George Herbert Mead, *Mind, Self, and Society from the Standpoint of a Social Behaviorist*, ed. Charles W. Morris (Chicago: University of Chicago Press, 1934); in reconstructing the development of Mead's conception of recognition, I have generally drawn on essays collected by Andrew J. Reck: George Herbert Mead, *Selected Writings*, (Indianapolis: Library of the Liberal Arts, 1964).

3   On this historical background, see Joas, *G. H. Mead*, esp. chs 2 and 3.

4   Mead, 'The definition of the psychical', in *Selected Writings*, pp. 25–59; here, p. 55.

5   'Social consciousness and the consciousness of meaning', in *Selected Writings*, pp. 123–33, here, p. 130.

6   Ibid., p. 131.
7   'The mechanism of social consciousness', in *Selected Writings*, pp. 134–41; here, pp. 136f.
8   Ibid., p. 139.
9   Ibid., p. 141.
10 Ibid., p. 140.
11 On this distinction, see Habermas, 'Individuation through socialization', esp. pp. 177ff. Here, Habermas is following an interpretation by Ernst Tugendhat in *Self-consciousness and Self-determination*, tr. Paul Stern (Cambridge, Mass.: MIT Press, 1986); with regard to Mead, esp. chs 11 and 12.
12 Mead, 'The social self', in *Selected Writings*, pp. 142–9; here, p. 146.
13 Mead, *Mind, Self, and Society*.
14 Ibid., pp. 153f. [Translator's note: In the first sentence, Morris's edition has 'latter' and 'former' inverted, something corrected in the German translation that Honneth uses.]
15 Ibid., p. 155.
16 Ibid., p. 196.
17 Ibid., p. 199; on Mead's conception of law in terms of a theory of recognition, see his *Movements of Thought in the Nineteenth Century* (Chicago: University of Chicago Press, 1972), pp. 21ff.
18 Ibid., pp. 204f.
19 If I understand him correctly, Ernst Tugendhat is pointing to this deficit at the relevant passage in his discussion of Mead: Tugendhat, *Self-consciousness and Self-determination*, p. 248.
20 Mead, *Mind, Self, and Society*, p. 196.
21 Ibid., p. 204.
22 Ibid., p. 199.
23 Ibid., p. 168.
24 Ibid., p. 221.
25 Ibid., p. 216.
26 Ibid., p. 205.
27 Ibid., p. 204.
28 In my view, one can use this to develop an argument, proceeding from Mead, against the widely held belief that, with his concept of ethical life, Hegel succumbed to the excesses of Romanticism in developing a theory of society; as an example of this line of thinking, see Charles E. Larmore, *Patterns of Moral Complexity* (Cambridge: Cambridge University Press, 1987), pp. 93ff.; to my mind, the best current defence of Hegel's concept of ethical life is Charles Taylor's contemporizing study, *Hegel and Modern Society* (Cambridge: Cambridge University Press, 1979), esp. ch. 2.8.
29 Mead, *Mind, Self, and Society*, p. 208.

Chapter 5 Patterns of Intersubjective Recognition

1   I have developed an initial overview of this thesis in my 'Integrity and disrespect'.
2   See Max Scheler, *Formalism in Ethics and Non-Formal Ethics of Values: A New Attempt toward the Foundation of an Ethical Personalism*, tr. Manfred S. Frings and Roger L. Funk (Evanston, Ill.: Northwestern University Press, 1973), esp. pp. 504ff.

3 Helmut Plessner, 'Die Grenzen der Gemeinschaft', in *Gesammelte Schriften*, vol. 5: *Macht und menschliche Natur*, ed. Günther Dux, Odo Marquard, Elisabeth Ströker (Frankfurt: Suhrkamp, 1981), pp. 7ff.

4 On this, see Niklas Luhmann, *Love as Passion: The Codification of Intimacy*, trans. Jeremy Gaines and Doris L. Jones (Cambridge, Mass.: Harvard University Press, 1986), ch. 13.

5 Hegel, *System of Ethical Life*, p. 110 [*System der Sittlichkeit*, 17].

6 See the outstanding overview by Morris N. Eagle, *Recent Developments in Psychoanalysis: A Critical Evaluation* (New York: MacGraw-Hill, 1989). See further J. R. Greenberg and Stephen A. Mitchell, *Object Relations in Psychoanalytic Theory* (Cambridge, Mass.: Harvard University Press, 1983).

7 Sigmund Freud, *Inhibitions, Symptoms, and Anxiety*, trans. Alix Strachey (New York: Norton, 1959).

8 René A. Spitz, *The First Year of Life: A Psychoanalytic Study of Normal and Deviant Development of Object Relations*, in collaboration with W. Godfrey Cobliner (New York: International Universities Press, 1965), esp. ch. 14.

9 Eagle, *Recent Developments in Psychoanalysis*, ch. 2.

10 H. F. Harlow, 'The nature of love', *American Psychologist* 13 (1958), pp. 673ff.

11 John Bowlby, *Attachment and Loss*, vol. 1: *Attachment* (London: Hogarth Press and the Institute of Psychoanalysis, 1969).

12 Daniel Stern, *The First Relationship: Mother and Infant* (London: Open Books, 1977). I have followed object-relations theorists here in using the term 'mother' to refer to a social role that traditionally has been – but need not be – fulfilled primarily by women. To emphasize the status of this concept as a technical term, it has been placed in quotation marks.

13 I refer in the following to: Donald W. Winnicott, *The Maturational Processes and the Facilitating Environment: Studies in the Theory of Emotional Development* (London: Hogarth Press and the Institute of Psychoanalysis, 1965); *Playing and Reality* (London: Tavistock, 1971). For a succinct account of Winnicott's particular role within psychoanalysis, see Greenberg and Mitchell, *Object Relations in Psychoanalytic Theory*, ch. 7.

14 Donald W. Winnicott, 'The theory of the parent–infant relationship', in *The Maturational Processes and the Facilitating Environment*, pp. 37–55.

15 See e.g. Couym Trevorthen, 'Communication and cooperation in early infancy: a description of primary intersubjectivity', in Margaret Bullowa (ed.), *Before Speech: The Beginning of Interpersonal Communication* (Cambridge: Cambridge University Press, 1979), pp. 321ff.; and 'The foundations of intersubjectivity: development of interpersonal and cooperative understanding of infants', in D. R. Olson (ed.), *The Social Foundations of Language and Thought: Essays in Honor of Jerome S. Bruner* (New York: Norton, 1980), pp. 316ff.

16 Donald W. Winnicott, 'From dependence towards independence in the development of the individual', in *The Maturational Processes*, pp. 83–92; here, pp. 84–7.

17 Winnicott, 'The theory of the parent–infant relationship', p. 52.

18 Ibid., pp. 44–5.

19 Winnicott, 'From dependence towards independence in the development of the individual', p. 87.

20   Ibid., pp. 87–9.
21   Donald W. Winnicott, 'The use of an object and relating through identifications', in *Playing and Reality*, pp. 86–94; here, p. 89.
22   See esp. ibid., pp. 104ff.; see with regard to this complex also Marianne Schreiber, 'Kann der Mensch Verantwortung für seine Aggressivität übernehmen? Aspekte aus der Psychologie D. W. Winnicotts und Melanie Kleins', in Alfred Schöpf (ed.), *Aggression und Gewalt: Anthropologisch-Wissenschaftliche Beiträge* (Würzburg: Königshausen & Neumann, 1983), pp. 155ff.
23   Donald W. Winnicott, 'Morals and education', in *The Maturational Processes*, pp. 95–105; here, p. 102.
24   Jessica Benjamin, *The Bonds of Love: Psychoanalysis, Feminism, and the Problem of Power* (New York: Pantheon, 1988) esp. pp. 36ff.
25   Donald W. Winnicott, 'Transitional objects and transitional phenomena', in *Playing and Reality*, pp. 1–25; here p. 12.
26   Ibid., p. 13.
27   Donald W. Winnicott, 'Playing: creative activity and the search of the self', in *Playing and Reality*, pp. 53–64, esp. pp. 54–6; see also 'The capacity to be alone', in *The Maturational Processes*, pp. 29–36.
28   Winnicott, 'The capacity to be alone', p. 33.
29   Ibid., p. 32.
30   Ibid., p. 33.
31   Jessica Benjamin, *The Bonds of Love*, esp. ch. 2.
32   Ibid., pp. 65ff.
33   Otto F. Kernberg, *Object-relations Theory and Clinical Psychoanalysis* (New York: Jason Aronson, 1984), chs 7 and 8.
34   See Jean-Paul Sartre, *Being and Nothingness: An Essay on Phenomenological Ontology*, tr. Hazel E. Barnes (New York: Washington Square Press, 1966), Part III, ch. 3, pp. 441–526.
35   On self-confidence as the result of the experience of love, see *inter alia*, John Bowlby, *The Making and Breaking of Affectional Bonds* (London: Tavistock, 1979), ch. 6; Erik H. Erikson, *Identity and the Life-cycle* (New York: Norton, 1980), pp. 57–67; less fertile, despite its promising title, is Nathaniel Branden's *The Psychology of Self-Esteem* (Los Angeles: Nash, 1969). Ch. 9 of the book carries the title 'Self-esteem and romantic love', but it remains utterly unclear in both its categories and its conception of the phenomenon. Paul Gilbert, by contrast, has recently made an important philosophical contribution to the analysis of primary relationships such as love and friendship in his *Human Relationships: A Philosophical Introduction* (Oxford: Blackwell, 1991), *inter alia* chs 2 and 4; in addition, for a recent psychoanalytically oriented presentation of love as a relational pattern, see Martin S. Bergmann, *The Anatomy of Loving* (New York: Columbia University Press, 1987), esp. Part II, pp. 141ff.
36   G. W. F. Hegel, *Hegel's Philosophy of Mind*, tr. William Wallace and A. V. Miller (Oxford: Oxford University Press, 1971), §432A, pp. 172f.
37   For a survey, see Leopold Pospíšil, *Anthropology of Law* (New Haven, Conn.: HRAF Press, 1974), ch. 3.
38   See Jürgen Habermas, 'Überlegungen zum evolutionären Stellenwert des modernen Rechts', in *Zur Rekonstruktion des historischen Materialismus* (Frankfurt: Suhrkamp, 1976), pp. 260–8.

39 Exemplary in this connection is Aron Gurewitsch, *Zur Geschichte des Achtungsbegriffs und zur Theorie der sittlichen Gefühle* (Würzburg, 1897).
40 Rudolph von Ihering, *Der Zweck im Recht*, vol. 2 (Leipzig, 1905).
41 Ibid., pp. 389ff.
42 Ibid., pp. 405ff.
43 Stephen L. Darwall, 'Two kinds of respect', *Ethics* 88 (1977/8), pp. 36ff.
44 In connection with Darwall's distinction, see Andreas Wildt, 'Recht und Selbstachtung im Anschluß an die Anerkennungslehren von Fichte und Hegel', in Michael Kahlo, Ernst A. Wolff, and Rainer Zaczyk (eds), *Fichtes Lehre vom Rechtsverhältnis* (Frankfurt: Klostermann, 1992), pp. 156ff.
45 In this connection, see Albrecht Wellmer, *The Persistence of Modernity: Essays on Aesthetics, Ethics, and Postmodernism*, tr. David Midgley (Cambridge, Mass.: MIT Press, 1991), pp. 195ff.
46 Darwall, 'Two kinds of respect', p. 254.
47 Robert Alexy, *Theorie der Grundrechte* (Frankfurt: Suhrkamp, 1986), esp. ch. 4; on Jellinek's theory of status, see ibid., pp. 229ff.
48 Thomas H. Marshall, 'Citizenship and social class', in his *Sociology at the Crossroads* (London: Heinemann, 1963), pp. 67ff.
49 Talcott Parsons, *The System of Modern Societies* (Englewood Cliffs, NJ: Prentice-Hall, 1971), esp. chs 2 and 5.
50 In connection with the following, see Marshall, 'Citizenship and social class', esp. pp. 73ff.
51 Ibid., p. 87.
52 See above, pp. 85ff.
53 Joel Feinberg, 'The nature and value of rights', in his *Rights, Justice, and the Bounds of Liberty: Essays in Social Philosophy* (Princeton, NJ: Princeton University Press, 1980), pp. 143ff.
54 Ibid., p. 151.
55 On this, see Wildt, 'Recht und Selbstachtung', 148ff.
56 For an overview, see e.g. Bernard R. Boxill, 'Self-respect and protest', *Philosophy and Public Affairs* 6 (1976/7), pp. 58ff. He supports his position on the basis of the documents collected in Howard Brotz (ed.), *Negro Social and Political Thought* (New York: Basic Books, 1966).
57 In what follows, I am drawing above all on Heinz Kluth, *Sozialprestige und sozialer Status* (Stuttgart: Enke, 1957) and Wilhelm Korff, *Ehre, Prestige, Gewissen* (Cologne: J. P. Bachem, 1966).
58 Max Weber, *Economy and Society: An Outline of Interpretive Sociology*, ed. Guenther Roth and Claus Wittich (New York: Bedminster Press, 1968), p. 932.
59 See Julian Pitt-Rivers, 'Honor', in *International Encyclopedia of the Social Sciences*, vol. 6, ed. David L. Sills (New York: Macmillan and Free Press, 1968), pp. 503–11. Empirical examples from traditionally constituted socieites can be found in J. G. Péristiany (ed.), *Honour and Shame: The Values of Mediterranean Society* (London: Weidenfeld & Nicolson, 1966); for historical illustration, see e.g. Richard van Dülmen (ed.), *Armut, Liebe, Ehre. Studien zur historischen Kulturforschung* (Frankfurt: Fischer, 1988).
60 On this concept, see Richard Sennett and Jonathan Cobb, *The Hidden Injuries of Class* (New York: Knopf, 1972).
61 Weber, *Economy and Society*, pp. 43ff., 932ff.
62 See Peter Berger, 'On the obsolescence of the concept of honor', *European Journal of Sociology*, 11 (1970).

63 On the process of individualization of social esteem, see Hans Speier, 'Honor and social structure', in *Social Order and the Risks of War* (New York: G. W. Stewart, 1952), pp. 36ff.; of fundamental importance for the historical thesis regarding a gradual individualization of 'honour' is, above all, Alexis de Tocqueville, *Democracy in America*, tr. George Lawrence, ed. J. P. Mayer (New York: Anchor Books, 1969), Part II, Book 3, ch. 18.

64 See Korff, *Ehre, Prestige, Gewissen*, ch. 3, pp. 111ff.

65 If I have correctly located its intent, Pierre Bourdieu's sociological theory is tailored to the analysis of this process. Combining Marx, Weber, and Durkheim, he undertakes to study the symbolic struggle in which different social groups try to reinterpret a society's system for classifying values, in order to raise their social prestige and, thereby, their power. See, *inter alia*, Pierre Bourdieu, *Distinction: A Social Critique of Aesthetic Judgement*, tr. Richard Nice (London: Routledge & Kegan Paul, 1984). To be sure, as I have tried to show elsewhere, Bourdieu tends to ignore the normative logic of this symbolic struggle for social esteem, because his analysis is based on an economic theory of action: see my 'Fragmented world of symbolic forms: reflections on Pierre Bourdieu's sociology of culture', *Theory, Culture, and Society*, 3 (1986), 55ff. [Reprinted in Honneth, *The Fragmented World of the Social*.]

66 This is also the conceptual proposal in Pitt-Riviers, 'Honor', p. 507: 'The reciprocal demonstrations of favor, which might be called mutual honoring, establish relationships of solidarity'.

67 Sartre's famous term the 'fused group' [*groupe en fusion*] is conceptually tailored to this phenomenon; see Jean-Paul Sartre, *Critique of Dialectical Reason*, vol. 1: *Theory of Practical Ensembles*, tr. Alan Sheridan-Smith and ed. Jonathan Rée (London: New Left Books, 1976), pp. 345–404.

68 See here – with the reservations already mentioned – Branden's study *The Psychology of Self-esteem*; in this connection, see also Helen M. Lynd, *On Shame and the Search for Identity* (New York: Harcourt, Brace, 1958).

Chapter 6   Personal Identity and Disrespect

1 On the danger of the breakdown of personal identity, see, as a whole, the collection edited by Glyris M. Breakwell: *Threatened Identities* (New York: Wiley, 1983).

2 For an excellent study of loss of reality as a result of torture, see Elaine Scarry, *The Body in Pain: The Making and Unmaking of the World* (Oxford: Oxford University Press, 1985), ch. 1.

3 See e.g. Boxill, 'Self-respect and protest'; and Feinberg, 'The nature and value of rights'.

4 Among the studies pointing in the direction of a category of 'psychological death' are those of Bruno Bettelheim, in *Surviving and Other Essays* (London: Thames & Hudson, 1979), esp. part I. On the category of 'social death', see, *inter alia*, Orlando Patterson, *Slavery and Social Death: A Comparative Study* (Cambridge, Mass.: Harvard University Press, 1992), and Claude Meillassoux, *Anthropologie de l'esclavage: le ventre de fer et d'argent* (Paris: Presses Universitaires de France, 1986), esp. part I, ch. 5.

5 See John Dewey, 'The theory of emotion', I, *Psychological Review* (1895), pp. 553ff., and 'The theory of emotion', II, *Psychological Review* (1896), pp. 13ff.

For a helpful presentation of Dewey's theory of emotions, see Eduard Baumgarten, *Die geistigen Grundlagen des amerikanischen Gemeinwesens*, vol. 2: *Der Pragmatismus: R. W. Emerson, W. James, J. Dewey* (Frankfurt, 1938), pp. 247ff.

6 For examples of this argument, see Gerhart Piers and Milton B. Singer, *Shame and Guilt: A Psychoanalytic and a Cultural Study* (New York: Norton, 1971), esp. pp. 23ff., and Lynd, *On Shame and the Search for Identity*, ch. 2; Georg Simmel also had a similar definition in mind in his brief 1901 essay 'Zur Psychologie der Scham', in his *Schriften zur Soziologie*, ed. J.-J. Dahme and O. Rammstedt (Frankfurt: Suhrkamp, 1983), pp. 140ff.

7 This aspect is underestimated by the otherwise excellent study by Sighard Neckel, *Status und Scham. Zur symbolischen Reproduktion sozialer Ungleichheit* (Frankfurt: Campus, 1991).

Chapter 7 Traces of a Tradition in Social Philosophy

1 On Marx's reception of Hegel's 'lordship and bondage' dialectic, see Thomas Meyer, *Der Zwiespalt in der Marxschen Emanzipationstheorie* (Kronberg im Taunus: Scriptor, 1973), *inter alia*, ch. A.2, pp. 44ff.

2 See my 'Labor and instrumental action: on the normative basis of critical theory', *New German Critique* (1982), pp. 31–54. [Reprinted in *The Fragmented World of the Social*.]

3 I owe this reference to Hans Joas, *Zur Kreativität des Handelns* (Frankfurt: Suhrkamp, 1992), pp. 131ff.

4 The full passage reads as follows: 'Supposing that we had produced in a human manner; each of us would in his production have doubly affirmed himself and his fellow men. I would have: (1) objectified in my production my individuality and its peculiarity and thus both in my activity enjoyed an individual expression of my life and also in looking at the object have had the individual pleasure of realizing that my personality was objective, visible to the senses and thus a power raised beyond all doubt. (2) In your enjoyment or use of my product I would have had the direct enjoyment of realizing that I had both satisfied a human need by my work and also objectified the human essence and therefore fashioned for another human being the object that met his need. (3) I would have been for you the mediator between you and the species and thus been acknowledged and felt by you as a completion of your own essence and a necessary part of yourself and have thus realized that I am confirmed both in your thought and in your love. (4) In my expression of my life I would have fashioned your expression of your life, and thus in my own activity have realized my own essence, my human, my communal essence.' *Karl Marx: Early Texts*, ed. David McLellen (Oxford: Basil Blackwell, 1971), p. 202.

5 For a criticism of this, see Ernst Michael Lange, *Das Prinzip Arbeit* (Frankfurt/Berlin/Vienna, 1980). A very interesting attempt to defend Marx's model of externalization can be found in Andreas Wildt, *Die Anthropologie des frühen Marx*, Studienbrief der Fern-Universität Hagen, 1987.

6 See Wildt, *Die Anthropologie des frühen Marx*.
7 On this transformation of the concept of labour, see my 'Work and instrumental action'.
8 Jeffrey C. Alexander has applied Parsons' critique of utilitarianism to Marx in a revealing, if quite one-sided, manner: *Theoretical Logic in Sociology*, vol. 2: *The Antinomies of Classical Thought: Marx and Durkheim* (Berkeley: University of California Press, 1982), chs 3 and 6. In this connection, see also Axel Honneth and Hans Joas, 'War Marx ein Utilitarist? Für eine Gesellschaftstheorie jenseits des Utilitarismus', in *Soziologie und Sozialpolitik. Erstes Internationales Kolloquium zur Theorie und Geschichte der Soziologie*, ed. Akademie der Wissenschaften der DDR (Berlin, 1987), pp. 148ff.
9 Andreas Wildt provides an excellent interpretation of these passages in 'Gerechtigkeit in Marx' Kapital', in E. Angehrn and G. Lohmann (eds), *Ethik und Marx. Moralkritik und normative Grundlagen der Marx'schen Theorie* (Königstein im Taunus: Athenäum, 1986), pp. 149ff.
10 See, *inter alia*, Albrecht Wellmer, 'Naturrecht und praktische Vernunft. Zur aporetischen Entfaltung eines Problems bei Kant, Hegel und Marx', in Angehrn and Lohmann, *Ethik und Marx*, pp. 197ff.; and Georg Lohmann, *Indifferenz und Gesellschaft. Eine kritische Auseinandersetzung mit Marx* (Frankfurt: Campus, 1991), ch. 6.
11 See Honneth and Joas, 'War Marx ein Utilitarist?'
12 Karl Marx, 'The Eighteenth Brumaire of Louis Bonaparte' and 'Civil war in France', in Karl Marx and Friedrich Engels, *Selected Works* (Moscow: Progress Publishers, 1969), vol. 1, pp. 398–487, and vol. 2, pp. 202–41.
13 An impressive interpretation of Marx's historical writings along this line is to be found in John F. Rundell's *Origins of Modernity: The Origins of Modern Social Theory from Kant to Hegel to Marx* (Cambridge: Polity Press, 1987), pp. 146ff.
14 On Sorel in general, see Michael Freund, *George Sorel. Der revolutionäre Konservatismus* (Frankfurt: Klostermann, 1972) and Helmut Berding, *Rationalismus und Mythos. Geschichtsauffassung und politische Theorie bei George Sorel* (Minden/Vienna: Oldenbourg, 1969).
15 That is the thesis of the fascinating study by Isaiah Berlin, 'Georges Sorel', in *Against the Current: Essays in the History of Ideas*, ed. Henry Hardy (London: Hogarth, 1979), pp. 296–332.
16 Georges Sorel, 'Was man von Vico lernt', *Sozialistische Monatshefte* 2 (1898), pp. 270ff.; here, pp. 271f.
17 Sorel, 'The ethics of socialism', in *From Georges Sorel: Essays in Socialism and Philosophy*, ed. John L. Stanley, tr. John and Charlotte Stanley (Oxford: Oxford University Press, 1976), pp. 94–110, here, p. 99. See Shlomo Sand, 'Lutte de classes et conscience juridique dans la pensée de Georges Sorel', in J. Julliard and Shlomo Sand (eds), *George Sorel et son temps* (Paris: Editions du Seuil, 1985), pp. 225ff.
18 Ibid., p. 97. [Translation modified.]
19 Ibid., p. 109.
20 Ibid., p. 102.
21 Ibid.
22 On Sorel's reception of Bergson, see Freund, *Georges Sorel*, ch. 9; and Hans Barth, *Masse und Mythos* (Hamburg: Rowohlt, 1959), ch. 3.

23 Sorel, *Reflections on Violence*, tr. T. E. Hulme and J. Roth (Glencoe, Ill.: Free Press, 1950), p. 151.
24 On this, see Berding, *Rationalismus und Mythos*.
25 Hendrik de Man, *Zur Psychologie des Sozialismus* (Jena, 1927); on Sorel, see p. 115.
26 See e.g. Sartre's Introduction to Frantz Fanon's *The Wretched of the Earth*, tr. Constance Farrington (London: MacGibbon, 1963), pp. 7–26; here, pp. 12f.
27 Sartre, *Being and Nothingness*, part III, ch. 1, pp. 271–370.
28 The most impressive are: Michael Theunissen, *The Other: Studies in the Social Ontology of Husserl, Heidegger, Sartre, and Buber*, tr. Christopher Macann (Cambridge, Mass.: MIT Press, 1984), ch. 6; and Charles Taylor, 'What is human agency?' in *Philosophical Papers*, vol. 1: *Human Agency and Language*: (Cambridge: Cambridge University Press, 1985), pp. 15–44.
29 Sartre, *Anti-Semite and Jew*, trans. George J. Becker (New York: Schocken Books, 1965); on this, see my 'Ohnmächtige Selbstbehauptung. Sartres Weg zu einer intersubjektivistische Freiheitslehre', *Babylon. Beiträge zur jüdischen Gegenwart*, 2 (1987), pp. 82ff.
30 Sartre, *Situations V: Colonialisme et néo-colonialisme* (Paris: Gallimard, 1964). [Translators' note: Few of these essays are available in English. See, however, along with the Introduction to Fanon's book, Sartre's Introduction to Albert Memmi, *The Colonizer and the Colonized*, tr. Howard Greenfield (New York, 1965).]
31 Sartre, Introduction to Fanon, pp. 16f.
32 Ibid., p. 17.
33 See e.g. ibid., pp. 18, 19.
34 Ibid., p. 21; see, by way of contrast, Sartre's reference to 'the latent universalism of bourgeois liberalism' in his 'Le Colonialisme est un système', *Les Temps modernes*, 123 (Mar.–Apr. 1956), pp. 1371–86. [Reprinted in *Situations V*.]
35 With regard to this thesis, see Mark Hunyadi, 'Sartres Entwürfe zu einer unmöglichen Moral', in Traugott König (ed.), *Sartre. Ein Kongreß* (Reinbek: Rohwohlt, 1988), pp. 84ff.

Chapter 8   Disrespect and Resistance

1 Frantz Fanon, *The Wretched of the Earth*; with regard to Fanon's reading of Hegel, see also his *Black Skin, White Masks*, tr. Charles Lam Markmann (New York: Grove Press, 1967), ch. 7.
2 Weber, *Economy and Society*, p. 38. [Translator's note: The Roth–Wittich edition has 'conflict' rather than 'struggle' as a translation of '*Kampf*'.]
3 Georg Simmel, *Conflict*, tr. Kurt H. Wolff (Glencoe, Ill.: Free Press, 1955). [Originally ch. 4 ('Der Streit') of Simmel's *Soziologie: Untersuchungen über die Formen der Vergesellschaftung* (Leipzig, 1908), pp. 247ff.]
4 Hans Joas provides a convincing re-valuation of the 'Chicago School' in 'Symbolischer Interaktionismus. Von der Philosophie des Pragmatismus zu einer soziologischen Forschungstradition', *Kölner Zeitschrift für Soziologie und Sozialpsychologie*, 40 (1988), pp. 417ff.
5 Robert E. Park and Ernest W. Burgess (eds), *Introduction to the Science of Sociology* (Chicago: University of Chicago Press, 1969), p. 241.

6   See e.g. Lewis A. Coser, *The Functions of Social Conflict* (London: Routledge & Kegan Paul, 1956).
7   I shall limit myself here to mentioning philosophical literature: Boxill, 'Self-respect and protest'; Thomas E. Hill, Jr., 'Servility and self-respect', in *Autonomy and Self-respect* (Cambridge: Cambridge University Press, 1991), pp. 4–18; Wildt, 'Recht und Selbstachtung'.
8   Markus Schwingel has recently shown this with admirable clarity – although with affirmative intent – with regard to Bourdieu's sociological theory: M. Schwingel, *Analytik der Kämpfe: Macht und Herrschaft in der Soziologie Bourdieus* (Hamburg: Argument Sonderband Neue Folge, 1993).
9   See Edward P. Thompson, *The Making of the English Working Class* (London: Gollancz, 1963).
10 Barrington Moore, *Injustice: The Social Bases of Obedience and Revolt* (White Plains, NY: M. E. Sharpe, 1978). See my review essay 'Moralischer Konsens und Unrechtsempfindung: Zu Barrington Moores Untersuchung über "Ungerechtigkeit"', in *Suhrkamp Wissenschaft. Weißes Programm. Almanach* (Frankfurt: Suhrkamp, 1984), pp. 108–14.
11 Andreas Griessinger, *Das symbolische Kapital der Ehre. Streikbewegungen und kollektives Bewußtsein deutscher Handwerksgesellen im 18. Jahrhundert* (Frankfurt: Ullstein, 1981).
12 See e.g. Arnold Gehlen, *Moral und Hypermoral. Eine pluralistische Ethik* (Frankfurt: Athenäum, 1969).

Chapter 9   Intersubjective Conditions for Personal Integrity

1   See e.g. Herbert Schnädelbach, 'What is neo-Aristotelism?', *Praxis International*, 7 (1987/8), pp. 225–37; Jürgen Habermas, 'Morality and ethical life: does Hegel's critique of Kant apply to discourse ethics?', in his *Moral Consciousness and Communicative Action*, tr. Christian Lenhardt and Shierry Weber Nicholsen (Cambridge, Mass.: MIT Press, 1990), 195–215; Larmore, *Patterns of Moral Complexity*.
2   See, among others, Alisdair MacIntyre, *After Virtue* (Notre Dame, Ind.: University of Notre Dame Press, 1981) Charles Taylor, 'Cross-purposes: the liberal–communitarian debate', in Nancy Rosenblum (ed.), *Liberalism and the Moral Life* (Cambridge, Mass.: Harvard University Press, 1989), pp. 159–82; and Michael Walzer, 'The communitarian critique of liberalism', *Political Theory*, 18: 1 (Feb. 1990), pp. 6–23.
3   In the formulation of this intermediate position, I have been inspired by Martin Seel's 'Das Gute und das Richtige', manuscript, 1991.
4   See Charles Taylor, 'What's wrong with negative liberty?', in his *Philosophical Papers*, vol. 2: *Philosophy and the Human Sciences* (Cambridge: Cambridge University Press, 1985), pp. 211–29.
5   Instructive here is Gabriele Neuhäuser, 'Familiäre Sittlichkeit und Anerkennungsformen bei Hegel' (MA thesis, University of Frankfurt, 1992).

Bibliography

Alexander, Jeffrey C., *Theoretical Logic in Sociology*, vol. 2: *The Antinomies of Classical Thought: Marx and Durkheim*. Berkeley: University of California Press, 1982.

Alexy, Robert, *Theorie der Grundrechte*. Frankfurt: Suhrkamp, 1986.

Bambey, Andrea, *Das Geschlechterdifferenz in feministischen Theorien*, Studientexte zur Sozialwissenschaften, Sonderband 5. Frankfurt, 1991.

Barth, Hans, *Masse und Mythos*. Hamburg: Rowohlt, 1959.

Baumgarten, Eduard, *Die geistigen Grundlagen des amerikanischen Gemeinwesens*, vol. 2: *Der Pragmatismus: R. W. Emerson, W. James, J. Dewey*. Frankfurt, 1938.

Benhabib, Seyla, *Situating the Self: Gender, Community, and Postmodernism in Contemporary Ethics*. New York: Routledge, 1992.

Benjamin, Jessica, *The Bonds of Love: Psychoanalysis, Feminism, and the Problem of Power*. New York: Pantheon, 1988.

Berding, Helmut, *Rationalismus und Mythos. Geschichtsauffassung und politische Theorie bei George Sorel*. Minden/Vienna: Oldenbourg, 1969.

Berger, Peter L. 'On the obsolescence of the concept of honor', *European Journal of Sociology*, 11 (1970).

Bergmann, S. Martin. *The Anatomy of Loving*. New York: Columbia University Press, 1987.

Berlin, Isaiah. 'Georges Sorel', in *Against the Current: Essays in the History of Ideas*, ed. Henry Hardy. London: Hogarth, 1979, pp. 296–332.

Bettelheim, Bruno, *Surviving and Other Essays*. London: Thames & Hudson, 1979.

Blasche, Siegfried. 'Natürliche Sittlichkeit und bürgerliche Gesellschaft. Hegels Konstruktion der Familie als sittliche Intimität im entsittlichten Leben', in M. Riedel (ed.), *Materialen zu Hegels Rechtsphilosophie*, Frankfurt: Suhrkamp, 1975, vol. 2, pp. 312ff.

Bloch, Ernst. *Natural Law and Human Dignity*, tr. Dennis J. Schmidt. Cambridge, Mass.: MIT Press, 1986.

Bobbio, Norberto, 'Hegel und die Naturrechtslehre', in M. Riedel (ed.), *Materialen zu Hegels Rechtsphilosophie*, ed. Frankfurt: Suhrkamp, 1975, vol. 2, pp. 81ff.

Borkenau, Franz, *Der Übergang vom feudalen zum bürgerlichen Weltbild*. Darmstadt: Wissenschaftliche Buchgesellschaft, 1971.

Bourdieu, Pierre, *Distinction: A Social Critique of Aesthetic Judgement*, tr. Richard Nice. London: Routledge & Kegan Paul, 1984.

Bowlby, John, *Attachment and Loss*, vol. 1: *Attachment*. London: Hogarth Press and the Institute of Psychoanalysis, 1969.

—— *The Making and Breaking of Affectional Bonds*. London: Tavistock, 1979.

Boxill, Bernard R., 'Self-respect and protest', *Philosophy and Public Affairs*, 6 (1976/7), pp. 58ff.

Branden Nathaniel, *The Psychology of Self-esteem*. Los Angeles: Nash, 1969.

Breakwell, Glyris M., *Threatened Identities*. New York: Wiley, 1983.

Brotz, Howard (ed.), *Negro Social and Political Thought*. New York: Basic Books, 1966.

Buck, Günther, 'Selbsterhaltung und Historizität', in Hans Ebeling (ed.), *Subjektivität und Selbsterhaltung. Beiträge zur Diagnose der Moderne*, Frankfurt: Suhrkamp, 1976, pp. 144ff.

Coser, Lewis A., *The Functions of Social Conflict*. London: Routledge & Kegan Paul, 1956.

Darwall, Stephen L., 'Two kinds of respect', *Ethics*, 88 (1977/8), pp. 36ff.

Dewey, John, 'The theory of emotion', I, *Psychological Review* (1895), pp. 553ff.

—— 'The Theory of Emotion', II, *Psychological Review* (1896), pp. 13ff.

Dülmen, Richard van (ed.), *Armut, Liebe, Ehre. Studien zur historischen Kulturforschung*. Frankfurt: Fischer, 1988.

Düsing, Edith, *Intersubjektivität und Selbstbewußtsein*. Cologne: Verlag für Philosophie J. Dinter, 1986.

Eagle, Morris N., *Recent Developments in Psychoanalysis: A Critical Evaluation*. New York: McGraw-Hill, 1989.

Erikson, Erik H., *Identity and the Life-cycle*. New York: Norton, 1980.

Fanon, Frantz, *The Wretched of the Earth*, tr. Constance Farrington. London: MacGibbon, 1963.

—— *Black Skin, White Masks*, tr. Charles Lam Markmann. New York: Grove Press, 1967.

Feinberg, Joel, 'The nature and value of rights', in *Rights, Justice, and the Bounds of Liberty: Essays in Social Philosophy*, Princeton, NJ: Princeton University Press, 1980, pp. 143ff.

Fichte, J. G., 'Grundlage des Naturrechts nach Prinzipien der Wissenschaftslehre', in *Fichtes Werke*, ed. Immanuel Hermann Fichte. Berlin: de Gruyter, 1971, vol. 3, pp. 1ff.

Freud, Sigmund, *Inhibitions, Symptoms, and Anxiety*, tr. Alix Strachey. New York: Norton, 1959.

Freund, Michael, *George Sorel. Der revolutionäre Konservatismus*. Frankfurt: Klostermann, 1972.

Freyer, Hans, *Machiavelli*. Weinheim: Verlagsgesellschaft, 1986.

Gehlen, Arnold, *Moral und Hypermoral. Eine pluralistische Ethik*. Frankfurt: Athenäum, 1969.

Gilbert Paul, *Human Relationships: A Philosophical Introduction*. Oxford: Blackwell, 1991.

Giusti, Miguel, *Hegels Kritik der modernen Welt*. Würzburg: Könighausen & Neumann, 1987.

Greenberg, J. R., and Mitchel, Stephen A., *Object Relations in Psychoanalytic Theory*. Cambridge, Mass.: Harvard University Press, 1983.

Griessinger, Andreas, *Das symbolische Kapital der Ehre. Streikbewegungen und kollektives Bewußtsein deutscher Handwerksgesellen im 18. Jahrhundert*. Frankfurt: Ullstein, 1981.

Gurewitsch, Aron, *Zur Geschichte des Achtungsbegriffs und zur Theorie der sittlichen Gefühle*. Würzburg, 1897.

Habermas, Jürgen, *Theory and Practice*, tr. John Viertel. Boston: Beacon Press, 1973.

——'Überlegungen zum evolutionären Stellenwert des modernen Rechts', in *Zur Rekonstruktion des historischen Materialismus*. Frankfurt: Suhrkamp, 1976, pp. 160–8.

——*The Philosophical Discourse of Modernity*, tr. Frederick G. Lawrence. Cambridge, Mass.: MIT Press, 1987.

——'Morality and ethical life: does Hegel's critique of Kant apply to discourse ethics?', in *Moral Consciousness and Communicative Action*, tr. Christian Lenhardt and Shierry Weber Nicholsen. Cambridge, Mass.: MIT Press, 1990, pp. 195–215.

——*Faktizität und Geltung: Beiträge zur Diskurstheorie des Rechts und des demokratischen Rechtsstaat*. Frankfurt: Suhrkamp, 1992.

——*Postmetaphysical Thinking: Philosophical Essays*, tr. William Mark Hohengarten. Cambridge, Mass.: MIT Press, 1992.

Harlow, H. F., 'The nature of love', *American Psychologist*, 13 (1958), pp. 673ff.

Hegel, G. W. F., *System der Sittlichkeit*, ed. Georg Lasson. Hamburg: Meiner, 1967.

——*Jenaer Realphilosophie*. Hamburg: Meiner, 1969.

——*Werke in 20 Bänden*, ed. Eva Moldenhauer and Karl Markus Michel. Frankfurt: Suhrkamp, 1971.

——*Hegel's Philosophy of Mind*, tr. William Wallace and A. V. Miller. Oxford: Oxford University Press, 1971.

——'The oldest systematic programme of German Idealism', in Henry S. Harris, *Hegel's Development: Toward the Sunlight*. Oxford: Clarendon Press, 1972, pp. 510–12.

——*Natural Law: The Scientific Ways of Treating Natural Law, its Place in Moral Philosophy, and its Relation to the Positive Sciences of Law*, tr. T. M. Knox. Philadelphia: University of Pennsylvania Press, 1975.

——*Phenomenology of Spirit*, tr. A. V. Miller. Oxford: Oxford University Press, 1977.

——*The Difference between the Fichtean and Schellingian Systems of Philosophy*, tr. H. S. Harris and Walter Cerf. Albany, NY: SUNY Press, 1977.

——'System of Ethical Life' (1802/03) and 'First Philosophy of Spirit' (Part III of the System of Speculative Philosophy 1803/04), ed. and tr. H. S. Harris and T. M. Knox. Albany, NY: SUNY Press, 1979.

——'Jena Lectures on the Philosophy of Spirit', in *Hegel and the Human Spirit: A Translation of the Jena Lectures on the Philosophy of Spirit (1805–6) with Commentary*, ed. and tr. Leo Rauch. Detroit: Wayne State University Press, 1983.

——*System der spekulativen Philosophie*. Hamburg: Meiner, 1986.

Henrich, Dieter. *Hegel im Kontext*. Frankfurt: Suhrkamp, 1971.

Hill, Thomas E., Jr., 'Servility and self-respect', in *Autonomy and Self-respect*. Cambridge: Cambridge University Press, 1991, pp. 4–18.

Hobbes, Thomas. *Leviathan*, ed. Richard Tuck. Cambridge: Cambridge University Press, 1991.

Honneth, Axel, 'Work and instrumental action', *New German Critique*, 26 (1982), pp. 31–54. [Reprinted in Honneth, *The Fragmented World of the Social*.]

——'Moral consciousness and class domination: some problems in the

analysis of hidden morality', *Praxis International*, 2 (Apr. 1982). [Reprinted in Honneth, *The Fragmented World of the Social*.]
—— 'Moralischer Konsens und Unrechtsempfindung: Zu Barrington Moores Untersuchung über "Ungerechtigkeit"', in *Suhrkamp Wissenschaft. Weißes Programm. Almanach*, Frankfurt: Suhrkamp, 1984, pp. 108–14.
—— 'Diskursethik und implizites Gerechtigkeitskonzept', in W. Kuhlmann (ed.), *Moralität und Sittlichkeit: Das Problem Hegels und die Diskursethik*. Frankfurt: Suhrkamp, 1985, pp. 183–93.
—— 'The fragmented world of symbolic forms: reflections on Pierre Bourdieu's Sociology of Culture', *Theory, Culture, and Society*, 3 (1986), pp. 55ff. [Reprinted in Honneth, *The Fragmented World of the Social*.]
—— 'Ohnmächtige Selbstbehauptung. Sartres Weg zu einer intersubjektivistische Freiheitslehre', *Babylon. Beiträge zur jüdischen Gegenwart*, 2 (1987), pp. 82ff.
—— Afterword to Charles Taylor, *Negative Freiheit? Zur Kritik des neuzeitlichen Individualismus*. Frankfurt: Suhrkamp, 1988, pp. 295–314.
—— *Critique of Power: Reflective Stages in a Critical Social Theory*, tr. Kenneth Baynes. Cambridge, Mass.: MIT Press, 1991.
—— 'Moral development and social struggle: Hegel's early social-philosophical doctrines', in Axel Honneth et al. (eds), *Cultural-political Interventions in the Unfinished Project of Enlightenment*, tr. Barbara Fultner Cambridge, Mass.: MIT Press, 1992, pp. 197–217.
—— 'Integrity and disrespect: principles of a conception of morality based on the theory of recognition', *Political Theory*, 20: 2 (May 1992), pp. 187–201.
—— *Desintegration: Soziologische Exkurse*. Frankfurt: Fischer, 1994.
—— *The Fragmented World of the Social: Essays in Social and Political Philosophy*, ed. Charles Wright. Albany, NY: SUNY Press, 1995.
—— and Joas, Hans, 'War Marx ein Utilitarist? Für eine Gesellschaftstheorie jenseits des Utililitarismus', in *Soziologie und Sozialpolitik. Erste Internationales Kolloquium zur Theorie und Geschichte der Soziologie*, ed. Akademie der Wissenschaften der DDR. Berlin, 1987, pp. 148ff.
—— *Human Nature and Social Action*. Cambridge, Mass.: MIT Press, 1988.
Horstmann, Rolf-Peter, 'Probleme der Wandlung in Hegels Jenaer Systemkonzeption', *Philosophische Rundschau*, 19 (1972), pp. 87ff.
—— 'Über die Rolle der bürgerlichen Gesellschaft in Hegels politischer Philosophie', in M. Riedel (ed.), *Materialen zu Hegels Rechtsphilosophie*. Frankfurt: Suhrkamp, 1975, vol. 2, pp. 276ff.
Hösle, Vittorio, *Hegels System*, vol. 2: *Philosophie der Natur und des Geistes*. Hamburg: Meiner, 1987.
Hunyadi, Mark, 'Sartres Entwürfe zu einer unmöglichen Moral', in Traugott König (ed.), *Sartre. Ein Kongreß*, Reinbek: Rohwohlt, 1988, pp. 84ff.
Ihering, Rudolph von, *Der Zweck im Recht*, vol. 22 Leipzig, 1905.
Ilting, Karl-Heinz, 'Hegels Auseinandersetzung mit der aristotelischen Politik', *Philosophisches Jahrbuch*, 71 (1963/4), pp. 38ff.
Jamme, Christoph, and Schneider, Helmut (eds), *Mythologie der Vernunft. Hegels 'ältestes Systemprogramm' des deutschen Idealismus*. Frankfurt: Suhrkamp, 1984.
Joas, Hans, *G. H. Mead: A Contemporary Re-examination of his Thought*, tr. Raymond Meyer. Cambridge, Mass.: MIT Press, 1985.
—— 'Symbolischer Interaktionismus. Von der Philosophie des Pragmatismus zu einer soziologischen Forschungstradition', *Kölner Zeitschrift für Soziologie und Sozialpsychologie*, 40 (1988), pp. 417ff.

——*Zur Kreativität des Handelns*. Frankfurt: Suhrkamp, 1992.

Kant, Immanuel, *The Metaphysics of Morals*, tr. Mary Gregor. Cambridge: Cambridge University Press, 1991. [*Metaphysik der Sitten*, Prussian Akademie edn, vol. 6 (Berlin: de Gruyter, 1968).]

Kernberg, Otto F., *Object-relations Theory and Clinical Psychoanalysis*. New York: Jason Aronson, 1984.

Kersting, Wolfgang, 'Handlungsmächtigkeit: Machiavellis Lehre vom politischen Handeln', *Philosophisches Jahrbuch*, 3: 4 (1988), pp. 234ff.

Kimmerle, Heinz, 'Zur Entwicklung des Hegelschen Denkens in Jena', in *Hegel-Studien*, suppl. 4 (1968).

Kluth, Heinz, *Sozialprestige und sozialer Status*. Stuttgart: Enke, 1957.

Kojève, Alexandre, *Introduction to the Reading of Hegel*, tr. James Nichols. New York: Basic Books, 1969.

Korff, Wilhelm, *Ehre, Prestige, Gewissen*. Cologne: J. P. Bachem, 1966.

Lange, Ernst Michael, *Das Prinzip Arbeit*. Frankfurt/Berlin/Vienna, 1980.

Larmore, Charles E., *Patterns of Moral Complexity*. Cambridge: Cambridge University Press, 1987.

Levinas, Emmanuel, *La Mort et le temps*. Paris, 1991.

Lohmann, Georg, *Indifferenz und Gesellschaft. Eine kritische Auseinandersetzung mit Marx*. Frankfurt: Campus, 1991.

Luhmann, Niklas, *Love as Passion: The Codification of Intimacy*, tr. Jeremy Gaines and Doris L. Jones. Cambridge, Mass.: Harvard University Press, 1986.

Lukács, Georg, *The Young Hegel*, tr. Rodney Livingstone. London: Merlin Press, 1975.

Lynd, Helen M., *On Shame and the Search for Identity*. New York: Harcourt, Brace, 1958.

Machiavelli, Niccolò, *The Prince*, ed. Quentin Skinner and Russell Price. Cambridge: Cambridge University Press, 1988.

——*The Discourses*, tr. Leslie J. Walker. London: Routledge & Kegan Paul, 1950.

Macho, Thomas H., *Todesmetaphern. Zur Logik der Grenzerfahrung*. Frankfurt: Suhrkamp, 1987.

MacIntyre, Alisdair, *After Virtue*. Notre Dame, Ind.: University of Notre Dame Press, 1981.

de Man, Hendrik, *Zur Psychologie des Sozialismus*. Jena, 1927.

Marquard, Odo, 'Hegel und das Sollen', in *Schwierigkeiten mit der Geschichtsphilosophie*. Frankfurt: Suhrkamp, 1973, pp. 37ff.

Marshall, Thomas H., 'Citizenship and social class', in *Sociology at the Crossroads*, London: Heinemann, 1963, pp. 67ff.

Marx, Karl, and Engels, Friedrich, *Selected Works*, 3 vols. Moscow: Progress Publishers, 1969.

Karl Marx: Early Texts, ed. David McLellen. Oxford: Blackwell, 1971.

Mead, George Herbert, *Mind, Self, and Society from the Standpoint of a Social Behaviorist*, ed. Charles W. Morris. Chicago: University of Chicago Press, 1934.

——*Selected Writings*, ed. Andrew J. Reck. Indianapolis: Library of the Liberal Arts, 1964.

——*Movements of Thought in the Nineteenth Century*. Chicago: University of Chicago Press, 1972.

Meillassoux, Claude, *Anthropologie de l'esclavage: le ventre de fer et d'argent*. Paris: Presses Universitaires de France, 1986.

Mercier-Josa, Solange, 'Combat pour la reconnaissance et criminalité', in *Hegels Philosophie des Rechts*, ed. Dieter Henrich and Rolf-Peter Horstmann. Stuttgart: Klett-Cotta, 1982, pp. 75ff.

Meyer, Thomas, *Der Zwiespalt in der Marxschen Emanzipationstheorie.* Kronberg im Taunus: Scriptor, 1973.

Moore, Barrington. *Injustice: The Social Bases of Obedience and Revolt.* White Plains, NY: M. E. Sharpe, 1978.

Münkler, Herfried, *Machiavelli: Die Begründung des politischen Denkens der Neuzeit aus der Krise der Republik Florenz.* Frankfurt: Europäische Verlagsanstalt, 1984.

Neckel, Sighard, *Status und Scham. Zur symbolischen Reproduktion sozialer Ungleichheit.* Frankfurt: Campus, 1991.

Neuhäuser, Gabriele, 'Familiäre Sittlichkeit und Anerkennungsformen bei Hegel'. MA thesis, University of Frankfurt, 1992.

Park, Robert E., and Burges, Ernest W. (eds), *Introduction to the Science of Sociology.* Chicago: University of Chicago Press, 1969.

Parsons, Talcott, *The System of Modern Societies.* Englewood Cliffs, NJ: Prentice-Hall, 1971.

Patterson, Orlando, *Slavery and Social Death: A Comparative Study.* Cambridge, Mass.: Harvard University Press, 1992.

Péristiany, J. G. (ed.), *Honour and Shame: The Values of Mediterranean Society.* London: Weidenfeld & Nicolson, 1966.

Piers, Gerhart, and Singer, Milton B., *Shame and Guilt: A Psychoanalytic and a Cultural Study.* New York: Norton, 1971.

Pitt-Rivers, Julian, 'Honor', in *International Encyclopedia of the Social Sciences,* vol. 6, ed. David L. Sills. New York: Macmillan and Free Press, 1968, pp. 503–11.

Plessner, Helmut, 'Die Grenzen der Gemeinschaft', in *Gesammelte Schriften,* vol. 5: *Macht und menschliche Natur*, ed. Günther Dux, Odo Marquard, and Elisabeth Ströker. Frankfurt: Suhrkamp, 1981, pp. 7ff.

Pospísvil, Leopold, *Anthropology of Law.* New Haven, Conn.: HRAF Press, 1974.

Riedel, Manfred (ed.), *Materialen zu Hegels Rechtsphilosophie*, 2 vols. Frankfurt: Suhrkamp, 1975.

——'Hegel's criticism of natural law theory', in *Between Tradition and Revolution: The Hegelian Transformation of Political Philosophy*, tr. Walter Wright. Cambridge: Cambridge University Press, 1984, pp. 76–104.

Ritter, Joachim, *Hegel and the French Revolution: Essays on the 'Philosophy of Right'*, tr. Richard Dien Winfield. Cambridge, Mass.: MIT Press, 1982.

Rose, Gillian, *Hegel contra Sociology.* London: Athlone, 1981.

Roth, Klaus, *Die Institutionalisierung der Freiheit in den Jenaer Schriften Hegels.* Rheinfelden/Berlin: Schäuble, 1991.

Rousseau, Jean-Jacques, *A Discourse on Inequality*, tr. Maurice Cranston. Harmondsworth: Penguin, 1984.

Rundell, John F., *Origins of Modernity: The Origins of Modern Social Theory from Kant to Hegel to Marx.* Cambridge: Polity Press, 1987.

Sachs, David, 'How to distinguish self-respect from self-esteem', *Philosophy and Public Affairs,* 10: 4 (1981), pp. 346–60.

Sand, Shlomo, 'Lutte de classes et conscience juridique dans la pensée de Georges Sorel', in J. Julliard and Shlomo Sand (eds), *George Sorel et son temps.* Paris: Editions du Seuil, 1985, pp. 225ff.

Sartre, Jean-Paul, 'Le Colonialisme est un système', *Les Temps modernes,* 123 (Mar.–Apr. 1956), pp. 1371–86.

——Introduction to Frantz Fanon, *The Wretched of the Earth*, tr. Constance Farrington. London: MacGibbon, 1963, pp. 7–26.

——*Situations V: Colonialisme et néo-colonialisme*. Paris: Gallimard, 1964.

——*Anti-Semite and Jew*, tr. George J. Becker. New York: Schocken Books, 1965.

——Introduction to Albert Memmi, *The Colonizer and the Colonized*, tr. Howard Greenfield. New York, 1965.

——*Being and Nothingness: An Essay on Phenomenological Ontology*, tr. Hazel E. Barnes. New York: Washington Square Press, 1966.

——*Critique of Dialectical Reason*, vol. 1: *Theory of Practical Ensemble*, tr. Alan Sheridan-Smith and ed. Jonathan Rée. London: New Left Books, 1976.

Scarry, Elaine, *The Body in Pain: The Making and Unmaking of the World*. Oxford: Oxford University Press, 1985.

Scheler, Max, *Formalism in Ethics and Non-Formal Ethics of Values: A New Attempt toward the Foundation of an Ethical Personalism*, tr. Manfred S. Frings and Roger L. Funk. Evanston, Ill.: Northwestern University Press, 1973.

Schnädelbach, Herbert, 'What is neo-Aristotelism?', *Praxis International*, 7 (1987/8), pp. 225–37.

Schreiber, Marianne, 'Kann der Mensch Verantwortung für seine Aggressivität übernehmen? Aspekte aus der Psychologie D. W. Winnicotts und Melanie Kleins', in Alfred Schöpf (ed.), *Aggression und Gewalt: Anthropologisch-sozialwissenschaftliche Beiträge*. Würzburg: Königshausen & Neumann, 1983, pp. 155ff.

Schwingel, Markus, *Analytik der Kämpfe: Macht und Herrschaft in der Soziologie Bourdieus*. Hamburg: Argument Sonderband Neue Folge, 1993.

Seel, Martin. 'Das Gute und das Richtige', manuscript, 1991.

Sennett, Richard, and Cobb, Jonathan, *The Hidden Injuries of Class*. New York: Knopf, 1972.

Siep, Ludwig, 'Der Kampf um Anerkennung. Zu Hegels Auseinandersetzung mit Hobbes in den Jenaer Schriften', *Hegel-Studien*, 9 (1974), pp. 155ff.

——*Anerkennung als Prinzip der praktischen Philosophie. Untersuchungen zu Hegels Jenaer Philosophie des Geistes*. Freiburg/Munich: Alber, 1979.

Simmel, Georg, *Conflict*, tr. Kurt H. Wolff. Glencoe, Ill.: Free Press, 1955.

——'Zur Psychologie der Scham', *Schriften zur Soziologie*, ed. J.-J. Dahme and O. Rammstedt. Frankfurt: Suhrkamp, 1983, pp. 140ff.

Smith, Steven B., *Hegel's Critique of Liberalism: Rights in Context*. Chicago: University of Chicago Press, 1989.

Sorel, Georges, 'Was man von Vico lernt', *Sozialistische Monatshefte*, 2 (1898), pp. 270ff.

——*Reflections on Violence*, tr. T. E. Hulme and J. Roth. Glencoe, Ill.: Free Press, 1950.

——'The ethics of socialism', in *From Georges Sorel: Essays in Socialism and Philosophy*, ed. John L. Stanley, tr. John and Charlotte Stanley. Oxford: Oxford University Press, 1976, pp. 94–110.

Speier, Hans, 'Honor and social structure', in *Social Order and the Risks of War*. New York: G. W. Stewart, 1952.

Spitz, René A., *The First Year of Life: A Psychoanalytic Study of Normal and Deviant Development of Object Relations*, in collaboration with W. Godfrey Cobliner. New York: International Universities Press, 1965.

Stern, Daniel, *The First Relationship: Mother and Infant*. London: Open Books, 1977.

Strawson, Peter, 'Freedom and resentment', *Proceedings of the British Academy*, 48 (1962), pp. 1–25.

Taminaux, Jacques, *La Nostalgie de la Grèce à l'aube de l'idéalisme allemand: Kant et les Grecs dans l'itineraire de Schiller, de Hölderlin et de Hegel*. The Hague 1967.

Taylor, Charles, *Hegel and Modern Society*. Cambridge: Cambridge University Press, 1979.

——*Philosophical Papers*, vol. 1: *Human Agency and Language*. Cambridge: Cambridge University Press, 1985.

——*Philosophical Papers*, vol. 2: *Philosophy and the Human Sciences*. Cambridge: Cambridge University Press, 1985.

——*Negative Freiheit? Zur Kritik des neuzeitlichen Individualismus*. Frankfurt: Suhrkamp, 1988. [= German edn of *Philosophical Papers*.]

——'Cross-purposes: the liberal–communitarian debate', in Nancy Rosenblum (ed.), *Liberalism and the Moral Life*. Cambridge, Mass.: Harvard University Press, 1989, pp. 159–82.

——*The Ethics of Authenticity*. Cambridge, Mass.: Harvard University Press, 1992.

——'The politics of recognition', in Amy Gutmann (ed.), *Multiculturalism and 'The Politics of Recognition'*. Princeton, NJ: Princeton University Press, 1992.

Theunissen, Michael, 'Die verdrängte Intersubjektivität in Hegels Philosophie des Rechts', in Dieter Henrich and Rolf-Peter Horstmann (eds), *Hegels Philosophie des Rechts*, Stuttgart: Klett-Cotta, 1982, pp. 317ff.

——*The Other: Studies in the Social Ontology of Husserl, Heidegger, Sartre, and Buber*, tr. Christopher Macann. Cambridge, Mass.: MIT Press, 1984.

Thompson, Edward P., *The Making of the English Working Class*. London: Gollancz, 1963.

——*Customs in Common*. New York: New Press, 1991.

Tocqueville, Alexis de, *Democracy in America*, tr. George Lawrence and ed. J. P. Mayer. New York: Anchor Books, 1969.

Trevorthen, Couym, 'Communication and cooperation in early infancy: a description of primary intersubjectivity', in Margaret Bullowa (ed.), *Before Speech: The Beginning of Interpersonal Communication*, ed. Cambridge: Cambridge University Press, 1979, pp. 321ff.

——'The foundations of intersubjectivity: development of interpersonal and cooperative understanding of infants', in D. R. Olson (ed.), *The Social Foundations of Language and Thought: Essays in Honor of Jerome S. Bruner*, New York: Norton, 1980, pp. 316ff.

Tugendhat, Ernst, *Self-consciousness and Self-determination*, tr. Paul Stern. Cambridge, Mass.: MIT Press, 1986.

Walzer, Michael, 'The communitarian critique of liberalism', *Political Theory*, 18: 1 (Feb. 1990), pp. 6–23.

Weber, Max, *Economy and Society: An Outline of Interpretive Sociology*, ed. Guenther Roth and Claus Wittich. New York: Bedminster Press, 1968.

Wellmer, Albrecht, 'Naturrecht und praktische Vernunft. Zur aporetischen Entfaltung eines Problems bei Kant, Hegel und Marx', in E. Angehrn and Georg Lohmann (eds), *Ethik und Marx. Moralkritik und normative Grundlagen der Marx'schen Theorie*. Königstein im Taunus: Athenäum, 1986, pp. 197ff.

——*The Persistence of Modernity: Essays on Aesthetics, Ethics, and Postmodernism*, tr. David Midgley. Cambridge, Mass.: MIT Press, 1991.

Wildt, Andreas, 'Hegels Kritik des Jakobinismus', in Oskar Negt (ed.), *Aktualität und Folgen der Philosophie Hegels*. Frankfurt: Suhrkamp, 1970, pp. 265–92.

——*Autonomie und Anerkennung. Hegels Moralitätskritik im Lichte seiner Fichte-Rezeption*. Stuttgart: Klett-Cotta, 1982.

——'Gerechtigkeit in Marx' *Kapital*', in E. Angehrn and G. Lohmann (eds), *Ethik und Marx. Moralkritik und normative Grundlagen der Marx'schen Theorie*, Königstein im Taunus: Athenäum, 1986, pp. 149ff.

——*Die Anthropologie des frühen Marx*, Studienbrief der Fern-Universität Hagen, 1987.

——'Recht und Selbstachtung im Anschluß an die Anerkennungslehren von Fichte und Hegel', in Michael Kahlo, Ernst A. Wolff, and Rainer Zaczyk, (eds), *Fichtes Lehre vom Rechtsverhältnis*. Frankfurt: Klostermann, 1992, pp. 156ff.

Williams, Robert R., *Recognition: Fichte and Hegel on the Other*. Albany, NY: SUNY Press, 1992.

Winnicott, Donald W., *The Maturational Processes and the Facilitating Environment: Studies in the Theory of Emotional Development*. London: Hogarth Press and the Institute of Psychoanalysis, 1965.

——*Playing and Reality*. London: Tavistock, 1971.

Young, Iris Marion, *Justice and the Politics of Difference*. Princeton, NJ, Princeton University Press, 1990.

Index

and different forms of recognition
94
and disrespect 131, 132, 135
ethical life 13, 14–30, 58–62, 68,
69, 87, 91, 121–2, 127, 170,
172–3, 175–6, 177–9
Jena writings xix–xx, 1, 5, 10, 14,
67, 71, 92, 121, 145, 158, 178–9
and legal recognition relations
107, 108, 109–10, 115, 118, 121
and love relationships 37–9, 69,
95–6, 98
and Marx 148, 149, 151
and Mead 71, 75–6, 78–9, 80, 87,
91, 92, 93, 94, 171
Phenomenology of Spirit xi, xx, 5,
30, 62–3, 145, 146, 147
Philosophy of Right 176
Realphilosophie xx, 57, 58, 59,
61–2, 69, 146
and Sorel 153, 155
System of Ethical Life xix–xx, 16,
18–29, 30, 33, 38, 40, 54, 56, 57,
58, 62, 69
Herder, Johann Gottfried 73
Hobbes, Thomas x, xxi, 5, 7, 9–10,
11, 17, 41, 43, 44, 67, 144, 145
Hölderlin, Friedrich 11, 12
honour xiv, 89
and social conflicts 167
and social esteem 123, 124–5, 126,
129, 134
in Sorel 160
struggle for 22–3, 24
human rights 119–20, 158
Husserl, Edmund xx

'I', Mead's concept of the xx–xxi,
74–5, 76–7, 80–5, 86, 88, 104
identity formation xix
and intersubjective conflict 69
in Mead 76–8, 80–3, 86, 92
and self-respect xi, xii
and social relations x–xi
see also personal identity
Ihering, Rudolph von 111–12, 113

independence, and love relationships
96, 99–102, 104, 107
individuality
growth of 18
liberalization of 84
individual rights
basic 115–18
and death 48–9
and self-respect 119–20
individuals
autonomy 5, 69, 108
and legal recognition relations
108, 109, 112, 117
intersubjective recognition
of human identity 1, 5, 63, 71, 83
patterns of 92–130
relationships of 69, 148
intersubjectivity
Hegel's theory of 11–30
Hegel's turn away from 31–3,
59–63, 67f.
Mead's theory of 71–91
primary 98
Sartre's theory of 156–7
intuition 24, 25
intellectual 58

James, William 81, 82, 136
Jellinek, Georg 115
Joas, Hans xx

Kant, I. xiv, 11, 12, 111, 112, 172,
173
Kernberg, Otto F. 106
Kierkegaard, S. 68
Kojève, Alexandre 48

labour
'alienated' 148
'anthropological' concept of 148
as medium of mutual recognition
158
self-realization through 146, 147,
148–9
and the Subjective Spirit 35